I0214410

The Nature of Doctrine in T. F. Torrance's Theology

Elmer M. Colyer

Wipf and Stock Publishers
150 West Broadway • Eugene OR 97401
2001

The Nature of Doctrine in T.F. Torrance's Theology

By Colyer, Elmer

ISBN: 1-57910-804-0

Contents

Contents

Foreword

I am delighted to write a Foreward to this book concerned with the nature of Christian doctrine, for it is a particularly discerning and faithful presentation of some of the important issues in Christian theology today which cry out for clarification. I refer particularly to the profound connections between Christian theology and modern science. I appreciate greatly what Professor Colyer does in this book to clarify the kind of integration of form, content and method which a genuine theological science involves. He has grasped and presented the all-important epistemological issues which an Evangelical doctrine today has to face in thinking out and reshaping its biblical and epistemological foundations after the manner of the great Greek theologians of the Early Church, so evident in the formulation of the Nicene creedal theology upon which all Christendom rests. Dr. Colyer discerns and gives cogent expression to the way in which Christian doctrine today takes issue with modern critical philosophy and the challenge of natural science, without depreciation of its evangelical thrust, and without cutting it adrift from the worship, biblical meditation and liturgical life of the Church, within which basic theological concepts are nourished and given intelligible contemporary expression. He sees clearly that doctrinal form, doctrinal content, doctrinal method and the mission of the Gospel, belong together and may not be divorced from one another without serious loss to their evangelical and theological integrity. I am happy that he has sought to do this through a careful examination of my own work, in which he has cleared away many misunderstandings, but has contributed to it the kind of spiritual insight and critical thrust which cannot but serve authentic Christian doctrine today.

Thomas F. Torrance
Edinburgh, Advent, 1997

Preface

This monograph arises out of my encounter with the theology of Thomas F. Torrance over the past fifteen years, first as a seminarian, then in a Ph.D. program, and more recently teaching and writing about Torrance's theology. Along with a growing number of scholars and pastors, I have come to the conclusion that Torrance is one of the most significant theologians of the past fifty years. He has made major contributions to the area of theological method, including the nature of theology, especially in relation to the dialogue between theology and natural science.

This monograph focuses on a subject closely related to theological method and the nature of theology: the nature of doctrine. I believe T. F. Torrance's understanding of the nature of doctrine (which I discuss in the chapters of this book) will significantly enrich the theological conversation about this topic in the academy and the church.

I wish to express my gratitude to Greg Schrimpf, my research assistant, for all of the editorial work he so faithfully completed during the process of moving the manuscript into print. Few professor are so fortunate to have a former professional copy editor, who is also a significant theologian in his own right, as a research assistant!

I also want to thank Jon Stock and Wipf & Stock Publishers for publishing this book. Wipf & Stock is an innovative, up-and-coming Christian publishing company that finds creative ways to bring books back into print and keep books in print beyond what most publishers are able to accomplish these days. Wipf & Stock has reprinted many of T. F. Torrance's own books and they were a natural choice when I finally decided to publish a rewritten version of my Ph.D. dissertation completed under Dr. Gabriel Fackre during my years in the Joint Doctoral Program at Boston College/Andover Newton Theological School.

This book is dedicated to Gab and to my other theological mentor from my seminary days, Dr. Donald G. Bloesch. I consider myself extremely blessed to have had two theologically astute, wise and godly mentors like Don Bloesch and Gab Fackre who have deeply enriched my life theologically and personally.

Introduction

The Current Debate on the Nature of Doctrine

The nature of Christian doctrine has been a topic of significant theological conversation and debate over the past fifteen years. George Lindbeck's influential book, *The Nature of Doctrine: Religion and Theology in a Postliberal Age,*[1] provided the initial stimulus for this discussion. *The Nature of Doctrine* is a ground-breaking work which lays the foundation for a "cultural-linguistic" approach to religion and a "rule theory" of doctrine. More than twenty book reviews and numerous articles, written in response, delineate perceived deficiencies and possibilities in Lindbeck's proposal.

According to Lindbeck, existing theories of doctrine can be categorized into one of four basic models. The "cognitive-propositionalist" theory emphasizes "the cognitive aspects of religion and stresses the ways in which church doctrines function as informative propositions or truth claims about objective realities."[2] Lindbeck is cautious about identifying particular theologians with propositionalism, though he says that this was the approach of "traditional orthodoxies" and names C. S. Lewis and Malcolm Muggeridge as examples of the cognitivist theory in the twentieth century, emphasizing that propositionalism is not simply a "pre-modern" phenomenon.[3]

The "experiential-expressive" model views doctrines as "noninformative and nondiscursive symbols of inner feelings, attitudes, or existential orientations."[4] Lindbeck associates experiential-expressive model with Friedrich Schleiermacher and subsequent "liberal theologies," though he admits that expressivism "comes in many varieties and can be given many names."[5]

A third theory of doctrine, "especially favored by ecumenically inclined Roman Catholics," combines the "cognitively propositional and expressively symbolic dimensions and functions of religion and doctrine" into a synthetic hybrid that is sustained, according to Lindbeck, only through "complicated mental gymnastics."[6] Here, Lindbeck points to Karl Rahner and Bernard Lonergan as examples of this way of synthesizing elements from the first two approaches. In the remainder of the book, however, Lindbeck generally subsumes his discussions of these hybrids under the first two approaches.[7]

Finally, there is Lindbeck's own proposal: a "cultural-linguistic approach," which he believes avoids certain anomalies latent in the other models. In Lindbeck's model "emphasis is on those respects in which religions resemble languages together with their correlative forms of life and are thus similar to cultures."[8] Doctrines, in turn, function not as expressive symbols or as truth claims, but "as communally authoritative rules of discourse, attitude and action."[9] His book delineates and defends this cultural-linguistic theory, particularly in contrast to the expressivist approach that Lindbeck sees as the dominant model in theology and religion in recent history.

Michael McCarthy, in his important book, *The Crisis of Philosophy*, speaks of the failure to discern alternatives as one of the problems in the recent crisis in epistemology and metaphysics.[10] This failure to discern alternatives is also a problem in Lindbeck's seductive typology regarding religion and the nature of doctrine.[11] Might there not be other theories concerning the nature of doctrine that not only escape Lindbeck's typology, but also remove, for example, the hiatus between the cognitive-propositionalist and cultural-linguistic models; other models more integrative, acknowledging and incorporating insights of the other approaches, while utilizing a more comprehensive and adequate orientation?

One recent attempt along these lines is that of Alister McGrath in his programmatic work presented in the 1990 Bampton Lectures at Oxford University and subsequently published (with considerable expansion) as *The Genesis of Doctrine: A Study in the Foundations of Doctrinal Criticism*.[12] McGrath's work is "a study in the foundations of doctrinal criticism," a discipline that "seeks to evaluate the reliability and adequacy of the doctrinal formulations of the Christian tradition, by identifying what they purport to represent, clarifying the pressures and influences which lead to their genesis, and suggesting criteria–historical and theological–by which they may be evaluated and, if necessary, restated."[13] McGrath's goal is the critical reappropriation of the doctrinal heritage of the

Christian faith and his book is a "tentative and provisional" study anticipating a more substantial subsequent treatment of the subject.[14]

McGrath engages in an extended conversation concerning Lindbeck's typology before outlining, in "four theses," what could be called an historical approach to understanding the nature of doctrine, since McGrath is anxious to assert "the right of living history over and against artificial theoretical constructions" (thus the emphasis in the title on the *Genesis* of doctrine versus Lindbeck's *Nature* of doctrine).[15] The suggestive proposal outlined in *The Genesis of Doctrine* is an advance beyond Lindbeck in the conversation about the nature of doctrine and represents a nuanced alterative deserving significant attention.

However, McGrath's book is not the final word in the ongoing discussion regarding the nature of doctrine, as he is quick to admit. His book is "tentative and provisional" and written with the hope that "it will stimulate further discussion."[16]

I find myself in essential agreement with McGrath's contention that the time is right–if not long overdue–for a careful reexamination of the nature of doctrine and related questions, and Lindbeck deserves credit for precipitating the debate. Nevertheless, without discounting the contributions of Lindbeck and McGrath, the debate regarding the nature of doctrine must continue for several reasons.

McGrath has effectively questioned the validity of Lindbeck's typology by showing its inability to schematize the complexity and differentiation within the field in question (there are significant anomalies, like Schleiermacher's view of the relation of doctrine to "Christian" experience, with which Lindbeck's categories are unable to cope[17]). In so doing, McGrath has cleared the ground for his own constructive and suggestive alternative. Yet, McGrath's own approach leaves many questions unanswered, a point I will return to in a moment.

In addition there are other approaches beyond that of McGrath, which effectively engage the issues he raises, and these alternatives and their merits need to be considered as well. That some of these other approaches, in Lindbeck's words, entail "complicated mental gymnastics" is a rather weak argument for dismissing them. One of the virtues of McGrath's book is that it documents the complex, polyvalent character and function of doctrine in the history of the Church.

Furthermore, McGrath rightly criticizes Lindbeck for his "studied evasion of the central question of revelation–in other words, whether the Christian idiom, articulated in scripture and hence in the Christian tradition, originates from accumulated human insight, or from the self-disclosure of God in the Christ-event."[18] However, while McGrath speaks of "epistemological realism," he engages in an equally studied evasion of grasping the epistemic nettle and telling his readers what he means by "epistemological realism" and how he integrates it in his understanding of the genesis and nature of doctrine. In addition, McGrath traces the genesis of Christian doctrine back to the rather undifferentiated "Christ-event" without precisely defining it for his readers or explaining why that genesis finally resides in the self-revealing Triune God who we come to know through Jesus Christ in the Holy Spirit.

In defense of McGrath, one must remember that his book is an intentionally introductory work to be more fully consummated in a future project. Yet, the point for this discussion is that McGrath has opened the door for further conversation concerning the nature of doctrine in the form of considering other alternative approaches beyond McGrath's and those outlined by Lindbeck.

The examination of one such alternative way of understanding the nature of doctrine is the subject of this monograph.

Thomas F. Torrance and the Nature of Doctrine

Thomas F. Torrance is considered by many to be the leading Reformed theologian in the English-speaking world in the last fifty years.[19] Because of his seminal work in theology and science, he was awarded the Templeton Foundation Prize for Progress in Religion in 1978, the equivalent of the Nobel Prize.[20] Torrance's important and difficult book, *Theological Science*, received the first "Collins Award" in Britain for the best work in theology, ethics and sociology relevant to Christianity for 1967-1969.[21] Torrance started the *Scottish Journal of Theology*, which he edited for over thirty years, founded the "Scottish Church Theological Society," and served as Moderator of the Church of Scotland in 1976-77. He has also been deeply involved in the ecumenical movement and was a pivotal figure in the dialogue between Orthodox and Reformed

Churches.

Within the field of systematic theology, Torrance has written on all the main loci and their interrelations. He has also carried on a dialogue with the major areas of the history of the Christian tradition and has made significant contributions to Patristic and Reformation studies and the history of hermeneutics. Torrance has published well over six hundred items.

In his important book, *Theology and the Gospel of Christ*, E. L. Mascall maintains that Torrance has been a controversial figure in theology today "largely because he insists on bringing out into the light of day many issues that others are content to brush under the carpet."[22] Torrance, himself, indicates that his "main concern has been to clear the ground for a...[theology] thought out and expressed...within the rigorous scientific context in which we work."[23]

David Ford notes that "apart from his [Torrance's] students' work there has been practically no comprehensive critique of his large corpus."[24] Only a few analyses of Torrance's theology have been published beyond short book reviews.[25]

It is clear that Torrance is a major figure in contemporary theology who has made significant contributions to many aspects of systematic theology in terms of breadth, depth and relevance within the modern scientific context. This suggests that Torrance's work could have important implications for the present discussion concerning the nature of doctrine.

However, Professor Torrance has not written a book or even an article explicitly devoted to the subject of the nature of doctrine. Furthermore, while there have been a few published articles and books and a number of unpublished dissertations have been written on various aspects of Torrance's theology, it appears that no one has dealt with his understanding of the nature of doctrine. This is the reason for the publication of this work on *The Nature of Doctrine in T. F. Torrance's Theology*.

The significance of the monograph is two-fold: 1.) it delineates an aspect of Torrance's theology which has not been studied; and 2.) it also contributes to the ongoing discussion concerning the nature of doctrine. Torrance's understanding of doctrine does not fit Lindbeck's typology and it is significantly different than McGrath's proposal, though it addresses many of the issues raised by McGrath's "four theses" and develops what McGrath neglects–an understanding of the nature of doctrine integrated with a critical, epistemic realism and a number of other important theological and philosophical issues.

A complete bibliography of Torrance's writings fills nearly forty single-spaced pages.[26] While I have read the majority of what he has written, it is necessary to limit the scope of material treated in this work. Therefore, I discuss only Torrance's mature position on the nature of doctrine. I do not trace the development of his theology or the development of his understanding of the nature of doctrine. Furthermore, my book is primarily descriptive because the complexity of the nature of doctrine in Torrance's theology requires extended analysis and exposition.

Thus, I do not enter into detailed discussions concerning the accuracy of Torrance's interpretation of important figures and movements in the history of theology. Nor do I deal with many other significant facets of Torrance's thought like his dependence on Karl Barth, or the relation of Torrance's understanding of the nature of doctrine in theology to his conception of the character of theory in natural science. I also do not engage in any detailed comparison of the nature of doctrine in Torrance's thought and that of other important figures in the history of Christian theology, though I do include some comments in this regard. To pursue any of these subjects would lead to a massive work, beyond the bounds of a monograph such as this one. The depth, integration and difficulty of Torrance's conception of the nature of doctrine can only be captured in an extended analysis such as the one that follows. Curtailing such analysis in favor of discussing other issues would prove detrimental to a careful and comprehensive delineation of Torrance's own position.

Method: Interpreting Torrance's Position

Several characteristics of Torrance's published materials have significant implications for interpreting and presenting his understanding of the nature of doctrine. As mentioned above, he has not written a book or even an article devoted to his understanding of the nature of doctrine. He does, however, discuss the nature of doctrine in many places, but always within a matrix of other questions and concerns.

Furthermore, almost all of Torrance's articles and books relevant to the nature of doctrine were originally given in the form of lectures. There is significant overlap in content between different sets of lectures, especially those published under the following titles: *The Ground and Grammar of Theology*,

Reality and Evangelical Theology, *Transformation and Convergence in the Frame of Knowledge*, and *Reality and Scientific Theology*.[27] Torrance has not fully systematized these various discussions of his theology and method, including the nature of doctrine, though he is probably a bit like Ernst Troeltsch who said, "I keep one [a system] in the back of my head...but only to correct it constantly."[28] In addition, Torrance's writing style has been repeatedly criticized for its difficulty and tendency toward over compressed exposition.[29] His theological perspective is integrative and holistic, and when combined with his difficult writing-style, it makes reading and comprehending his work a formidable task.

A common consequence of these characteristics of Torrance's publications is that he is often grossly misunderstood, as in the case of Ronald Thiemann's discussion of Torrance's epistemology and charge that Torrance is a foundationalist.[30] A further consequence is that there is no easy method for gaining a comprehensive understanding of Torrance's theology other than carefully working through all of his major works. This is, undoubtedly, one of the reasons why his theology has not had as great an impact as one might expect. The result is that Torrance's understanding of the nature of doctrine only comes into view after a significant immersion in, and comparison of, his various writings.

Furthermore, in order to understand the nature of doctrine in T. F. Torrance's theology, one must see how doctrine is related to other elements within his theology. Charles Hefling, in his perceptive book, *Why Doctrines?*, follows a similar procedure in outlining his understanding of the nature of doctrine: "The following chapters aim at clarifying what doctrines are...what Christian doctrines are...not in words but by their relations to other things; not just verbally, that is, but functionally."[31] A similar procedure is needed in order to properly present Torrance's understanding of the nature of doctrine. Only by seeing the interrelation of doctrine and a number of other important facets of Torrance's theology will the nature of doctrine in his theology gradually come into view.

Thus, the structure of my book in not that of a progressive, sequential argument. Rather, the five chapters that follow discuss different facets of an integrated whole. The components of Torrance's theology treated in these five chapters are deeply integrated in Torrance's own thought and writings. This is intentional, for Torrance is a unitive or integrative thinker.

In the order of chapters that follows, each chapter will build upon those that precede it as the discussion progresses from one aspect of Torrance's theology to another in relation to the nature of doctrine. However, the order could have been different, though the sequence utilized here has certain strengths over others.

In any case, the order of chapters does not mirror steps in the development of Torrance's position. In fact, Torrance argues that questions of method, which are treated in chapters 1 and 2, cannot be settled prior to theological investigation, but only as theological inquiry progresses.[32] However, one has to enter the circular character of T. F. Torrance's theology somewhere and dealing with his basic assumptions and method is as good an access point as any.

Content: An Overview of Torrance's Position

Therefore, chapter 1 discusses some of Torrance's fundamental assumptions before outlining his epistemology, his understanding of how form is integrated or how concepts are derived. After recounting Torrance's analysis of the shift in the integration of form from Newton through Hume to Kant, Torrance's own position is analyzed in relation to Einstein and Michael Polanyi.

This section is of critical importance for understanding the nature of doctrine in Torrance's theology, for according to Torrance doctrine is, at least in part, an instance of a successful integration of form. The way Torrance conceives of the integration of form is pivotal for grasping a series of other significant elements of his thought including the social coefficient in knowing, the relation of language to being and the character of truth, all also crucial themes that further delineate the nature of doctrine in his theology.

The second chapter carries the discussion of the integration of form into the field of theology and doctrine. The opening section outlines Torrance's critique of certain trends in modern biblical and theological hermeneutics as a foil for developing Torrance's own position in the section that follows. Then the discussion is related to Torrance's "axiomatic dogmatics" and doctrine as an instance of the integration of form. The chapter closes with sections on the structure of belief in Torrance's thought and some critical questions regarding Torrance's proposal.

Torrance is convinced that there are no final, culturally-invariant categories in the Kantian sense that make up the structures of understanding.[33] Yet, he also argues that we never apprehend anything without a conceptual framework and without "engaging at once in forming judgements and developing interpretations about it."[34] This forces Torrance to address the importance of (and problems associated with) sociology of knowledge, to which Lindbeck and McGrath have rightly called attention. Chapter 3 treats Torrance's understanding of this "social coefficient" in knowledge of God and doctrine, and the way in which it can either impede or aid knowledge of God and the development of doctrine.

In Torrance's perspective, it is in the living Christian community that we learn the skills and develop a certain pattern of life and thought that is so important to theological inquiry. Doctrine is (and doctrines are) rooted in interrelated forms of life in social-conceptual fields.[35]

Thus the Christian community plays an indispensable role in all of theological inquiry, including doctrinal formulation. All real knowledge has a personal and social coefficient that cannot be eliminated and this coefficient conditions doctrine and the nature of doctrine. There is a certain similarity between this aspect of Torrance's theology and Lindbeck's notion of a "quasi-transcendental" *a priori*,[36] but with several critical differences which lead to quite different conceptions of the nature of doctrine.

However, since the Church interacts with the habits of thought and life of the surrounding culture, it can come to reflect those habits, assimilating them into its presuppositional framework, which, in turn, regulates its interpretation and appropriation of the Gospel from behind. In such a condition, the social coefficient can adversely affect the Church's life and thought, including its understanding of particular doctrines and also the nature of doctrine. Thus Torrance argues that theology must come to terms with the social conditioning of its concepts and doctrines.

Here Torrance's Reformed emphasis comes to the fore-front as he calls for repentant readiness to submit the Church's doctrinal heritage to critical scrutiny. The positions of Torrance and McGrath are very close on this point.

Despite this critical edge, Torrance sees doctrine as having an essentially positive role to play in the life of the Church, helping the people of God properly refer their thought beyond themselves to God. As part of the Church's total response to God, doctrine plays a role in establishing the Church as a community of reciprocity with God and with humanity. Doctrine guides and interprets, as well as generates, experience in Christian community and life.

However, Christian life and thought have a history arising out of the realities and events of God's self-revelation which doctrine must serve. This is the subject of chapter 4.

According to Torrance, God singled out Israel from among the nations for vicarious service in which Israel, through its long ordeal in history, became the "womb" for the incarnation of the Word of God, a "matrix" of appropriate forms of thought and speech for the reception and expression of God's ultimate self-revelation in Jesus Christ. Christ also established a nucleus of interpersonal reciprocities within the speaker-hearer relations of his disciples which became the controlling basis or apostolic foundation out of which the New Testament Scriptures were born and took shape within the Church.

Torrance maintains that doctrine is related to God through the biblical witness as the Church attends from that witness to the vicarious humanity of Jesus Christ himself as the "real text" through which the Word and Truth of God in its primary objectivity is known. Torrance's view of revelation as trinitarian cannot be understood without discussing the role of the Holy Spirit in the mediation of revelation through Scripture in the Church.

This discussion of the mediation of revelation and reconciliation influences how Torrance construes the character of Holy Scripture that serves as the source and norm of doctrine, for the Bible is only properly understood and authoritative as it points beyond itself to Jesus Christ who is the Truth of God. Chapter 4 outlines the relation of doctrine to the various facets of Torrance's "realist" interpretation of God's self-revelation.

The nature of doctrine in Torrance's theology cannot be understood without discussing the way he conceives of the nature of truth. This is the subject of Chapter 5.

Torrance operates with a stratified structure in our knowledge of God, a structure that he believes our knowledge assumes on the ground of God's self-revelation. This stratified structure helps clarify Torrance's understanding of the doctrine as disclosure model, for he maintains that one cannot state in statements how statements are related to reality, since this would substitute a logical or linguistic relation for a real relation. However, though the relation between language and reality cannot be precisely stated, reality shows through. When doctrine is appropriately integrated, it becomes "disclosive" of the reality to which it is a response.

Thus, for Torrance, doctrines are neither propositions, nor nondiscursive symbols of inner experiences, nor second-order rules governing first-order discourse. Rather doctrines are "paradigmatic media," "disclosure models," conceptual patterns through which a fuller disclosure of the Truth of God in Jesus Christ witnessed to in Scripture can take place.

This leads to a discussion of Torrance's understanding of doctrine in relation to the character of truth. Torrance rejects a strictly propositionalist or correspondence theory of truth.[37] In contrast, Torrance develops a stratified notion of truth in which the truth of statement, the truth of created reality, and the ultimate Truth of God reflect different levels of reality related and coordinated with one another. Doctrines can serve the Truth of God, but their truth is not to be found in themselves, but in a disclosive relation to the realities they signify.

Here Torrance, like his mentor Karl Barth, wants to guard (or better, acknowledge) the majesty and sovereignty of the Truth of God over all human conception and formulation of it. This imparts a certain open quality to doctrinal formulation that acknowledges doctrinal inadequacy and continuous revisability in light of further disclosure of the Truth of God.

The chapter closes with a treatment of Torrance's understanding of the justification of truth and authority in theology and doctrine. For Torrance, doctrine is authoritative only as it points beyond itself to the "*autousia*" and "*autexousia*" of God.[38] Thus, Torrance argues that the truth and authority of doctrine is cast back upon the Truth and Authority of God in Jesus Christ. This implies that, in the end, justification by faith is applied to the justification of truth in theology and doctrine as well. Yet, this does not discount, but rather establishes, the authority and freedom of the Church and doctrine to serve the Truth of God.

The concluding section draws various elements in Torrance's understanding of the nature of doctrine together in a final restatement of the salient features of his position.

Notes

1. George Lindbeck, *The Nature of Doctrine: Religion and Theology in a Postliberal Age* (Philadelphia: Westminster Press, 1984).

2. Ibid., p. 16.

3. Ibid.

4. Ibid.

5. Ibid., pp. 16 and 21.

6. Ibid., p. 17.

7. Ibid., p. 16. Lindbeck also states that, "The currently most familiar theological theories of religion can, for our purposes, be divided into three types." Ibid. He discusses these three types and then asserts that, "This book proposes an alternative." Ibid., p. 17. This alternative–Lindbeck's own–becomes the fourth type. Yet in the "Foreward" Lindbeck refers to his own approach as "a third, a postliberal, way" of conceiving religion and doctrine. Ibid., p. 7. Though somewhat confusing, readers can grasp Lindbeck's intent by remembering that he subsumes the third synthetic hybrid under the earlier approaches (cognitive-propositionalism and experiential-expressivism). In so doing, Lindbeck's own proposal then becomes the "third" model.

8. Ibid., pp. 17-18.

9. Ibid., p. 18.

10. Michael H. McCarthy, *The Crisis of Philosophy* (Albany: State University of New York Press, 1990), pp. xvii-xx, 60-66, 226 and 227-28.

11. While Lindbeck's typology is helpful in illuminating his own cultural-linguistic paradigm, it is unable to cope with the complexity and differences within the field it seeks to schematize. His book has been criticized repeatedly for its inadequate characterization of rival theories, especially the cognitivist approach. See Alister E. McGrath, *The Genesis of Doctrine: A Study in the Foundations of Doctrinal Criticism* (Cambridge, Mass.: Basil Blackwell Inc., 1990), pp. 14-34 for a sensitive criticism of Lindbeck's typology, and pp. 237-259 for a comprehensive bibliography of the debate concerning Lindbeck's book and the nature of doctrine. In defense of Lindbeck, it should be noted that he is dealing with *ideal types* which by their very nature are not rigidly embodied in particular theological perspectives.

12. See the previous note (11).

13. See ibid., pp. vii-viii. McGrath is developing an agenda suggested by G. F. Woods' paper, "Doctrinal Criticism," found in *Prospect for Theology*, ed. F. G. Healey (London: James Nisbit, 1966), pp. 73-92. See McGrath, *Doctrine*, p. 204.

14. Ibid., p. viii.

15. Ibid., p. ix. McGrath grants considerable concessions to historical consciousness. See chapter 4-6.

16. Ibid., p. viii.

17. See ibid., pp. 25-26 for McGrath's criticism of Lindbeck on this point.

18. Ibid., p. 28. Ronald Thiemann forthrightly argues for "theology without revelation" in his important book, *Revelation and Theology: The Gospel as Narrated Promise* (Notre Dame, Ind.: University of Notre Dame Press, 1985). The kind of narrative theology of Thiemann and Lindbeck, which seems to eschew the concept of revelation, is in part a reaction against the perceived revelational "actualism" of Barth.

19. I. John Hesselink, "A Pilgrimage in the School of Christ–An Interview with T. F. Torrance," *Reformed Review* 38, no. 1 (1984): 47.

20. Ibid..

21. Thomas F. Torrance, *Theological Science* (London: Oxford University Press, 1969).

22. E. L. Mascall, *Theology and the Gospel of Christ* (London: SPCK, 1977), p. 49.

23. See Hesselink, "Pilgrimage," p. 22.

24. See Ford's review of Thomas F. Torrance, *Reality and Scientific Theology* in the *Scottish Journal of Theology* 41 (July 1988): 276. For an initial analysis and evaluation of Torrance's work, see the essays written by various theologians from Europe and North America in Elmer M. Colyer, ed., *The Promise of Trinitarian Theology: Theologians in Dialogue with T. F. Torrance* (Lanham, Md.: Rowman & Littlefield, 2001).

25. See "Secondary Sources" in the Bibliography at the end of this monograph. There are two book-length introductions to Torrance's theology published to date: Alister E. McGrath, *T. F. Torrance: An Intellectual Biography* (Edinburgh: T & T Clark, 1999) and Elmer M. Colyer, *How to Read T. F. Torrance: Understanding His Trinitarian and Scientific Theology* (Downers Grove, Ill.: InterVarsity Press, 2001).

26. See McGrath, *Torrance*, pp. 250-96.

27. *The Ground and Grammar of Theology* (Charlottesville: The University of Virginia Press, 1980); *Reality and Evangelical Theology* (Philadelphia: Westminster Press, 1982); *Transformation and Convergence in the Frame of Knowledge* (Grand Rapids: Eerdmans, 1984); and *Reality and Scientific Theology* (Edinburgh: Scottish Academic Press, 1985).

28. See Ernst Troeltsch, "Meine Bücher" in *Gesammelte Schriften*, vol. IV. (Tubingen: J. C. B. Mohr, 1925), p. 4.

29. See, for example, Daniel Hardy's article, "Thomas F. Torrance" in *The Modern Theologians: An Introduction to Christian Theology in the Twentieth Century*, ed. David F. Ford (New York: Basil Blackwell Inc., 1989), I:86. Torrance acknowledges the difficulty of his writing style. See Michael Bauman, *Roundtable: Conversations with European Theologians* (Grand Rapids: Baker Book House, 1990), pp. 117-8.

30. See Thiemann, *Revelation*, pp. 32-45. Part of Thiemann's problem is his highly selective reading of Torrance, treating only three of Torrance's books. This kind of approach to understanding Torrance is inadequate to the character of Torrance's publication.

31. Charles C. Hefling, Jr., *Why Doctrines?* (Cambridge, Mass.: Cowley Publications, 1984), p. 2.

32. See Torrance, *Theological Science*, pp. 2, 9, and 10.

33. Ibid., p. 92.

34. Ibid., p. viii.

35. See Thomas F. Torrance, *God and Rationality* (New York: Oxford University Press, 1971), pp. 16-17.

36. Lindbeck, *Doctrine*, pp. 33 and 36-37.

37. Those who link Torrance closely with the tradition of Scottish "Common Sense" realism should consider this point carefully. Torrance's realism is quite different than that of fundamentalism and evangelical rationalism.

38. See Thomas F. Torrance, "Theological Realism," in *The Philosophical Frontiers of Christian Theology*, eds. B. Hebblethwaite and S. Sutherland (New York: Cambridge University Press, 1982), pp. 180-81.

Chapter 1

Method and the Integration of Form

The Fundamental Axiom of Torrance's Theology

The fundamental axiom that runs throughout Thomas F. Torrance's theological writings is that it is the nature of the object or subject matter under investigation which determines the methods utilized in examining it, the mode of rationality employed in conceptualizing what is disclosed, and the form of verification in accordance with it.[1] Torrance describes theology "as a dogmatic, or positive and independent, science operating on its own ground and in accordance with the inner law of its own being, developing distinctive modes of inquiry and its essential forms of thought under the determination of its given subject-matter."[2] It is the strict application of this axiom to all aspects of theological endeavor which leads to a rigorous *scientific* theology.

Torrance operates with a refined understanding of science and readers who fail to grasp it often misread his work. A scientific theology, in Torrance's perspective, does *not* conform to the presuppositions and/or procedures of a universally applicable science, a *scientia universalis* (there is no universal science according to Torrance, despite certain philosophies that claim otherwise). Nor does theology conform to other specific sciences (*scientiae speciales*) like natural science. Theological science, for Torrance, like every special science, *has its own particular scientific requirements and material procedures determined by the unique nature of its object or subject matter.*

Thus there are simply various special sciences with various formal similarities (like Torrance's basic axiom) because they are human inquiries in space and time. The special sciences can and should learn from one another, as Torrance has from natural science. Yet each science must be rigorous in faithfulness to the nature of the object or subject matter in its investigation. So for Torrance, theology can be scientific if God is in fact knowable and when theology allows actual knowledge of God (the nature of theology's object/subject matter) to determine all aspects of theology, including generating the form of life and conceptual structures (doctrines) appropriate to that knowledge.

In fulfilling its task, scientific theology "seeks to unfold and present the content of the Word of God within the limits of the Church prescribed for it by the incarnation and apostolic foundation, and to articulate that content today through an examination of the doctrinal decisions in the past."[3] Such theology investigates the essential interrelations of the various constitutive elements of the Christian faith and brings them to articulation in doctrine.

However, it is the task of "Philosophy of Theology" (which is analogous to philosophy of science in the sphere of natural science) to "clarify the processes of scientific activity in theology, to throw human thinking of God back upon God as its direct and proper Object, and thus to serve the self-scrutiny of theology as a pure science."[4] The fact that method must be apposite to the nature of the reality under investigation implies four further points concerning Torrance's understanding of "philosophy of scientific theology" (theological method).

First, method can be distinguished, but never separated, from content. One cannot lay down the conditions upon which valid knowledge is possible in detachment from the actual knowing relation, for to do so is to risk the danger of allowing habits of mind uncritically formed or acquired from some other field of inquiry to influence and distort the apprehension and expression of the reality in question.[5]

Therefore, second, Torrance argues that an adequate account of theological epistemology cannot be developed apart from substantial exposition of the knowledge of God. "This means that all the way through theological inquiry we must operate with an *open* epistemology in which we allow the way of our knowing to be clarified and modified *pari passu* with advance in deeper and fuller knowledge of the object."[6] As Daniel Hardy has pointed out, this explains why Torrance has given so much attention to the reality with which theology is concerned, while at the same time carefully attending to the philosophy of theology (theological method).[7]

This implies, third, that there is a delicate dialectical relationship between positive theology and philosophy of theology which acknowledges the difficulty posed by the fact that "the act of observing interferes...with our knowledge of it [the real]," while also maintaining "that it is possible to gradually refine and elaborate methods that will carry within themselves self-correcting devices so that we may always be directed away from ourselves to the compulsive force of the objective connections in the real world."[8] Reality is capable of human apprehension and linguistic expression, an assumption that Torrance believes is continuously operative in everyday human experience and in every field of inquiry, despite the problems raised by modernity's turn to the subjective pole of knowledge, and postmodernity's rejection of all foundationalist epistemologies which claim to render entirely explicit the conditions under which genuine knowledge is possible.[9]

Torrance rejects epistemological dualisms which presuppose a chasm between the human knower and what we seek to know.[10] Epistemological dualism asserts that the human knower cannot know "reality" or the thing-in-itself (Kant's infamous *Ding an sich*) because human knowing is always influenced by culture, language and the structures/activities of the mind operative in the process of knowing.

In place of epistemological dualism between subject and object, Torrance embraces a critical realist epistemology in which there is a *potential* correlation, an achievable isophormism, a *possible* continuity between subject and object presupposed by everyone in everyday life in the world and confirmed by successful scientific endeavor. For Torrance, reality (contingent and Divine) discloses itself in such a manner that it is *possible* for human beings to apprehend it. Scientific knowledge, natural and theological, is "a rigorous and disciplined extension" of ordinary ways of knowing and "as such applies to every area of human life and thought."[11]

Fourth, this means that Torrance is a realist but only in a qualified sense.[12] If realism means a *necessary* correspondence or *inherent* isomorphism between reality and the human mind/thought (a static analogy of being, for instance), then Torrance is not a realist.[13] However, in another sense Torrance is a realist, for he argues, as Hardy points out, that there can be "an *actual* correspondence between reality and thought or language *if* the thinker is conformed to the mode of rationality afforded by reality....Scientific knowledge might therefore be described as proceeding within a 'double activity,' wherein reality actively gives itself, together with the appropriate mode of knowing it, and we actively responding by knowing it in the fashion it provides."[14] When this takes place there is real knowledge and a correlation or transparence between the human mind/thought and reality.[15] For Torrance genuine knowledge is neither impossible not inevitable since the human mind plays an active role in knowing which requires the generation (discovery *and* creation) of the appropriate forms of thought, speech and life in order for authentic knowledge of reality in its interrelations to take place.

It is the struggle to overcome our "artificiality" (humanity's tendency impose preconceived conceptual structures upon reality), to generate appropriate methods and fitting conceptual patterns, which leads to the proper formation of the human subject in relation to the object of knowledge, whether it is the world of nature or God.[16] Torrance also suggests that this struggle is one of the factors that accounts for a certain commonality between theological science and other special sciences, for they share a similar problem: "how to refer our thoughts and statements genuinely beyond ourselves, how to reach knowledge of reality...and yet how to retain the full and integral place of the human subject in it all," since we never "apprehend anything without engaging at once in forming judgements and developing interpretations about it."[17]

This, of course, is the age-old problem in philosophy, theology, and science of the relationship between the discovery of form or intelligibility and the creation/imposition of it in human rational activity. These last statements show that Torrance accepts the essential point in the rise of historical consciousness as formulated by James Brown in his important study, *Subject and Object in Modern Theology*, that "we are inevitably and inseparably inside the knowledge relation, from the start to the end, and so cannot step outside of ourselves to an indifferent standpoint from which to view and adjust the relations of thought and being."[18]

Torrance sees the issues and problems surrounding the integration of form (how concepts are derived or how appropriate categories are generated in human knowing) in the modern period as of critical importance for theology and theological method. A major part of Torrance's work in the area of theological method deals with issues and problems related to the integration of form.

In a sense, doctrine for Torrance is, in part, an instance of the successful integration of form or intelligibility in human knowledge of God. Thus understanding how Torrance conceives of the integration of form provides significant insight into his conception of the nature of doctrine. It also illumines many other aspects of Torrance's theology in relation to doctrine and its character.

In order to understand Torrance's formulation of how form is integrated in theology it is important to understand his analysis of the shift in the integration of form from Newton through Hume to Kant, for Torrance argues that

> this is the great story of modern thought, whether in theology, science, or philosophy: the struggle for fidelity, for the appropriate methods and apposite modes of speech, and therefore for the proper adaptation of the human subject to the object of his knowledge, whether it be God or the world of nature or man; but it is also the story of the struggles of man with himself, for somehow the more he comes to know, the more masterful he tries to be and the more he imposes himself upon reality, the more he gets in the way of his own progress.[19]

Here we see the connection between the fundamental axiom that runs through Torrance's writings and his discussion of the integration of form in the modern world from Newton to Kant.

Integration of Form From Newton To Kant

There are many places in Torrance's writings where he deals with the basic shift in epistemological orientation from Newton through Hume to Kant or the "making of the modern mind," as he calls it.[20] But the most fully developed discussion of it appears in chapter 1 of *Transformation and Convergence in the Frame of Knowledge.*[21]

Torrance sees two "fateful forces" at work shaping the "modern" mind: 1.) the transposition of intelligibility from the objective to the human subjective pole in the knowing relation (and the subsequent loss of the idea of inherent intelligibility in nature); 2.) the developing notion that humanity can understand and verify only what it creates for itself.[22] In other words, the modern turn to the subject, when combined with the notion of autonomous reason and a dualistic epistemology, with its isolation of the human subject over against nature, leads to what

F. A. Hayek calls "constructivist rationalism" that has infected many aspects of modern technological society and has had a dramatic impact on biblical studies and theology.[23]

According to Torrance, Descartes and Newton, in unique but parallel ways, "built into the fabric of Western thought a fundamental dualism between subject and object on the one hand and between God and the world on the other hand."[24] The hiatus between subject and object tended to restrict the human subject to inner states of consciousness over against the world of nature as the object of knowledge.[25] This led to a notion of *representative perception* (subjective representations or sense data between the objective material world and the immaterial human mind) controlling the relation between the human subject and nature as the object of knowledge.

The result over time of this kind of representative perception has been the modern turn to the mental processes and inner consciousness of the human subject, rather than the intelligible intrinsic interrelations in the objective world of nature.[26] The goal, of course, of the modern analysis of human subjectivity was the development of an account (a foundation) of how the human mind achieves knowledge of the material world through the subjective representations or sense data which mediate between the material world of nature and the human mind. Herein lies the modern quest for (and more recently critique of) an epistemology which renders entirely explicit the conditions for real knowledge (epistemological foundationalism).

Newton

Torrance argues that Newton accepted Descartes' dualism and "subjective representations" between the human mind and the objective structure of the natural world, including a sharp distinction between mind and matter.[27] He thought that sense data was somehow related to the mind through a particular part of the brain (the *sensorium*). Newton, however, was far more convinced than Descartes that these notorious "secondary qualities" which "arise in the sensorium are in some sense properties of nature, for they are sensations of motions or dispositions in the external world."[28]

Yet, while Newton emphasized the discovery of form in nature and a close connection between scientific concepts/theories and sensory experience, Torrance contends that

Newton never really solved Descartes' fundamental dualism, but rather built it into the structure of Western science.[29] However, Torrance believes that it was also Newton's understanding of the process by which form is discovered and integrated in scientific inquiry (how concepts are derived) that led to significant problems in both science and philosophy.

Newton conceived of natural science, Torrance suggests, as an inquiry into "the causal inter-action between corporeal things in terms of 'manifest principles' which it derives from phenomena."[30] Scientific concepts are deduced from phenomena or derived by a process of abstraction from observation or from sense data. Newton asserted the point in his famous *hypotheses non fingo* (I frame no hypotheses) for "whatever is not deduced from phenomena, is to be called an hypothesis; and hypotheses, whether metaphysical or physical, whether occult qualities or mechanical, have no place in experimental philosophy. In this philosophy particular propositions are inferred from the phenomena, and afterward rendered general by induction."[31] Torrance concurs with E. A. Burtt who contends that science for Newton is a form of inquiry yielding laws deducible from phenomena which state the mathematical behavior of nature. Science becomes absolutely certain truth about the characteristics of the natural world.[32]

The human subject, thus, plays a minor part in the integration of form (derivation of concepts) and is understood as discovery, rather than construction and/or imposition of form. For this reason, Einstein said of Newton that, "Nature to him was an open book, whose letters he could read without effort. The conceptions which he used to reduce the material of experience to order seemed to flow spontaneously from experience itself, from the beautiful experiments which he ranged in order like playthings and describes with affectionate wealth of detail."[33]

However, the problem, which Hume soon so pointedly exposed, is that this was not how Newton actually conducted his scientific endeavor. Newton was cognizant of the issue, for he did not–and could not–derive absolute space and time, theoretical concepts so crucial for his conceptualization of laws of motion, from observation nor could he abstract them from experience. Thus Newton said that "It is a matter of great difficulty to discover and effectually to distinguish the true motions of particular bodies from the apparent, because the parts of that immovable space in which those motions are performed do by no means come under the observation of our senses."[34]

Torrance notes that at precisely this point, Newton had to utilize theoretical components that he did not develop by abstraction from observation in order make sense of the empirical. Thus Torrance argues that

> in the last resort what Newton did was to fall back upon his profound belief that the universe, far from being arbitrary, has been so constructed that in the simplicity and uniformity of its natural order it is accessible to our theoretical analysis and synthesis; and then in light of that conviction to posit the concepts of absolute time and space, independent of the empirical processes that fall within their embrace...[as] the simplest way of linking together the manifold features of nature...to form a comprehensive system of the world that was logically coherent and complete.[35]

In addition, it was the amazing success of Newton's work, for example in the presentation of a consistent and precise account of motion, that rendered plausible absolute time and space and the theoretical explanation of his scientific procedure. Torrance points out that this actually blinded Newton's successors to "the fictitious character" of absolute space and time and also misled them into believing that scientific theories and concepts must be abstracted from phenomena or deduced from sense data.[36] The basic question is *how* concepts are generated and integrated with the empirical world around us, for Newton's actual practice did not follow his theoretical account of his methodology.

Hume

However, Torrance argues that Hume, who had accepted the picture of passive perception and active reason from empiricists like Locke, uncovered this difficulty in Newton's account of how form is integrated by revealing that crucial theoretical components like space, time and causality are not simply "given" in sensory experience. Hume's analysis demonstrated that the relation between one observed fact and another is simply contingent in an account purely based on sense perception. As Hume states the point: "Objects have no discoverable connection together; nor is it from any other principle but custom operating upon imagination, that we can draw inference from the appearance of one to the existence of another."[37] When a stone shatters a glass what we actually "see" is a stream of impressions. We assert that the stone is the "cause" of the breaking glass. But what the senses give is only a series of perceptions of the stone and the glass.[38] In light of his analysis, Hume defines a cause as, "an object followed by another, and whose appearance always conveys the thought to that other."[39]

In spite of the fact that Hume's account seems to contradict our human experience, his critique created a major impasse for the empirical conceptualization of human knowledge, for as Torrance notes, "If no intrinsic or necessary connection is perceivable between one observed factor and another, then some of the most important components of scientific knowledge, e.g. in Newton's system of the world, such as substance, relation, causality, are not reached through sense experience, and cannot be employed in inductive operations from phenomena."[40] Hume's critique provided the shock that awakened Kant from his "dogmatic slumber," for Hume demonstrated the inadequate character of a exclusively empirical account of the integration of form.

Kant

Immanuel Kant, who was a mathematician and astronomer himself, realized that a different and more satisfactory account had to be developed outlining how form is integrated in everyday human knowing and in scientific inquiry, an account in which theoretical elements, not abstracted or deduced from observation, operate along with empirical ingredients in scientific inquiry and ordinary experience. Thus, Torrance sees Kant's significant contribution to the development of European thought to be the construction of an epistemology in which the empirical perspective of Locke, Berkeley and Hume is synthesized with the more rationalist method of Descartes and Leibniz. It is an epistemology in which purely theoretical *a priori* components operate together with empirical *a posteriori* ingredients in all knowing, whether in ordinary human life or in scientific inquiry.[41]

Since Kant's *a priori* categories and structures of the human mind are the necessary condition for the possibility of intelligible experience, Kant contends that human beings cannot know the thing-in-itself (*Ding an sich*), but only how things appear through the conceptual grid we bring to all cognitive activity. Furthermore, in light of the fact that Kant's categories are unchanging, they cannot be criticized or modified by experience.

This means, Torrance maintains, that the accent is no longer on the *discovery* form, as it was for Newton. In stark contrast, intelligibility and all theoretical components in knowledge are moved to the subjective pole of the knowing relation (the human mind categorizes sense data so that it becomes intelligible) which, in turn, leads to the idea that humanity can only really understand that which it creates.[42] This is an "inversion of the knowing relation and a constructivist mentality" which Torrance contends is all too characteristic of "the modern mind."[43]

In Kant's view the human mind projects patterns upon what is external to it, since this was the only alternative that he could see (in light of Hume's skepticism) which could stabilize the astonishing advances of Newtonian science. Thus we find Kant's famous statement in his *Critique of Pure Reason*: "Hitherto it has been assumed that all our knowledge must conform to objects....We must...make trial whether we may not have more success in the tasks of metaphysics, if we suppose that objects must conform to our knowledge."[44] Torrance also argues that the concept of the inherent intelligibility in nature also began to recede, since Kant was compelled to concede that "the understanding is itself the source of the laws of nature, and so for its formal unity."[45]

The shift was now complete and the accent is almost entirely upon the *imposition* of form rather than the discovery of form. Torrance goes on to trace the deep problems this created for Protestant theology of the nineteenth and early twentieth centuries that accepted Kant's basic epistemological orientation.[46] Similar problems occurred in natural science impacted as it was by this making of the modern mind.[47] The effect of the shift in understanding in reference to the integration of form is clearly evident in the way in which theology and doctrine came to be conceived.

Schleiermacher, Lindbeck and Doctrine

It is at just this point that George Lindbeck locates the genesis of what he calls the "experiential-expressivist" understanding of religion and doctrine. Lindbeck maintains that Kant, "helped clear the ground for its [expressivism] emergence by demolishing the metaphysical and epistemological foundations of the earlier regnant cognitive-propositional views...[a] ground-clearing that was later completed for most educated people by scientific developments that increased the difficulties of accepting literalistic propositional interpretation of such biblical doctrines as creation, and by historical studies that implied the time-conditioned relativity of all doctrines."[48]

Lindbeck also observes that Kant's "reduction of God to a transcendental condition (albeit a necessary one) of morality seemed to the sensibilities of most religious people to leave religion intolerably impoverished."[49] This breach was filled by Schleiermacher (and the many forms of experiential-expressivism which followed) who moved the ground of religion to the one place that Kant's critiques had not touched: the specific "the feeling of utter dependence" (*das schlechtinnige Abhängigkeitsgefühl*) at the center of religion.[50]

Thus early in his systematic theology, *The Christian Faith*, Schleiermacher suggests that, "The common element in all howsoever diverse expressions of piety, by which these are conjointly distinguished from all other feelings, or, in other words, the self-identical essence of piety, is this, the consciousness of being utterly dependent, or, which is the same thing, of being in relation with God."[51] God is the "Whence" or "Co-determinant" in this feeling.[52]

In Schleiermacher's perspective, doctrines are not propositions communicating cognitive information about the religious thing-in-itself (God). Doctrines express the human prereflective religious experience of absolute dependence on something (God) beyond the human self.

Schleiermacher, according to Lindbeck, it the father of experiential-expressivism in its various forms. Expressivism views religions, including Christianity, as culturally-conditioned manifestations of a common pre-linguistic core experience at the center of all religion. In Lindbeck's own words: "Various religions are diverse symbolizations of one and the same core experience of the Ultimate."[53] Doctrines are simply cultural-specific expressions of aspects of a homogeneous experience.

I will not rehearse Lindbeck's damaging critique of expressivism. When combined with Alister McGrath's additional criticism,[54] Lindbeck's case against this stream of modern theology is quite damaging. However, does Schleiermacher fit Lindbeck's description of expressivism? I agree with McGrath and Charles Hefling[55] that Schleiermacher does not neatly fit Lindbeck's typology.[56] As McGrath points out, "Christian doctrine according to Schleiermacher, does not concern some 'prereflective experience' common to all religions but concerns the distinctively Christian experience of Jesus of Nazareth." Second, this experience is not private, but communal, related to Jesus through the actual history of the Christian community "constituted by an ongoing tradition of faith and worship, and perhaps, of theology as well," as Hefling points out.[57]

Still, when one examines some of Schleiermacher's actual doctrinal discussions, one is left with the uneasy feeling that there is more than a grain of truth in Lindbeck's criticism. There is no doubt that Schleiermacher radically reconceived the nature of doctrine in light of the problems created for the cognitive-propositionalist understanding by Hume and Kant, among others. Schleiermacher's grounding of religion and doctrine in immediate self-consciousness (*Gefühl*) has provided a paradigm exceedingly attractive to many intellectuals throughout the modern period.

Nevertheless, Schleiermacher's brilliant reconstruction does not really solve the problems latent in Kant's epistemology. Rather, Schleiermacher simply adjusts Christian faith and the nature of doctrine as to avoid those problems.

We must ask whether Lindbeck's own "cultural-linguistic" alternative has really made all that much progress beyond expressivism in overcoming the problems posed for religion and doctrine by Kant's "solution" regarding the integration of form (how concepts are derived). While Lindbeck's position is in many respects an improvement, it still does not surmount the basic epistemic difficulties latent in Kant's proposal.

According to Lindbeck, religions are cultural-linguistic frameworks which precede experience. Thus he asserts that, "a religion can be viewed as a kind of cultural and/or linguistic framework or medium that shapes the entirety of life and thought....It is not primarily an array of beliefs...or a symbolism expressive of basic attitudes, feelings, or sentiments....Rather, it is similar to an idiom that makes possible the description of realities, the formulation of beliefs, and the experiencing of inner attitudes, feelings, and sentiments."[58]

In a sense, what Lindbeck does is historicize Kant's *a priori* by employing a "cultural-linguistic" paradigm as the theoretical framework for understanding religion and doctrine. Religion, for Lindbeck, becomes a "kind of cultural and/or linguistic framework....It functions somewhat like a Kantian *a priori*...,"[59] though rather than innate in the human mind (as in Kant), it is socially acquired. But make no mistake, though only "quasi-transcendental (i.e., culturally formed)," it is still an "*a priori* for the *possibility* of experience."[60]

At certain points in his discussion Lindbeck seems to admit a more dialectical relation between the cultural-linguistic framework and experience, between the theoretical and experiential, than is evident in this last quotation. But then there are many other places where he simply asserts that "it is necessary to have the means for expressing an experience in order to have it."[61]

In light of the quasi-transcendental (culturally-formed) character of the Christian idiom (the Christian cultural-linguistic framework), McGrath raises a rather disconcerting question for Lindbeck's project: "How does the Christian idiom come into being?"[62] McGrath accuses Lindbeck of "a studied evasion of the central question of revelation...whether the Christian idiom, articulated in scripture and hence in the Christian tradition, originates from accumulated human insight, or from the self-disclosure of God in the Christ-event."[63] McGrath may be a bit unfair toward Lindbeck on this point, forgetting that Lindbeck explicitly states that his argument and his proposed paradigm are designed to be doctrinally and religiously neutral, and therefore not aimed at the kind of *material* question McGrath poses.[64]

Nevertheless, when Lindbeck says that technical theology and official doctrine are second-order discourse (doctrines are rules–sort of like the grammar–of Christian discourse) that seldom if ever succeed in making affirmations of ontological import and when one considers the philosophical commitments of his cultural-linguistic paradigm, it is difficult to see how Lindbeck can avoid the central point of McGrath's criticism. Without a doctrine of revelation and an element of critical realism in his construal of the relation between the Christian language and form of life, and the realities that Christian faith intends (Jesus Christ, the Triune God, etc.), it seems that the

Christian idiom is dangerously near to some form of conventionalism or fideism.[65] Or, to put it another way, is Lindbeck able to transcend his fateful identification of religion (and every cultural-linguistic framework) with a quasi-transcendental Kantian *a priori* and provide an adequate construal of how form is integrated in theology? Lindbeck simply assumes the existence of religious cultural-linguistic frameworks without ever dealing with their genesis or adequacy. While illuminating and helpful, Lindbeck leaves all too many questions unanswered, especially epistemological ones.

These criticisms, however, in no way invalidate the significance of Lindbeck's book and its many germinal insights, including the importance of a cultural-linguistic framework in the discussion of how form is integrated, a subject to which we will return in chapter 3.

Integration of Form: Einstein, Polanyi & Torrance

It is clear from the earlier discussion of the integration of form from Newton to Kant that Torrance believes there were deep and unresolved difficulties in the way these important modern thinkers construed basic epistemological issues. Furthermore, Torrance also sees the basic tendencies operative within the "modern mind" affecting theology and natural science. Those theologians or biblical scholars who have remained within the general horizon of what Torrance calls "the modern mind" tended to perpetuate those difficulties in their own fields, including the way doctrine was conceived.[66] The same could be said of natural science.[67]

Or to state the point positively, Torrance sees Newton, with his stress on the discovery of form, and Kant, with his emphasis on the constant coordination of theoretical and empirical ingredients, as both partially correct and partly mistaken. Kant took a major step forward in conceptualizing how form integrated by demonstrating that Newton had operated with a constant coordination of empirical and theoretical elements of knowledge in such a way that the theoretical components were not directly abstracted from observation or deduced from sense data.[68]

However, Kant was mistaken in his conception of the *manner* in which these ingredients are fused, since he conceptualized this relation as necessary and legislative cognitive structures imposed upon all our experience of the world in order to render sense data intelligible.[69] There is "a profound element of truth here," Torrance maintains, since "in all our knowing there is a real interplay between what we know and our knowing of it" and since "we do not apprehend things apart from a theoretic structure."[70] Nevertheless, Torrance argues that if our conceptual elements determine what we apprehend, then what we seek to know can provide no control over our understanding it.[71] Human "knowledge" becomes almost exclusively constructive.

Newton was correct on this point: that form must be correlated with the intelligibility of what we attempt to know.[72] However, Torrance contends that Newton did not fully realize that theoretical ingredients exert a considerable influence in our apprehension of the world and these ingredients are not abstracted from observation or deduced directly from sense data.[73]

Without dismissing either Newton nor Kant, Torrance maintains that, "The one way out of that impasse requires a theoretic structure which, while affecting our knowledge, is derived from the intrinsic intelligibility of what we seek to know, and is open to constant revision through reference to the inner determinations of things as they come to view in the process of inquiry."[74] It is at this point that Torrance finds the work of Einstein and Polanyi (and Karl Barth) helpful in his attempt to articulate a more adequate understanding of the way in which form can be integrated in everyday experience and in scientific inquiry. Here, Torrance claims to be following the horizon-shift in the fundamental conception of reality and in the integration of form inculcated through the astonishing discoveries of Faraday, Maxwell, Einstein, Michael Polanyi, and others (including, Torrance would argue, Karl Barth).[75]

According to Torrance, it was not until these discoveries that the deep and unresolved epistemological difficulties latent in modern thought began to be surmounted. As Torrance sees it, Faraday, Maxwell, Einstein and Polanyi in natural science, and Karl Barth in theology, were all struggling against the modern mind or "general frame of knowledge" conditioned by the intellectual history from Descartes and Newton through Hume and Kant and the brilliant European culture with which they are associated.[76]

This does *not* mean that Torrance borrows his epistemology from modern Einsteinian and post-Einsteinian science and philosophy of science–a common misunderstanding of his position.[77] Rather, in examining modern science and philosophy of science Torrance discovered that Christian theology (as renewed through the work of Karl Barth) and natural science (Faraday, Maxwell, Einstein and Polanyi) were both struggling with similar sets of epistemological problems arising out of the received framework of thought.[78]

I will first discuss several elements of this horizon-shift in natural science (from Faraday and Maxwell through Einstein, Polanyi and others) relevant to Torrance's understanding of the integration of form before outlining Torrance's position in relation to Einstein and Polanyi.

A Horizon-shift in Natural Science

What Torrance has in mind when he refers to this horizon-shift in how reality is conceived and how form is integrated is clarified in his important article, "The Integration of Form in Natural and Theological Science," though Torrance discusses the matter in other places.[79] Torrance points out that

> In recent years a distinct shift has been taking place in the philosophy of science, which is now becoming very noticeable. Not long ago when one asked a natural scientist to give an account of his scientific method, it often became evident that he had not reflected very deeply about it, and just as often he tended to put forward a theory of science which did not seem to accord very well with the empirico-theoretical steps he had taken in making his discoveries, but in which he fell back into earlier positivist ideas derived through his own theoretical upbringing, not least the uncritical assumption that all things in the last analysis are capable of logico-causal explanation in purely physico-chemical terms.[80]

What Torrance sees in the older science (positivism, for example) is an inadequate method interconnected with a reductionist ontology in which higher levels of created reality are explained downward in terms of logico-causal interconnections at the purely physico-chemical level.

In order to disclose this horizon-shift in how reality is

conceived (no longer simply in logico-causal categories) and how form is integrated, Torrance discusses Sir John C. Eccles' work on the interaction of brain and conscious mind, an interaction that reveals "the emergence of properties which are of a different kind from anything that has been as yet related to matter with its properties as defined in physics and chemistry."[81] What Torrance (and Eccles) is suggesting is that a higher level of reality–conscious mind–displays properties that are not completely amenable to physico-chemical, causal explanation. In other words, this higher level of reality (conscious mind), by its very character as it has come to view in the forward movement of Eccles' scientific inquiry, cannot be adequately explained by the properties of physics and chemistry and therefore may not be reduced to the terms of that lower level.[82] The older modern science with its hard mechanistic, instrumentalist character is unable to match the actual modes of relation (disclosed by Eccles's work) found to exist in reality.[83]

The same is true of quantum theory, relativity theory and the kinds of relations that obtain in the biological field, for each require more subtle and elastic forms of conceptualization in order to appropriately express the dynamic relations found to inhere in reality.[84] Torrance also suggests that sociological and historical fields of inquiry are likewise not amenable to the restrictive methods and conceptualities in what he calls "causalist science" or "modern instrumentalist science."[85] Whatever else this new science–that of Eccles and others–is, it is a kind of science concerned with relations where the real relations in the world of space and time are brought to articulation through appropriate conceptual relations.[86]

Torrance is pointing to the shift from modern observationalist and positivist science, with its explanatory "reduction downwards" of all reality to the level of atomic particles and with its conceptual structures viewed as pragmatic and instrumentalist in character,[87] to the "new conception of science" resulting from the work of Maxwell, Einstein and others, including Eccles, with its "dynamic and open field-structures" and "multivariable, many-layered" understanding of the character of the universe. This new science entails integrative methods of inquiry that are needed in order to bring to articulation the coherences and interrelations found actually embedded in the stratified levels of the universe.

As Torrance sees it, natural science is entering "a third era" beyond Greek-essentialist and modern-instrumentalist views of science; a third era which "starts from a unitary approach to the universe...and an integration of form which transcends the limits of analytical methods with their disintegrating effects,"[88] though this is an arduous and complex transition ongoing for close to a century rather than a sudden conversion.[89]

Science has only been able to advance more deeply in its understanding of the universe as it has broken free from the artificial limitations of the older science, for example in the repeated failure of Newtonian mechanics to account for the electromagnetic field of Faraday and Maxwell.[90]

This massive shift in science precipitated by the work of Faraday and Maxwell on the electromagnetic field, Einstein's relativity theory, and the work of people like Eccles thus led to: 1.) a different conception of reality; 2.) a change in the way concepts are derived or the way form is integrated (or at least a change in the way we think we derive or integrate form); and 3.) an alteration in the relation of science to ordinary human experience and knowledge, each of which Torrance discusses in some detail.[91] The second of these changes is of special interest for the present discussion of the nature of doctrine.

Integration of Form in Einstein, Polanyi & Torrance

Throughout this horizon-shift in science, Torrance argues that, "It is more and more apparent that the proper nature of the rational subject and the true functioning of his understanding are revealed only as we break through the subject-object bifurcation and allow our minds to function as they must under the constraint of objective reality and the compelling claims of its inherent intelligibility."[92] Here Torrance thinks "modern" science stemming from Newton repeatedly misled scholars into supposing that scientific concepts are derived by abstraction or observation directly from phenomena or sense date.[93]

Einstein

It was Einstein who put his finger on the real obstacle to understanding how form is integrated: Newton's idea that concepts/theories are derived by logical abstraction or deduction from sense data or experience.[94] Yet Einstein did not view form as a Kantian *a priori* imposed upon the sensory experience in scientific inquiry. Torrance sees Einstein's work as putting an end to the notions of the integration of form (how concepts/theories are derived) stemming from Newton, Kant and others not just by criticizing them, but because Einstein's achievement advanced our knowledge of the universe in an unprecedented manner (his theories of relativity, for example).[95]

Yet, Torrance notes that Einstein, himself, asserted that "nothing can be said concerning the manner in which concepts are to be made and connected, and how we are to coordinate them with experience."[96] Einstein sees the human knower engaged in the process of inquiry as, "helpless...until principles he can make the basis of deductive reasoning have revealed themselves to him."[97] Torrance points out that there are some indications of how Einstein developed his concepts and theories.

Though Einstein describes his ideas as "free creations" and "freely chosen conventions," Torrance notes that, "he did not mean that they were mere fictions or empty fantasies....They arose out an intimacy with and a sympathetic understanding of experience, under the belief in the intelligibility or comprehensibility (*Verständlichkeit*) of the world external to the percipient."[98] Thus, the concepts and theories that Einstein utilized were in one sense freely chosen. Yet, in another sense, they were shaped via Einstein's apprehension of the intrinsic structure of the universe and are confirmed by the applicability those concepts and theories to the universe.[99] This means that for Einstein, "there is...a real harmony between our concepts and experience....But it is easier to speak of this harmony negatively...since we are not concerned with a logical but a trans-logical or an extra-logical relation between concepts and experience."[100] This is a crucial point since Torrance is convinced that there are no logical bridges between reality and the human mind.

While he agrees with Einstein's critique of earlier conceptualizations of integration of form in scientific inquiry, Torrance argues that we have to press beyond Einstein at this point.[101] We can say more concerning this epistemic process than Einstein allowed and Daniel Hardy is correct when he notes that Torrance finds Michael Polanyi's work helpful at this point.[102]

Polanyi

More than any other philosopher of science, Torrance thinks that Michael Polanyi has rightly conceptualized how form is integrated in scientific inquiry and has also demonstrated that creative scientific discovery is not fully formalizable.[103]

At the center of Polanyi's epistemology is the claim that "we know more than we can tell," for as Torrance points out, "in addition to our 'focal awareness' and the explicit knowledge to which it gives rise, we always operate with a 'subsidiary awareness' and an implicit knowledge on which we rely in all our explicit operations."[104] Polanyi calls this the "tacit dimension" whereby the human mind, through a heuristic leap from the parts to the whole, can discern *Gestalten*, patterns of intelligibility in a particular field of inquiry which have not been discovered before.[105]

However, it is important to note at this juncture that Polanyi and Torrance do not advocate beginning with discrete particulars or sense data and then combining them into wholes, for the interrelations between the particulars (which are constitutive of the whole) have to be grasped together, simultaneously.[106] The kind of integration Polanyi and Torrance call for is far more complex and holistic than beginning with particulars and then aggregating them into a whole.[107]

The tacit dimension is comprehensive and complex, and entails the basic knowledge we gained in our earliest years, knowledge that we presuppose throughout life. As Torrance points out, "A child by the age of five, for example, has learned more 'physics' than he could ever bring to explicit understanding and expression even if he turned out to be a bright physicist....It is in reliance upon that implicit understanding and knowing that all our explicit thought and formulation, and all genuine advance, take place in any science, physical, social or theological."[108]

This implicit understanding or tacit dimension is inevitably shaped by the language and culture in which we live, a point we will take up in chapter 3.[109] of this monograph. In theology the tacit dimension is shaped within the worship and life of the Christian community. Thus, for Polanyi and Torrance, the tacit dimension is informal, undefined and in large measure inarticulate, yet still of critical significance in explicit thought and formulation.

Torrance argues that since it is on the basis of the tacit dimension that scientific theory bears upon experience, this seems to demand "a significant modification in what we understand by knowledge, for knowledge cannot then be defined merely in terms of what is explicit, and also in what we understand by reality, for correspondingly, reality cannot be defined in terms of what is only correlated with explicit concepts and statements."[110] "Tacit knowing" is central to the integration of form in scientific inquiry and everyday knowledge.[111]

From Torrance and Polanyi's perspective, form is integrated on the basis of a "tacit foreknowledge," an "intuitive insight," a "*prolepsis*" which "takes shape in our understanding under the imprint of the internal structure of that into which we inquire, and develops within the structural kinship that arises between our knowing and what we know as we make ourselves dwell in it and gain access to its meaning. Far from being, therefore, an *a priori* conception, or preconception, the foreknowledge with which scientific inquiry operates is an intuitive anticipation of a hitherto unknown pattern."[112] How is it that we move from a disparate jumble of seemingly unrelated particulars to an integrated understanding of the whole? How can we gain an integrated view of Torrance's theology from the discussions of various aspects of his position scattered about in a number of different publications?[113]

In Torrance's perspective, we begin with the various parts (that make up the corpus of his writings), which we "indwell" until we achieve an insight into the structure of his thought–we make an intuitive leap from scattered particulars in their interrelations to an integrated whole which we test and refine through our ongoing research. The process includes an ineradicable element of creative imagination, but it is an imagination that must be molded by the reality we are investigating. A structural kinship develops between our knowledge and what we seek to know, a kinship that is not, however, inherent or necessary (as in Kant), but contingent upon the all-important dynamic, integrative interaction between the knower and the known.[114] Yet the insight, prolepsis or structural kinship is also not abstracted from phenomena nor deduced from sense data (as with Newton), but arises within the knower's heuristic, informal indwelling of the field of inquiry: there is a dynamic, integrative extra-logical interaction between the knower and the known.[115]

Hardy correctly indicates that for Polanyi and Torrance, "this is a *personal* and *informal* integrative process...not limited to the initial moment of discovery, but persists in scientific work and–through its alternation with analytic and deductive procedures–produces a deepening awareness of the object."[116] Torrance does not discount the importance of analytic and deductive operations "by means of which we test a theory's coherence and draw out its implications."[117] However it does mean that the integrative element predominates.

It is this integrative element that Polanyi spells out so carefully while refusing any displacement of it by analytic and discursive modes of thought utilizing purely explicit, formal connections.[118] Behind the explicit hypothetico-deductive processes arising out of "hunches," "guesses," "intuitions," is "an implicit integrative activity of the *mind* that is at work in the epistemic process of scientific discovery."[119] Furthermore, no matter how successful a theoretical construction may be at mediating insight into the inherent organization or intelligibility of any field, Torrance contends that there is *no logical bridge* between concepts/theories and the objective structures of nature.[120]

Polanyi utilizes as a model the "logic of perceptual integration" to clarify this integrative character of the human mind beyond purely inferential and/or analytical procedures.[121] Visual perception entails both *focal* and *subsidiary* awareness. In Torrance's words, "They operate conjointly in such a way that we are subsidiarily aware of the marginal elements with a functional bearing on the object we know focally. This functional relation is a product of an integration carried out tacitly...linking the subsidiary elements to the focal centre in such a way that our apprehension of the clues is transformed into an apprehension of the objective reality to which they point."[122] This is an astonishing feat when you stop to think about it, one which a child learns only gradually and with great difficulty.

The popular *Magic Eye* pictures provide a concrete example of focal and subsidiary awareness. The *Magic Eye* appears to be merely a mass of tiny images with no discernable interrelations. But if we gradually move the *Magic Eye* away from our faces and avoid focusing on the detail, a three-dimensional picture appears. The human mind is able to integrate clues which the creators of the *Magic Eye* embed in the interrelations of the details of the small images.

It is this matrix of interrelations that is constitutive of the 3-D image and the human mind integrates subtle clues embedded in the detail. Because the 3-D image is intrinsic in the interrelations of the details, we can only perceive it by an holistic, simultaneous perceptual integration of subsidiary elements with a focal bearing on the 3-D image. There is no way to perceive the 3-D image by analyzing the isolated tiny images and then attempting to aggregate them into a whole.

Polanyi also utilizes the experiments with inverting spectacles to illustrate the integrative activity of the human mind in everyday experience. When one uses inverting spectacles, which make things appear upside-down, or reversed from right to left, one becomes completely disoriented. Even the most simple tasks become nearly impossible. It takes about eight days of tacit learning and active experimentation before one can see "properly" again.[123] This is not unlike the process by which a child first learns to coordinate vision with her surroundings. With the inverting spectacles, which change the visual image, it is the *conceptual image* that changes during those eight painful days.

The very fact of this change, Torrance notes, "reveals how the visual and the conceptual images operate inseparably together in our orientation to the objective structure of the world around us."[124] The change takes place not simply through active experimentation, but on the basis of tacit learning. The conceptual image is not imposed upon the visual image, nor is it deduced from the visual image. What takes place is a complex integrative activity that cannot be stated in wholly explicit procedures. Yet though the integration is tacit, it is none the less real because normal vision is restored after the eight days of tacit learning.

Torrance and Polanyi find a similar pattern in the integration form in scientific inquiry:

> Active scientific inquiry relies tacitly upon indefinable, integrative powers of thought through which the clues of which we are subsidiarily aware are brought to bear upon the object of our focal attention in such a way as to enable us to apprehend it as a comprehensive entity in its own coherent features and intrinsic structure. The clues with which we operate...and the intuitive apprehension of reality we gain from them, arise under the impact of that reality and its intrinsic structure upon our minds, so that what is distinctive here in the conjoint functioning of subsidiary and focal awareness is the way in which empirical and theoretical, or ontological and formal, elements are fused inseparably together.[125]

But note once again that this structural isomorphism that develops between our knowledge and that which we seek to know is neither inherent nor necessary, but contingent upon the dynamic, integrative, interactive indwelling of the known by the human knower, as is evident with the inverting spectacles experiment.

It is the fusion of form in being (nature entails intrinsic interrelations), which demands an integrative form of knowing that combines empirical and theoretical ingredients. Since form and being are fused in nature (nature is intrinsically interrelational), form cannot be grasped by analytic activity that first isolates sense data and then attempts to deduce concepts/theories from it, any more than the conceptual image can be conformed to the visual one in the inverting spectacles experiment by such a process (or the *Magic Eye* can be perceived by such a process).

Thus, Polanyi and Torrance argue that "the epistemic process in scientific discovery is essentially an *integrative activity*, rather than an analytical or an abstractive activity."[126] For this reason Polanyi and Torrance are skeptical regarding the possibility that the integration of form can be rendered in an entirely explicit procedure, for to do so discounts the dynamic and creative character of this kind of integrative activity that utilizes tacit dimensions.[127]

In the end therefore, in the words of Polanyi, with which Torrance agrees (and here we see another distinctive characteristic of their epistemologies), "any critical verification of a scientific statement requires the same powers for recognizing rationality in nature as does the process of scientific discovery."[128] This does not discount the importance of analytic and logical/deductive procedures that are also a part of scientific endeavor. But it does mean that the actual way scientific concepts and theories are applied to nature (which is the crucial test for Torrance) "is not basically different from the way in which they are discovered by the scientist in the first place."[129] Thus, in the end the "meaning, the success and the validity of a scientific theory," Torrance argues, "depend on its *ontological import*, i.e., its *power of objective reference* to point to and reveal the hidden structure in the world to which it is correlated, and which determines its cognitive and heuristic values."[130]

The proper integration of form rests on "personal knowledge" and "personal judgement," but these are for Polanyi–and emphatically(!) for Torrance–made "under the judgement of the hidden reality he seeks to uncover, which exists independently of his knowing of it and is as such the external pole of his personal judgement."[131] For Torrance, reality itself is the judge of the truth or falsity of our concepts and theories.[132]

Torrance asserts that "only persons are capable of distinguishing what they know from their knowing of it, and of engaging in sustained self-critical operations in the interest of objectivity and consistency."[133] Understood in this light, for Torrance and Polanyi, it is personal participation rooted in the process of indwelling that enables human knowledge to rise above purely subjective imposition of form as with Kant. Torrance speaks of an "epistemological inversion" in which, though we begin with a framework of thought, we pose our questions and proceed with our inquiry in such a way that we come to question our initial questions and then pose them again so that the ongoing inquiry constantly inverts the determining factor in our knowledge away from our own constructive activity to the intrinsic intelligible interrelations in that which we seek to know.[134]

The personal element is not–and should not–to be eliminated, but rather molded and shaped by constant reference back to the reality under investigation. It is rigorous personal acts of self-criticism and judgement that curtail the imposition of ourselves and our constructions upon what we seek to know.[135] For Torrance (and Polanyi), personal agency in knowing cannot be placed in contra-position to genuine objectivity, for personal being "is the bearer of objectivity."[136] We will take up these issues again in chapter 5 of this monograph.

That personal being is the bearer of objectivity points up what Torrance calls the most startling feature of the new science: the astonishing fact that humanity cannot be separated from the structure of the universe of which humanity is a constituent element, but rather humanity is that highest level or boundary point through which the astonishing intelligibility of the created universe comes to articulation in praise of its Creator.[137] Humanity is thus the "priest of creation," the "mouth through which the whole universe gives voice to the glory and majesty of the living God," a universe with a "stratified structure" and "ascending hierarchy of relations" that are "open upward" in a "dimension of depth...that cannot be flattened downward by being reduced to connections all on the same level."[138]

One final point remains before summing up Torrance's understanding of the integration of form and then turning to how all of this is related to theology and doctrine in the next chapter. This is Polanyi's and Torrance's emphasis on the need for and element of indeterminacy/openness in our conceptions and theories correlated with the ability of reality to constantly take us by surprise.[139] There must be a place for wonder in all scientific inquiry that keeps the human mind open to the astonishing ability of reality (created and Divine) to take us by surprise.[140]

Summary

In summary, for Torrance the way in which form is properly integrated begins within the knowing relation, and therefore within a cultural-linguistic framework or a framework of belief with a tacit dimension. Form is neither deduced from the data, nor is form simply an *a priori* (intrinsic or quasi-transcendental) imposed upon data, even though the framework of the knower plays a role in the apprehension of reality. Rather in Torrance's perspective, form arises through a prolepsis, an insight or foreknowledge, which takes shape in our understanding under the imprint of the internal structure of that into which we inquire as we indwell it.

Thus while the knower begins within a framework of belief, it is one that is open to revision or radical transformation as the process of inquiry and discovery moves forward. Even the tacit dimension suffers constant modification in the ongoing dynamic relation between the knower and the known. We seek to clarify and expand what we know through radical self-criticism in which we drag our preconceptions and unexamined presuppositions out into the open and allow the ongoing inquiry to question and modify them.

This is a dynamic, personal and informal integrative process, not limited to the initial moment of discovery, but persistent throughout scientific inquiry, though analytic and deductive procedures have an important place. While the insights that arise are never completely displaced by analytic or hypothetical-deductive procedures, they are not for that reason any less rational.

For Torrance, the dynamic integrative process is rather the intelligent manner in which the human mind creatively and personally adapts itself to that which it seeks to know so that form is integrated–the theoretical is fused with the empirical–in such a way as to reflect the unity of form and being in reality itself; first brokenly, then more clearly, though never fully, for reality (contingent and especially Divine) always seems to retain a depth of comprehensibility and multi-dimensionality that eludes, astonishes and baffles us in our inquiry.

Despite his optimistic tone in discussing the integration of form that he advocates, Torrance admits the limited character of human knowing. We know only in part and imperfectly. But for Torrance we do know, for properly developed theoretical formulations (doctrines in theology) can be progressively disclosive of the realities to which they point. This means that reality (Divine and contingent) is simultaneously the ground both of the objectivity and the revisability of our conceptualization of it.

This is the point at which Torrance believes that the kind of integration of form he advocates can transcend, at least to a degree, the problem he sees in Kant of imposing theoretical formulations upon reality in our knowing of it, while at the same time moving beyond Newton's notion that form must be deduced from the empirical or abstracted from observation.

For Torrance, proper theoretical formulations must repeatedly redirect our attention to reality. They must be open formulations which allow for their own revision and even transformation. Only then do they serve their purpose as disclosive of the realities they signify.

Notes

1. In the "Preface" to *Theological Science,* Torrance points to the Gifford Lectures of his "revered teacher," A. E. Taylor, as inculcating this principle. See Thomas F. Torrance, *Theological Science* (London: Oxford University Press, 1969), p. xii. Also Thomas F. Torrance, *The Ground and Grammar of Theology* (Charlottesville: University of Virginia Press, 1980), p. 8 and Thomas F. Torrance, *God and Rationality* (New York: Oxford University Press, 1971), p. 93.

2. Torrance, *Theological Science*, p. 281.

3. Thomas F. Torrance, *Theology in Reconstruction* (Grand Rapids: Eerdmans, 1975), p. 146. For Torrance this means that Jesus Christ, God incarnate for us in our world, is the "living dynamic Object" of our faith and of scientific theology. See Thomas F. Torrance, *Reality and Evangelical Theology*, (Philadelphia: Westminster Press, 1982), p. 138. This, in turn, calls for a living theology and personal participation in the Gospel. Ibid.

When interviewed by *Faith and Life*, the magazine of the Church of Scotland, Torrance suggested that the real heart of his theology is "that it is deeply Nicene and doxological (theology and worship going inextricably together), with its immediate focus on Jesus Christ as Mediator, and its ultimate focus on the Holy Trinity." See Robert J. Palma, "Thomas F. Torrance's Reformed Theology," *Reformed Review* 38, no. 1 (Autumn, 1984), p. 3. Theology, in Torrance's perspective, ought always to be the rational worship of God. This means that theology has its place in the Church's total response in worship, obedience and mission, and is simply one aspect of that holistic response to God.

It should also be noted that while Torrance makes a significant place for "practical" theology, he is wary of a primarily "functional" view of theology and says that dogmatic theology should be "pursued as a pure science for its own sake, or rather for the sake of God Himself." See Torrance, *Rationality*, p. viii. Yet Torrance sees genuine theology as intensely practical, for by revealing the real relation which God has established with us in Jesus Christ, humanity's real needs are disclosed and addressed. Torrance, *Reconstruction*, p. 16.

4. Torrance, *Theological Science*, p. xiii.

5. Thus critical questions about the possibility of knowledge cannot be raised "*in abstracto*" but only "*in concreto*," not "*a priori*" but only "*a posteriori*." See Ibid., p. 1.

6. Ibid., p. 10.

7. See Hardy's article, "Thomas F. Torrance," in *The Modern Theologians: An Introduction to Christian Theology in the Twentieth Century*, ed. David F. Ford (New York: Basil Blackwell Inc., 1989), 1:72.

8. Torrance, *Theological Science*, p. xii.

9. See Torrance, *Theological Science*, pp. 3, 10, and 286. Also see Torrance, *Rationality*, pp. 93 and 196.

10. See Elmer M. Colyer, *How to Read T. F. Torrance: Understanding His Trinitarian and Scientific Theology* (Downers Grove, Ill.: InterVarsity Press, 2001), pp. 57-60, for a fuller discussion of Torrance's rejection of epistemological and cosmological dualisms.

11. Torrance, *Rationality*, pp. 9-10 and 91. Also see ibid., p. 114 and Torrance, *Ground and Grammar*, p. 8.

12. Torrance suggests that his book, *Divine and Contingent Order*, "is an essay in the tradition of Scottish realist theological and epistemological thought which goes back at least as far as John Duns Scotus." See Thomas F. Torrance, *Divine and Contingent Order* (Oxford: Oxford University Press, 1981), p. x. Also see Torrance, *Theological Science*, p. xvi and Thomas F. Torrance, *Space, Time and Resurrection* (Grand Rapids: Eerdmans, 1976), p. 6.

13. Hardy, "Torrance," p. 77.

14. Ibid.

15. Ibid.

16. Torrance, *Theological Science*, p. xiii.

17. Ibid.

18. James Brown, *Subject and Object in Modern Theology* (New York: Macmillian, 1955), p. 170. See Torrance, *Theological Science*, p. 1. This is reminiscent of Heidegger's concept of the "thrownness" (*Geworfenheit*) of human life.

19. Torrance, *Theological Science*, p. xiii.

20. See Thomas F. Torrance, "The Making of the 'Modern Mind' From Descartes and Newton to Kant," chapter 1 of *Transformation and Convergence in the Frame of Knowledge* (Grand Rapids: Eerdmans, 1984), pp. 1-59. Also see Torrance, *Ground and Grammar*, chapter 2, "Emerging From the Cultural Split," pp. 15-43 and Thomas F. Torrance, *Reality and Scientific Theology*, vol. 1 *Theology and Science at the Frontiers of Knowledge* (Edinburgh: Scottish Academic Press, 1985), chapter 1, "Classical and Modern Attitudes of Mind," pp. 1-31.

21. See Torrance, *Transformation*, pp. 1-59. A minor problem regarding Torrance's publications can be cleared up at this juncture. In his book, *Space, Time and Resurrection,* Torrance refers his readers to his "forthcoming book, *Integration and Interpretation in Natural and Theological Science.*" See Torrance, *Resurrection*, p. 5. However, Torrance never published *Integration and Interpretation in Natural and Theological Science.* What happened was that Torrance excerpted the chapters dealing with hermeneutics, gave them as the Payton Lectures at Fuller Theological Seminary in 1981, and published them under the title, Reality and Evangelical Theology. *Transformation and Convergence in the Frame of Knowledge* was then published (minus the chapters on hermeneutics) in place of *Integration and Interpretation in Natural and Theological Science.* See Torrance, *Transformation*, p. xiv.

22. Torrance, *Transformation*, p. 6.

23. Ibid., p. 5.

24. Ibid., p. 6.

25. Ibid.

26. Ibid.

27. See ibid., pp. 13-14.

28. See ibid.

29. Ibid., p. 14.

30. Ibid.

31. Isaac Newton, *Philosophiae Naturalis Principia Mathematica*, trans. by A. Motte (1729), rev. and ed. by Florian Cajori (Chicago: Encyclopedia Britannica, 1955), p. 547. See Torrance, *Transformation*, p. 17. It is however true that Newton did in fact advance speculative hypotheses, as Torrance points out. Ibid.

32. See ibid., p. 18.

33. See Albert Einstein's foreword to Isaac Newton, *Optics*, 4th ed. (New York: Dover, 1952), p. vii. Also see Torrance, *Transformation*, p. 16.

34. Newton, *Principia Mathematica*, p. 12. See Torrance, *Transformation*, p. 22. Thus Einstein points out that "We can see indeed from Newton's formulation of it that the concept of absolute space, which comprised that of absolute rest, made him feel uncomfortable; he realized that there seemed to be nothing in experience corresponding to this last concept." Albert Einstein, *The World as I See It*, trans. Alan Harris (London: John Lane, 1935), p. 135. See Torrance, *Transformation*, p. 52.

35. Torrance, *Transformation*, pp. 22-23.

36. Ibid., p. 23.

37. David Hume, *A Treatise of Human Nature* (London: Longmans, Green, 1909), I.iii.8, pp. 403-4. See Torrance, *Transformation*, p. 35. Torrance points out that Hume's position was not as skeptical as it appears.

38. This illustration is found in Colin Gunton, *Enlightenment and Alienation* (Grand Rapids: Eerdmans, 1985), p. 22.

39. David Hume, *An Enquiry Concerning Human Understanding*, ed. L. A. Selby-Biggs (Oxford: Clarendon, 1962), 7.2, p.77. Also see Gunton, *Enlightenment*, p. 22.

40. Torrance, *Transformation*, p. 36.

41. Ibid.

42. In hermeneutics, this line of thought has led to the idea that the Bible does not portray a "followable world." When Kant's categories of the mind are historicized, as they have been since the rise of "historical consciousness" in the nineteenth and twentieth centuries, it has tended to lead in the direction of a "reader-response" hermeneutic.

This can take a decidedly "individualistic" turn, as in the case of Edgar McKnight who goes so far as to say that, "The principle of fantasy is involved because readers use materials taken in from literary work to create the wish-fulfilling fantasy characteristic of themselves." See Edgar McKnight, *The Post-Modern Use of the Bible* (Nashville: Abingdon Press, 1988), p. 159. However, thus far this trend seems more often to lead to a "community of hermeneutical privilege" which can properly construe the meaning of the biblical text. But with both there is a loss of the intrinsic intelligibility (perspicuity) of the biblical text which parallels the loss of the intrinsic intelligibility of nature in Kant's synthetic *a priori*.

43. See Torrance, *Transformation*, p. 37.

44. Immanuel Kant, *Critique of Pure Reason*, trans. N. Kemp Smith (London: Macmillian, 1933), p. 22.

45. Torrance gives this quotation from Kant. See Torrance, *Transformation*, p. 38.

46. See Torrance, *Transformation*, pp. 43-46 and Torrance, *Ground and Grammar*, pp. 15-43.

47. See Torrance, *Transformation*, pp. 61-71.

48. George Lindbeck, *The Nature of Doctrine* (Philadelphia: Westminster Press, 1984), pp. 20-21.

49. Ibid., p. 21.

50. It should be noted that Schleiermacher's understanding of feeling (*gefühl*) is more like what we might designate by "immediate self-consciousness." Furthermore, "the feeling of absolute dependence" (*das schlechtinnige Abhängigkeitsgefühl*) is more like one's self-consciousness of the self's "non-self-causedness" (*Sichselbstnichtsogesetzhaben*), than an "emotion" of absolute dependence. See Charles Hefling's article, "The Meaning of God Incarnate According to Friedrich Schleiermacher," *Lonergan Workshop*, vol. 7 (Atlanta: Scholars Press, 1988), pp. 111-12.

51. Friedrich Schleiermacher, *The Christian Faith*, ed. and trans. H. R. Mackintosh and J. S. Stewart (Edinburgh: T & T Clark, 1989), p. 12-13.

52. Ibid., pp. 16-17.

53. Lindbeck, *Doctrine*, p. 23.

54. Alister E. McGrath, *The Genesis of Doctrine: A Study in the Foundations of Doctrinal Criticism* (Cambridge, Mass.: Basil Blackwell Ltd., 1990).

55. See Charles Hefling, "Turning Liberalism Inside-Out" in *Method: Journal of Lonergan Studies* 3, no. 2 (1985), pp. 51-69.

56. See McGrath, *Doctrine*, p. 25.

57. See Hefling, "Friedrich Schleiermacher," p. 117.

58. Lindbeck, *Doctrine,* p. 33.

59. See ibid., p. 33.

60. Ibid., p. 36.

61. Ibid., p. 37. Lindbeck points to certain groups of people whose tribal language does not discriminate between green and blue and indicates that lacking the linguistic *a priori* for experiencing the difference between the two colors, they find it difficult to recognize the difference between the two colors. See ibid., p. 37. On this particular point, I fear that Lindbeck fails to distinguish between "focal awareness" and "differentiated experience." There are many things in life that we are not consciously aware of because our focal awareness is directed to something else. This, however, does not mean that our experience is homogeneous until we have achieved categorical differentiation. Is this not the point of many of the questions of small children? They perceive differences in things and are looking for categorical expression with which to render them explicit. Does not the whole learning process that every child passes through indicate a far more dialectically complex relation between language and experience that Lindbeck's discussion suggests?

62. McGrath, *Doctrine*, p. 28.

63. Ibid.

64. Lindbeck, *Doctrine*, p. 10.

65. There is no question that Lindbeck wants to make ontological truth claims for the Christian idiom within his cultural-linguistic paradigm, as Bruce Marshall has pointed out in his brilliant article, "Aquinas as Postliberal Theologian," *The Thomist* 53, no. 3 (July 1989): pp. 353-402. However, that is not the point.

The question is whether, in the end, there is any *warrant* for making such claims within Lindbeck's theory. Lindbeck, himself, concedes that, "a crucial theological challenge of a cultural-linguistic approach is whether it can...do so [make such truth claims]." See Lindbeck, *Doctrine*, p. 63. In differentiating his cultural-linguistic theory so sharply from cognitive-propositionalism one is left with an uneasy feeling concerning the relationship between the "followable world" depicted by the biblical narrative, embodied in the idiom of Christian life and belief, and the reality of God.

Marshall has outlined Lindbeck's position and stated the issues regarding ontological truth claims with astonishing clarity–one which I judge to be true to Lindbeck's position, as Lindbeck seems to grant. See Lindbeck's, "Response to Bruce Marshall," *The Thomist* 53 no. 3 (1989): pp. 403-6. Marshall carefully distinguishes between the way truth is *defined* and the way truth claims are *justified*. See Marshall, "Aquinas," pp. 354ff. Marshall contends that Lindbeck has a "correspondence definition of truth," but a "coherentist account of justification." Ibid.

Marshall outlines Lindbeck's differentiation of "categorical truth" (categories adequate to reality) and "intrasystematic truth" (the right use of categories as coherent with the wider network of Christian belief and life within the cultural-linguistic framework). See ibid., pp. 357-66. Each is a *necessary* condition for ontological truth. But only together do they constitute the *sufficient* conditions for ontological truth. Ibid., pp. 366-70.

Marshall sees this as very *near* to Aquinas' position. However, there is a pivotal difference which Marshall notes in footnotes 28 and 49 on pp. 367 and 376. In the first, Marshall maintains that Lindbeck "needs to make it more clear how...adequate categories and intrasystematic coherence are not only necessary, but sufficient conditions for the truth of religious utterances....But it seems crucial to the kind of position articulated by Lindbeck to hold that...*no further step is necessary* in order to ascertain whether a given utterance is true." Ibid., p. 367. In contrast to Lindbeck, Marshall argues that Aquinas has an "explicitly theological way of dealing with" this issue, namely a "**crucial link** between [God as] *prima veritas* and *a Deo revelatum*," (Ibid., p. 373.) something that Lindbeck does not explicitly state, as McGrath astutely observes. For Aquinas, "since God as *prima veritas* is the source and measure of all truth, and since God's revelation in Scripture and creed is the linguistic embodiment of his being as *prima veritas*, whatever propositions cohere with Scripture and creed must be true." Ibid., p. 376.

Lindbeck never treats this critical point and without it, or something that serves the same role, it is difficult to see how his position can sustain the ontological claims that he wants to retain within his theory. The closest Lindbeck ever comes to addressing this is the following statement: "I am not sure that this is possible for those who exclude any reference to an ideal observer or knower (whether real or hypothetical) when defining truth, but for the theist for whom God is *prima veritas*, as he was for Aquinas, the answer is clearly in the affirmative." See Lindbeck, "Response," p. 404. Yet notice that for Marshall the issue is not simply God as *prima veritas*, but also *a Deo revelatum,* Scripture as the linguistic embodiment of that *prima veritas*!

However, Aquinas was a "pre-modern" who lived before Kant's "ground-clearing that was later completed for most educated people by the scientific developments that increased the difficulties of accepting literalistic propositional interpretations of such biblical doctrines as creation, and by historical studies that implied the time-conditioned relativity of all doctrines." Lindbeck, *Doctrine*, pp. 20-21. It seems that the Bible as the embodiment of the *prima veritas* is a real problem for moderns (and postliberals like Lindbeck) and while Lindbeck mentions Aquinas with reference to God as the *prima veritas*, he does not mention the Bible as a *Deo revelatum*, nor does he tell us his own position with regard to all this. Until Lindbeck clarifies his perspective in this area, the question of ontological truth claims within his cultural-linguistic theory remains a very real one, as Bruce Marshall has documented with such precision and fairness. Torrance, however, does address this and offers a very different solution, as we shall see in chapter 4.

66. See Torrance's discussions of how theology and biblical studies were adversely affected by the impact of "the modern mind" in *Ground and Grammar*, pp. 26-43 and Thomas F. Torrance, "The Historical Jesus: From the Perspective of a Theologian," in *The New Testament Age: Essays in Honor of Bo Reicke*, ed. William C. Weinrich (Macon, Ga.: Mercer University Press, 1984) Vol. II, pp. 511-26.

67. See Torrance's discussion in *Transformation*, pp. 61-71. Torrance indicates that Einstein struggled twenty years to think his way out of Newtonian and Kantian habits of mind and develop relativity theory. See Thomas F. Torrance, *Scientific Theology*), p. 75.

68. See Torrance, *Transformation,* p. 41. Torrance sees Kant's synthetic *a priori* in which empirical and theoretical components operate together as an improvement over naive empiricism in which thought is controlled by observational facts which are independent of the theoretical element of our scientific constructions. Ibid., p. 73.

69. Kant said of the geometer that, "The true method was not to inspect what he discerned in the figure, or in the bare concept of it, and from this, as it were, to read off its properties; but to bring out what was necessarily implied in the construction by which he presented it to himself. If he is to know anything with *a priori* certainty he must not ascribe to the figure anything save what follows from what he himself set into it in accordance with his concept." Quoted by Torrance in ibid., p. 41. Here, the human inquirer is no longer viewed as a pupil ready to learn from the object, but as a judge who compels witnesses to answer questions which the judge poses.

70. Ibid., p. 42. Torrance grants Lindbeck's point that the theoretical components with which we operate, often uncritically, in everyday experience and in scientific inquiry are in a significant measure culturally and linguistically formed and important in all apprehension and significant in shaping experience, though Torrance would argue that there is a strong empirical element involved, since as children, our conceptual components were repeatedly integrated with our experience. Lindbeck unfortunately gives too little attention to this element. The relation between the theoretical and experiential are far more complex than his account allows. This is part of Torrance's point. We need an account of the integration of form that grants the complexity of this integration as it actually occurs.

71. Ibid.

72. Ibid., pp. 22-23.

73. Ibid.

74. Ibid., p. 42. There are severe difficulties inherent in assimilating Torrance's epistemology. First of all there is no one place in his writings where he carefully sets out the different elements of his position in a clear and organized manner. Daniel Hardy has pointed out that part of the problem is Torrance's tendency toward over compressed exposition. Hardy also acknowledges that the problem is also rooted in the difficulty of the subject-matter with which Torrance deals. See Hardy, "Torrance," p. 86. A further reason is simply that Torrance adopts a position that by its very nature is not fully formalizable, as will become clear in course of discussing Torrance's position.

75. See ibid., pp. 61-87. Torrance sees Karl Barth as doing for theology something similar to what Einstein did for science, though Torrance has some reservations with Barth, especially regarding the issue of Barth "restricting the relation between God and man, grace and nature, to the *event* of grace without working out, at any rate in a way that satisfies his critics, the *ontology* of the creaturely structures which it assumes." See "Natural Theology in the Thought of Karl Barth," in Thomas F. Torrance, *Karl Barth: Biblical and Evangelical Theologian* (Edinburgh: T & T Clark, 1990), p. 156. This article was published three different times. See *Religious Studies* 6, (1970): pp. 121-35 and *Transformation*, pp. 285-302.

76. Ibid., pp. viii-xi. Torrance asserts that this general frame of knowledge arises whenever an accepted philosophical or scientific tradition melds with a culture and society. Torrance's "framework of knowledge" and Lindbeck's cultural-linguistic framework are quite similar. Torrance also notes that these culture-linguistic frameworks are often extremely resistant to new ideas and the reconstruction those ideas call for. See ibid., p. xi.

77. Torrance claims to have developed his theological position in terms of content and epistemology in dialogue with the Greek fathers (and Karl Barth) before he deliberately set out to make room within the world of

modern science for Christian theology, taking issue with modern critical philosophy. It was at that time that he came into contact with Michael Polanyi. Alister McGrath is correct on this point. See McGrath's effective criticism of Colin Weightman's characterization of Torrance as embracing a Polanyian epistemology. See Alister E. McGrath, *T. F. Torrance: An Intellectual Biography* (Edinburgh: T & T Clark, 1999), pp. 228-32. Also see Colin Weightman, *Theology in a Polanyian Universe: The Theology of Thomas F. Torrance* (New York: Peter Lang, 1994).

78. Torrance, *Transformation*, p. xii.

79. Thomas F. Torrance, "The Integration of Form in Natural and Theological Science," was initially a lecture presented at the Jubilee Symposium of the Academie Internationale de Philosophie des Sciences, at Drogen-Gent, Belgium, September 12, 1972, and published in *Science, Medicine and Man* 1 (1973): pp. 143-72. It has been reprinted in Torrance, *Transformation*, pp. 61-105. Also see Torrance, *Scientific Theology*, pp. 64-81.

80. See Torrance, "Integration," p. 143.

81. Torrance cites this passage from Eccles' book, *Facing Reality: Philosophical Adventures of a Brain Scientist* (London: Heidelberg Science Library, 1970), p. 59 in Torrance, "Integration," p. 62.

82. See Torrance, "Integration," pp. 143-45. This is also an example of Torrance's fundamental axiom that the reality or subject-matter under investigation must be allowed to determine the method of inquiry, the mode of rationality, and the form of verification.

83. See Torrance, *Scientific Theology*, pp. 72-76.

84. See ibid. and Torrance, "Integration," pp. 143-55.

85. See Torrance, *Scientific Theology*, p. 72 and Torrance, "Integration," p. 143.

86. Torrance, *Scientific Theology*, pp. 66-67.

87. See ibid., pp. 64-71. Torrance suggests that the older science was being undermined in the nineteenth century by Faraday's discover of the electromagnetic field and Maxwell's account of it through partial differential equations. Ibid.

88. Ibid., pp. 70-71. Torrance notes that it was with relativity theory and quantum theory that this revolution actually began to forcefully unfold, for neither Newton's classical laws of motion nor his account of the integration of form are able to cope with the changes demanded by these scientific advances. See ibid., p. 66. Torrance would also say that this is true with integration of form in patristic theology embodied in Nicea and Chalcedon which Torrance sees as not being *deduced* from Scripture, but rather integrated in a far profounder manner. See ibid., pp. 90-96.

89. Ibid., p. 71. Also see Thomas F. Torrance, *Christian Theology and Scientific Culture* (New York: Oxford University Press, 1980), pp. 26-27.

90. See Torrance, *Scientific Theology*, p. 75.

91. See ibid., pp. 71-87.

92. Torrance, *Transformation*, p. 73. Here we see the fundamental axiom of Torrance's theology discussed above embodied as he develops his own understanding of the integration of form.

93. Torrance, *Transformation*, p. 76. Torrance suggests that it was modern science's emphasis upon "direct contact with experience" and its giving "full place to empirical factors in respect to both the content and the control of knowledge" that was the source of this misunderstanding. See

ibid.

The result of this notion, when subjected to Humean critique was that Kant transferred intelligibility to the human pole of the knowing relation and conceived the integration of form involved as one of necessary and legislative, *a priori* structures imposed upon the flux of sense experience in order to render it intelligible to human subjectivity, as discussed earlier in this chapter. All of which led to a mechanistic and causalist outlook upon the universe that is hostile to human freedom and Divine interaction, except within some "transcendentalist" realm existing parallel to the world of space and time. See Torrance, *Scientific Theology*, p. 76. This is the real root of the repeated attempts of modern theology to find some respectable place in Western culture for the Christian message and to relocate religion and theology in a transcendental realm exempt from the mechanistic and causalist conception of Newton's universe. But in removing the ground of religion and theology from the universe of space and time, this also tends to remove religion and theology from humanity's mundane life in space and time. The result is that religion and theology are all too often ghettoized as they often have been in Western culture in the modern period.

However, the other problem for a theology that relocates its ground in a transcendental realm beyond the categorical is that, by definition, this makes it extremely difficult for theology to remain "rational," for one still has to prescind from transcendentality in order to rationally reflect on its subject matter and articulate it. But this is a problem, for as soon as one prescinds, all the problems associated with the categorical realm come rushing back into play, and then one faces the perplexing task of attempting to make intelligible the relation between that reflection and its transcendental ground, something that has repeatedly proved to be a problem for theologies which are grounded in the transcendental realm.

94. Torrance, *Transformation*, p. 76.

95. See Torrance, *Scientific Theology*, p. 77. Also see Torrance, *Transformation*, pp. 66-72 and 76-78. Einstein, himself, said with reference to the idea that scientific theories are directly derived from experience that "A clear recognition of the erroneousness of this notion [that concepts are deduced from experience] really only came with the general theory of relativity, which showed that one could take account of a wider range of empirical facts, and that too in a more satisfactory and complete manner, on a foundation quite different from the Newtonian than was possible with it." See Einstein, *The World*, p. 135. See Torrance, *Transformation*, p. 76.

96. Albert Einstein, *Out of My Later Years* (New York: Philosophical Library, 1950), p. 61. See Torrance, *Transformation*, p. 77. There is an interesting parallel here between Einstein on discovery and Karl Barth on revelation. Whereas Einstein says we can not say how concepts are formed in the process of scientific discovery and we are helpless until principles have "revealed" themselves to the scientist, Barth, in developing his understanding of the subjective reality and possibility of revelation, argues that one cannot say "how" the Holy Spirit is the subjective reality of revelation. It might not be far from the truth to say that as Polanyi attempted to explain the process of discovery in science more fully than did Einstein, so Torrance has attempted to treat theological method, particularly epistemology in relation to revelation, more fully than Barth.

97. Einstein, *The World*, p. 138. See Torrance, *Transformation*, p. 115.

98. Torrance, *Scientific Theology*, pp. 77 and 79.

99. Ibid. Also see Torrance, *Transformation*, pp. x-xii and 77-79, Torrance, *Ground and Grammar*, pp. 30-31, and Torrance, *Theological Science*, pp. 117-19.

100. Torrance, "Integration," p. 77. Einstein could speak of the sense of "religious awe" at the astonishing fact that the universe is comprehensible to the human mind. See Torrance, *Scientific Theology*, p. 53.

101. Torrance, *Scientific Theology*, p. 132.

102. See Hardy, "Torrance," p. 78. It should also be noted that Hardy is one of the few commentators on Torrance's theology who has rightly understood Torrance's position regarding the integration of form and the structure of belief, though there are several points where Hardy fails to grasp the full implications of Torrance's understanding of the integration of form.

Torrance was Polanyi's "Literary Executor." See Thomas F. Torrance, ed., *Belief in Science and in Christian Life: The Relevance of Michael Polanyi's Thought for Christian Faith and Life* (Edinburgh: Handsel Press, 1980), p. 148.

103. See Torrance, *Scientific Theology*, p. 77 and also p. 50. Also see Torrance's article, "The Place of Michael Polanyi in the Modern Philosophy of Science" in *Ethics in Science and Medicine* 7 (1980): 57-95. The article was reprinted in Torrance, *Transformation*, pp. 107-73. Also see Torrance, *Scientific Culture*, pp. 62-69.

104. Torrance, "Polanyi," p. 60.

105. Ibid., p. 116. This is not wholly new, for a similar idea appears at least as far back as Schleiermacher's seminal work in the field of hermeneutics, though without clear expression of the tacit dimension so critical to Polanyi's work. Schleiermacher spoke of a "divinitory method" which enables interpreters to "leap" into the hermeneutical circle (hermeneutical spiral might be a better image since it is in moving repeatedly, and often simultaneously, back and forth from the parts to the whole that an accurate understanding of the parts in relation to the whole is achieved). It is possible for interpreters "to construct for themselves a complete image" of the whole of a text or a person's thought "from only scattered traces" or parts. See Friedrich Schleiermacher, *Hermeneutics: The Handwritten Manuscripts*, ed. H. Kimmerle, trans. J. Duke and J. Forstman (Missoula, Mont.: Scholars Press, 1977), p. 207.

106. Torrance, *Transformation*, p. 78.

107. Ibid.

108. See Torrance, *Scientific Culture*, p. 13.

109. Ibid. However, Torrance maintains that "this does not imply that we must operate uncritically within the knowledge and wisdom accumulated in our cultural tradition, just because we are unable to extricate ourselves from involvement in it. On the contrary, it is because our thought is so powerfully influenced by culture that we must bring its latent assumptions out into the open and put them to the test." See ibid. Thus, if the tacit dimension constitutes an epistemological "foundation," it is a foundation affected by one's cultural-linguistic framework and therefore by all the problems of sociology of knowledge. Furthermore, it is clear from Torrance's statement that the tacit dimension is open to critical modification as inquiry proceeds. This would seem to indicate that if Torrance is a foundationalist, it would have to be some form of what some have called "soft foundationalism." Torrance explicitly rejects the Greek notion of science "where the stress is upon unchanging *foundations*

of knowledge." See Torrance, *Transformation*, p. 65.

However, Torrance is certainly not the kind of foundationalist Ronald Thiemann contends that he is. See Ronald Thiemann, *Revelation and Theology: The Gospel as Narrated Theology* (Notre Dame, Ind.: University of Notre Dame Press, 1985), pp. 32-42. According to Thiemann, Torrance is a foundationalist, for "Torrance uses the term *intuition* to signify the indubitability and incorrigibility of this *causally imposed knowledge*." See ibid., p. 40. Yet, Torrance maintains that, "no rational knowledge is merely *per modum causalitatis*...[for] even though I think rationally as I am compelled to think...I am free and not a puppet." Torrance, *Rationality*, p. 198. Furthermore, in rejecting the "mechanization of knowledge," Torrance argues that history, human knowing, and reality at all levels of the created universe are "found to be much too subtle and flexible...to be open to explanation or understanding within the old framework of 'necessity and chance.'" See Thomas F. Torrance, *The Christian Frame of Mind* (Colorado Springs: Helmers & Howard, 1989), pp. 43-46 and 48-50. Torrance also maintains that "if beliefs were causally imposed on our minds...that would eliminate freedom to believe or not to believe as we judge we must and so relieve us of personal responsibility for our belief...if beliefs were causally imposed on us that would also eliminate the possibility of error." See Torrance, ed., *Belief in Science*, p. 14.

It seems that Thiemann, himself, has not moved all that far beyond the problematic dichotomy of chance and necessity, for he presents the reader with an unhelpful disjunction: either foundationalism with its appeal to "non-inferential" intuitive apprehension of the real *or* a "narrated promise" awaiting an "eschatological justification" and a "person-specific act" of faith "with reasons and causes related to that person's individual history" (Feuerbach would have fun with this!), the explanation of which "lies beyond theology's descriptive competence." See Thiemann, *Revelation*, pp. 94 and 147-48.

If Thiemann would have examined a wider selection of Torrance's writings, and read those he did consult more carefully, he might have noticed that Torrance is very close to Polanyi in epistemology on this point. There is a certain irony in this, since, in a sense, Thiemann fails to heed the fundamental axiom that runs throughout Torrance's writings: that it is the nature of that which one is investigating that determines how it is to be understood. Thiemann has imported the foundationalist/anti-foundationalist debate into his reading of Torrance, rather that interpreting Torrance on his own terms and in relation to Einstein and Polanyi. The result is that Thiemann misunderstands Torrance on rather basic and important issues.

110. See Torrance, "Polanyi," p. 60. Thus, Torrance maintains that, "If that is the case–and it is increasingly being granted on both sides of the Atlantic that this is the case–then Polanyi's discovery about the structure of tacit knowledge is a contribution to modern philosophy of science of quite fundamental importance." Ibid., pp. 60-61.

111. Torrance, *Transformation*, pp. 114 and 122. Torrance can say of this tacit dimension that outstanding scientists have made great discoveries in natural scientific on the basis of "an epistemic awareness of the mind more deeply grounded than any set of scientific evidence, without which scientific inquiry would not be possible." See Thomas F. Torrance, "Ultimate Beliefs and the Scientific Revolution," *Cross Currents* 30, no. 2 (1980): p. 132.

112. Torrance, "Polanyi," p. 61. Torrance describes the process as circular:

> We develop a form of inquiry in which we allow some field of reality to disclose itself to us in the complex of its internal relations. As we do that we come up with a significant clue in light of which all evidence is then re-examined and reinterpreted and found to fall into a coherent pattern or order. In a scientific inquiry the fundamental insight we have discovered may have to be revised as all the pieces of evidence come together and throw light upon each other, but nevertheless it is under the direction of that insight that the discovery is made. Once the insight has put us on the track of that discovery, something irreversible has taken place in our understanding: a pattern of truth has been built into our minds on which we cannot go back, and which we cannot rationally deny.

See Thomas F. Torrance, *The Mediation of Christ* (Grand Rapids: Eerdmans, 1983), pp. 13-14. Also see Torrance, *Resurrection*, pp. 11-13.

113. Or can we only impose a form or create our own meaning from a text, a meaning that bears only a tangential relation to the meaning the author intended, as McKnight seems to indicate in his book, *The Post-modern Use of the Bible*, when he calls for a radical reader-response approach to biblical interpretation.

114. See Torrance, *Transformation*, p. 78.

115. Ibid.

116. Hardy, "Torrance," p. 78. Hardy has also astutely observed that Torrance's understanding of the structure of belief parallels the structure of scientific inquiry just outlined. See ibid., pp. 80-81.

117. Torrance, *Transformation*, p. 80.

118. See Torrance, *Transformation*, p. 116. Here we see a parallel between Polanyi and Torrance and Narrative theology in that both entail, in the words of Gabriel Fackre, "well-founded doubts about the inordinate claims of discursive thought." See Gabriel Fackre's insightful article, "Narrative Theology: An Overview," in *Interpretation* 37, no. 3 (1983): p. 340.

119. Torrance, "Polanyi," p. 63.

120. Torrance, *Transformation*, p. 80.

121. Ibid., pp. 117-18.

122. Torrance, "Polanyi," p. 63.

123. See Torrance, *Scientific Theology*, p. 43

124. Torrance, "Polanyi," p. 64.

125. Ibid.

126. Ibid. To construe the epistemic process of scientific discovery in abstractive terms "would open up a fatal gap between the explicit and the tacit in which the all-important clues pointing to coherences in nature would vanish with the disintegration of the matrix in which they are born." Ibid.

127. Ibid.

128. See Michael Polanyi, *Personal Knowledge* (Chicago: University of Chicago Press, 1958), p. 13.

129. See Torrance, *Scientific Theology*, p. 77. Also see Torrance, *Theological Science*, pp. 161-203 and 222-80, where Torrance distinguishes between "existence-statements" and "coherence-statements" and the logic

of both. Here Torrance clarifies many of the important functions of the logico-deductive processes in natural and theological science.

130. Torrance, "Integration," p. 155. Torrance also asserts that, "Hence, just as it was not through any logical nexus that the basic concepts (out of which the theory was built) were derived from experiences, so likewise there is at the conclusion no logical nexus by means of which it can be demonstrated or verified: the all-important connection at the end must be just as empirical and intuitive as it was at the start." Ibid. He also says that "all knowledge of reality begins with experience and ends in experience, even though it many involve arduous intellectual activity throughout." Ibid., p. 153.

131. Torrance, "Polanyi," p. 67. Torrance disagrees with Polanyi on the details of this point, seeing a certain "phenomenalist" tendency in Polanyi's thought stemming from the influence of the Vienna school on Polanyi. See Torrance, *Scientific Theology*, pp. 133-35.

132. Torrance, *Transformation*, p. 123.

133. Torrance, "Polanyi," p. 72.

134. Torrance, *Scientific Theology*, p. 26.

135. Ibid., p. 27. At this point, the next step would be to incorporate a communal element in this self-criticism in which we listen to the insight and criticism of others along the lines of Gabriel Fackre's understanding of the role of the whole Church in theological conversation. Torrance grants this, as will become clear in chapter 3.

136. Ibid., pp. 133-34.

137. Torrance, *Transformation*, p. 84.

138. See Torrance's address, "Man the Priest of Creation," delivered when he received the Templeton Foundation Prize for Progress in Religion in March 1978, reprinted in Torrance, *Ground and Grammar*, pp. 1-14.

139. See Torrance, *Transformation*, pp. 135-36. and Torrance, *Scientific Theology*, p. 80.

140. Torrance, *Transformation*, pp. 77-78.

Chapter 2

The Integration of Form and Doctrine

In this chapter, we must develop the implications regarding Torrance's conceptualization of the integration of form (how concepts and theories are derived) from the foregoing discussion in chapter 1 for his understanding of doctrine as an instance of the integration of form in theology. This will require examining his understanding of biblical and theological hermeneutics so as to discern how doctrine arises as an integration of form in relation to the biblical witness. The chapter will also provide some examples of particular doctrines which Torrance recognizes as instances of the successful integration of form. The final section of the chapter will deal with Torrance's understanding of the structure of belief and will answer some of the most pointed criticisms of Torrance's epistemology to date.

Once again, it is important to note that Torrance is not attempting to ground theology upon natural science. In fact, a scientific theology cannot be built upon the methodology of natural science because theology requires a significantly different kind of personal participation since it is concerned with the living Triune God whom human beings cannot know without being reconciled to God at the very core of their being. Revelation and reconciliation are inseparable. Theological epistemology and method have to be shaped by the character (Torrance's fundamental axiom) of theology's "Object" (the living God).

Nevertheless, theology and physical science face parallel epistemological problems because of the received framework of thought and its dualist, phenomenalist and mechanistic habits of mind within which theology and science operate. In fact, Torrance finds the same kinds of habits of mind (as in the intellectual history from Descartes to Kant) and epistemological (and cosmological) dualism infecting modern historical-critical biblical studies and theology as well.

Torrance's Critique of Modern Hermeneutics

What happens when the historical Jesus is investigated with the kind of "observationalist and analytical methods" Torrance thinks are inadequate for the integration of form in theology?[1] In Torrance's view, this kind of approach "begins with a phenomenological bracketing off of the evangelical material from any realm of things in themselves and their internal relations, i.e., quite independent of a compelling structure beyond themselves."[2]

What Torrance means by this is that modern historical-critical biblical studies proceed in a similar manner to Newton who argued that his concepts and theories were deduced from sense data or abstracted from observing phenomena. First the "empirical data" has to be isolated and analyzed. Then the scientist deduces or abstracts scientific concepts and theories (natural laws) from that isolated data.[3]

Critical biblical studies also attempts to isolate the real (probable) historical data by piercing through the biblical text to its various textual and pre-textual sources that are regarded as more historically authentic. The reason this is necessary is because the natural theological coherence of the biblical witness as it stands (of a Gospel, for instance) was imposed upon the original historical data by the early church.[4] The doctrines of classical Christian faith, as it came to expression in the ecumenical councils of Nicea and Chalcedon, are still further removed from the real historical Jesus and reflect a theological framework influenced by non-Christian Greco-Roman culture and philosophy

According to critical biblical studies, what we see in the early Church and already in the New Testament is a constructivist epistemology in which the human mind imposed form upon what it sought to know not unlike the epistemological process described by Kant. The difference is that while Kant's categories of the mind are *a priori*, with the rise of historical consciousness, the framework of thought operative in the early Church is socially-acquired from the cultural matrix of that time-period.[5]

The modern biblical scholar, therefore, has to work back

behind the theological accretions that the early Church imposed upon the historical Jesus in order to arrive at the "real" historical data upon which to construct an accurate picture of the historical Jesus.[6] Of course, the resulting construal of the historical Jesus is not very close to that of Nicea and Chalcedon.

The actual problem, Torrance maintains, is the presuppositions and methods with which modern historical-critical biblical studies operate. Torrance sees the "modern" world view as one which rejects the idea of God acting directly in history. Thus, those who accept assumptions like this

> rule out of court from the very start all miracles and, of course, the incarnation and resurrection, and indeed any genuine revelation. Because they reject out of hand any idea that God interacts with our world, they can only interpret the New Testament accounts of the saving Acts of God in Christ as oblique, indirect, poetic, symbolic or mythological ways of speaking which are, strictly, not true for they have no direct ground in reality.[7]

Hence, the New Testament witness regarding "miracles, atonement, resurrection, and so on" are ascribed "to the creative imagination of early Christian piety–even to a sort of religious hysteria."[8]

The result, according to Torrance, is that the "ontological reference of biblical statements" to such an active self-revelation of God is by definition or presupposition cut short: "Thus the Bible is treated, and interpreted, in such a way as to bracket off the surface of the text and the phenomenal events it may describe from the objective, intelligible depth of God's active self-revelation, as though it were not academically respectable to take God or his self-revelation into account."[9]

Then, in turn, the historical-critical method, operating out of these assumptions, is deployed to sift through the New Testament documents in order to trace down the various forms and sources, and in the process, distinguish what can really be known about what the historical Jesus did and said from what is only the subsequent extrapolation of the early Church.[10] (This is what Torrance means by "analytical and abstractive methods.") Theology is then to be pursued on the basis of the resulting "data" regarding the historical Jesus that remain, for some kind of theoretical framework is required to take the place of the one "imposed" by the early Church.

Torrance argues that,

> Here we evidently have at work in modern biblical scholarship the constructivist rationalism with which we are familiar elsewhere in the history of phenomenalist thought in the ambiguous game of piecing together what has already been disintegrated through its basic assumptions and analytic methods, so that one artificially contrived framework after another is thought up in order to "save the appearances."[11]

Yet, Torrance thinks that "it is we who create the impasse by our failure to understand the material in the light of the conceptual organization it derives from its own natural ground–by failing to interpret the narratives in terms of their own latent or inherent patterns."[12] Our problem is that we "persist in tearing apart what has already been joined on a natural ontological basis, and then complain that the New Testament account of Jesus is inconsistent or paradoxical, since we cannot now put the empirical and theoretical factors together."[13] Despite the immense amount that has been learned about the Bible, its language, and its history through the modern historical-critical study–all of which Torrance grants–Torrance questions how much ground has been gained theologically through this approach.[14]

Remember that these same kind of methods proved problematic in natural science. Hume demonstrated that Newton did not and could not deduce his concepts and theories from sense data. Kant's analysis revealed that the human mind operates with a continuous coordination between empirical and theoretical elements in all human knowledge.

Furthermore, Maxwell and Einstein demonstrated that the analytic isolation of "empirical data" actually breaks up the very intrinsic interrelations (form in being) of an electromagnetic field (or space-time continuum) into discrete particles (atoms externally related to one another) and in so doing destroys the natural cohesion that is characteristic or defining of what those intrinsically interconnected realities are. Torrance thinks that the analytic and deductive methods of critical biblical studies do the same thing to the biblical text.

Picture the Bible (or the Gospels) as a kind of literary *Magic Eye* with clues embedded in the interrelations of the details to a three-dimensional image (God's *oikonomia*, the divine realities and events in God's saving activity in Israel, in Jesus Christ, and in the apostolic Church).[15] If the Bible is examined piecemeal by analytically isolating data, the very interrelations (and clues) of the detail, which have to be integrated in order to perceive the pattern embedded in the detail, are effaced.

While we could learn a lot about the *Magic Eye* by isolating the tiny figures and analyzing them separately, this will not take us very far toward perceiving the 3-D image. So Torrance argues that we have to indwell the conjoint and multifaceted character of the biblical witness in order to assimilate it and thereby grasp the pattern of God's self-revelation. This is not wholly unlike the way we are able to integrate a subsidiary awareness of the clues embedded in the *Magic Eye* so that we see in our focal awareness the 3-D image imprinted in the interrelations of the detail.

Though there are many limitations in this comparison, it helps indicate that Torrance views theological interpretation of the Bible as primarily an integrative activity that approaches the Bible holistically. Methods and/or presuppositions which do not permit this kind of holistic, integrative theological procedure are questionable in Torrance's mind, if for no other reason than that parallel methods and presuppositions have been set aside in natural science (as we see in Maxwell, Einstein, Polanyi and others) because they proved to be inadequate and actually detrimental to advance in scientific inquiry. If an electromagnetic field requires a sophisticated holistic and integrative approach in order for the human mind to assimilate its intrinsic interconnected kind of order, then should we not expect that the even more subtle order with which theology is concerned will also require modes of inquiry beyond analytic, abstractive, deductive and similar methods which tear the fabric of Scripture into pieces?[16]

Of course, Torrance is not opposed to source, form and redaction criticism.[17] He admits there are inconsistencies between the Gospel accounts and tensions in the theological perspectives of various books of the Bible. Yet these are often the actual clues to a deeper coherence and intelligibility in the interrelations in the biblical witness.[18]

However, what if we set aside the assumptions of critical biblical studies and operate with a different method of integrating form; one which pays close attention to the original and natural integration of the empirical and theoretical, historical and theological, factors of the biblical witness; an integrative approach which operates simultaneously at both levels, thinking them conjointly?[19] This is what Torrance proposes. How does it take place?

Hermeneutics and the Integration of Form

Torrance argues that there is no logical, analytical or abstractive way to enter the dynamic pattern of God's revelatory and saving activity in Israel and Jesus Christ imprinted upon the ordered series of events (*oikonomia*, form inherent in being) to which the biblical documents bear witness. We cannot deduce or abstract the incarnation, atonement or the Trinity (the intrinsic form inherent in God's activity) by isolating and analyzing "historical data" because these procedures are incapable of integrating form in the holistic manner appropriate to the nature of the field under investigation (Jesus Christ has to be interpreted in light of the Old Testament in order for his death on the Cross to make sense as an atonement for sin, for example). Torrance proposes another approach that he believes is more adequate.[20]

Cultivation of Insights

The first step in the procedure Torrance advocates is formally similar to Einstein and Polanyi's work in the sphere of natural science, for we cultivate insights by *indwelling* the field of inquiry (in theology, the biblical witness). As we indwell Scripture and assimilate its witness to the relations and patterns of God's revealing and saving activity, a structural kinship or isomorphism develops between the human mind (an integration of form in knowing) and the intrinsic structure (intelligibility) of the saving events and divine realities (form in being) to which the Bible bears witness.[21] Since the order with which theology is concerned is of such a character that it must be grasped holistically (we have to consider the entire Gospel depiction of Jesus Christ, not just the "probable data" unearthed by critical biblical studies),the method employed must be one that enables us to enter that order holistically.[22] This informal movement of thought (indwelling) permits us to attend to all that the field entails until we gain the "clues" which, in turn, enable us to begin to grasp the order of the field of inquiry.

These clues arise only out of an ongoing and intimate contact with the field of inquiry. This is an informal process, since we cannot anticipate all that the field will embrace before the inquiry begins. There is real discovery and the first glimpses of the intelligibility of the field arise as insights or clues.

The isomorphism that develops (often in the form of a concept/theory) is not necessary and inherent in the mind prior to the process of indwelling, as in Kant. It only arises out of that process (and the participation the process entails) so that the concept/theory (assimilation of form in knowing) comes to reflect and disclose the intrinsic relations in the field of inquiry (the doctrine of the Trinity reflects and discloses the threeness-in-oneness of God's revealing and saving activity). In addition the integration of form that takes place is dynamic (it "happens," it is an event that arises out of the process of indwelling), but also ontological (it is not simply constructed and imposed by the human mind on that which the mind seeks to know).

The kind of clue that arises out of the process is what Clement of Alexandria called a *prolepsis*, Torrance contends, the forward leap of the mind to a hitherto unknown aspect of reality, "an authentically heuristic process of inquiry and knowledge (*heuretike ekzetesis/episteme*) leading through scientific perception (*epistemonike theoria*) to accurate faith (*akribepistis*), i.e., a rational assent that corresponds precisely to the nature of the reality apprehended."[23] Because theology is concerned with a redemptive self-communication by the living God, theological inquiry requires evangelical and doxological participation, if it is to reflect the redemptive character of God and God's activity in the biblical witness.[24]

Of course, this is what makes theology rather different than natural science, since theological inquiry deals with the living God who comes to us in *Self*-revelation that demands a participation with characteristics different than what is found in natural science. Torrance often asserts that we cannot know God behind God's back or apart from God's purposes for our lives.[25]

In Torrance's perspective, the place where we find the conditions which provide participatory access to the order theology investigates and develop clues or anticipatory insights is the Church, the people of God in worship, fellowship and commitment to the Gospel: "It is through religious experience, in the context of tradition in the continuity of the life of the

Church where learning through others, meditation upon the message of Holy Scripture, prayer and worship regularly take place, that these basic convictions and primary concepts take their rise."[26]

Thus Torrance argues that as a child learns more about physics in her first five years than she will ever be able to fully comprehend even as a brilliant physicist, so we come to know "far more than we can ever tell about God within the fellowship of the Church," if the Church is responsibly participating in the Gospel.[27] Here we learn the basic insights that are needed to develop knowledge of God in explicit theological formulation.

There is a social coefficient, Torrance contends, in all human knowledge, including knowledge of God. The structures of thought and life embodied in the habits of a community influence all scientific endeavor, including theology. This is simply another way of saying that Torrance grants that there are no *a priori* categories in the Kantian sense, but that we are always within the knowing relation in which we apprehend realities through a cultural-linguistic framework. We will deal with this at length in the next chapter. For Torrance, theology is always faith seeking understanding within the Christian community, though it includes rigorous intellectual activity throughout.[28]

In addition, Torrance contends that this is, in fact, what happened in the early church. In his examination of classical conciliar patristic theology as it comes to expression in the Niceno-Constantinopolitan Creed, Torrance finds this same kind of theological process of tacit knowing by indwelling of biblical witness within the worshiping life of the Christian community.[29] Through this process of indwelling and tacit knowing the empirical and theoretical, the historical and theological, are fused in participatory Christian experience and knowledge.[30]

Only in this manner can we adequately (holistically), apprehend the kind of complex order with which we are concerned in theology–the kind of relations that obtain in the realities which are witnessed to by the biblical text. If the historical-critical method is unable to arrive at these clues, which are developed into refined theoretical components (doctrines) in our theological knowledge (like the hypostatic union, *homoousion*, and the Trinity, for example), it is because the analytic and abstractive tendencies of the historical-critical method hinder it from entering the all-important integrative process that enables theology to attend to all that the biblical texts embrace in their witness to God's self-revelation and grasp at least something of the complex of relations underlying the biblical message. The intelligibility or order inherent in God's revealing and saving activity (*oikonomia*) is of such a complex and interrelated character that it cannot be grasped by analytic, deductive modes of discursive reason (as important as they are for theology), but only through an integrative movement of thought.[31] Without this informal integrative process that occurs within the Church as the community of reciprocity in relation to God, these basic clues or insights cannot arise and the biblical text becomes theologically baffling, as it has, in Torrance's mind, for all too much of modern biblical scholarship, despite the tremendous advance that scholarship has made in so many other respects.[32]

Scientific Theological Inquiry

The specific scientific activity in theology, Torrance contends, is not all that different from the way knowledge arises out of this informal or tacit process, but is rather a rigorous refinement of it.[33] In fact, for Torrance, scientific theology is always a development or refinement of the basic knowledge of God that arises out of God's self-revelation through the grace of Jesus Christ in the communion of the Holy Spirit within the evangelical and doxological life of the Christian community as the Church indwells the biblical witness.[34] Theology simply refines, extends, corrects and unifies this knowledge and tests the Church's life and witness in light of it.

The theologian returns to the biblical witness with the clues discussed above. Torrance maintains that this demands "theological exegesis and interpretation" of the biblical text in which we attempt to "indwell" the biblical witness, consider the whole apostolic witness in its various strata in such a way so as to be directed through it to the objective realities (God's revealing and saving activity through Israel and in Jesus Christ) under which the apostolic tradition arose and took shape in the primitive Church.[35] In Torrance's words:

> Evangelical theology is built up not through systematic construction out of biblical propositions, but through such a cognitive indwelling of theologians

> in the Holy Scriptures that the objective truths of divine revelation become steadily imprinted upon their minds. It is then on the ground of those truths and their inner connections to which the Scriptures refer, and under the guidance of the theological instinct they generate, that theologians must think it all out for themselves and bring it to coherent expression.[36]

In this way, indwelling the conjoint focus of the multiple strata of the biblical witness in its reference to God's self-revelation, the basic insights or clues discussed above are tested and extended or maybe questioned and subjected to revision.

Torrance never develops all that this indwelling includes, since it cannot be rendered entirely explicit because it is an holistic and integrative activity dependent on a tacit dimension. To attempt to do so is to sever the immediate relation between the mind and reality which is of a personal participatory character, and to replace it with some other type of relation, often a logical one, as in the case of Newton who said we deduce our concepts/theories from sense data.

It is, however, at this juncture that all the normal hermeneutical apparatus come into play, including the historical-critical method which Torrance maintains is "scientifically obligatory,"[37] despite its limitations, as already noted.

General Guidelines for Biblical Interpretation

Torrance never provides a detailed discussion of the more mundane tools or exegetical procedures of biblical and theological interpretation because his emphasis is on what he sees as the neglected integrative aspect of proper hermeneutical and epistemological activity. He does however discuss four "general guidelines" for theological interpretation of the biblical witness faithful to the actual pattern of saving events in God's activity in Israel and Jesus Christ out of which the Bible arose. Theological interpretation must

> (1) attend to the "scope" of divine revelation in the Scriptures, (2) respect the objective grounding and ordering of Scriptural statements in the "economic" reality of the Words and Acts of God himself, (3) be guided by an interpretive framework of thought

> derived from the connections and coherences in the biblical subject matter, and (4) clarify and check interpretation in accordance with "canon of truth."[38]

By the "scope" of divine revelation in the Scriptures, Torrance has in mind "the general perspective" or "frame of reference" within which Scripture is correctly interpreted. It denotes the basic pattern of meaning that comes into view when we look not simply at the words of the biblical witness, but look through the text to God's redemptive self-revelation out of which the text arose and to which it directs us.[39] We attempt to follow the "semantic reference" of Scripture so that we encounter and apprehend the living Words and Acts of God through the biblical text for ourselves.[40]

We will discuss what Torrance means by the "objective grounding and ordering" of the biblical witness in the "economic" (*oikonomia*) activity of God in chapter 4 which discusses the material content of the integration of form in relation to doctrine. However, basically what Torrance has in mind by this second hermeneutical guideline is that if we are to interpret and understand Scripture appropriately we have to trace what we learn back to its source in God's patterned redemptive activity in the history of Israel and in Jesus Christ, for Torrance maintains that the Scriptures are grounded in and structured by God's *oikonomia* so that the interpretation of the biblical witness must be guided by it.[41]

Furthermore, since the primary function of the biblical reference beyond itself depends upon the secondary reference of biblical statements to one another in coherent sequences, Torrance argues that biblical statements have to be read within the syntactical or formal-logical structures and whole context in which they are embedded.[42] This point is very similar to Hans Frei's contention that the biblical narratives convey their meaning and depict their meaning only through the complex chronological sequences and interaction of the entire narrative. This is why approaches which fragment the text (the quest the "real" historical "data" behind the text) are doomed to failure, for they destroy the very interconnections that are the clues to the texts real meaning.

Here the full arsenal of exegetical procedures is utilized in order to discern the meaning of the many images, analogies, figures, idioms, etc. of Scripture and the orderly connections built up by the words, sentences and narratives of the Bible.[43]

This must all be organized in such a way so as to disclose the "inner rational sequence" or the "inner logic" of the biblical message. This is what Torrance means by his third "guideline," the interpretive framework of thought derived from the connections and coherences in the biblical subject matter. I suspect that Torrance has something like the Niceno-Constantinopolitan Creed in mind.

The fourth guideline for the task of biblical interpretation, according to Torrance, is that one must clarify and check interpretations in accordance with "the canon of truth," which he also calls "the rule of faith," or "the Truth of God itself" in Jesus Christ.[44] Here, Torrance's intent is that we allow the Truth of God in Christ to maintain its majesty and authority over all our interpretations and formulations of it.[45] This point will be discussed more fully in chapter 5.

Thus, through the interpretive process, with the help of these four guidelines and all that they imply, the theologian's mind "becomes assimilated to the *integration* of the different strata [of the Bible] in their bearing upon the objective events and realities they intend, and...there arises a structural kinship between his knowing and what he seeks to know."[46] For Torrance–and this is the absolutely crucial point for grasping his theological method, especially his hermeneutics and his understanding of the nature of doctrine–this involves an integration of form "which operates at a profounder level than any formal deduction...and which cannot be reproduced or replaced by any explicit processes of a logical or inferential kind..."[47] as significant as those explicit procedures are for theological inquiry.

There is a circularity to this hermeneutical activity in which exegesis and interpretation of Bible is guided by a theological articulation of the realities and truths which the Bible mediates, though those realities and truths are only accessible to us through our ongoing exegesis of the biblical witness.[48] Furthermore, Torrance argues that this "inevitably has the effect of allotting to the Scriptures a subsidiary status" to the realities they intend.[49] This is why Torrance is willing to grant "the network of difficulties and contradictions..., for example, in the New Testament presentation of the accounts of the resurrection,"[50] and yet not be terribly concerned by it. Here again we see a distinct difference between Torrance's position and that of Protestant fundamentalism.

This does not diminish the importance of Scripture in

Torrance's theology, for "without all that the Scriptures in the saving purpose of God have come to embody, we would not be able to know God or to have intelligible communion with him within our continuing human and historical existence."[51] Rather for Torrance this has meant "an exciting rethinking and deepening of the doctrine of Holy Scripture"[52] which we will discuss in chapter 4.

For now, however, it should be noted that one of the reasons why Torrance is not particularly bothered by difficulties and contradictions regarding the details of the resurrection, for example, is his understanding of the nature of memory: "Does the way of thinking which gives primacy to written language not operate with a different organization of recall, on a linear, word-for-word basis, rather than employing in-depth structures which characterize the natural memory or the ongoing informal, tacit coefficient of explicit thought?"[53] Scripture is a faithful witness to the realities it intends despite the difficulties and inaccuracies in the text as it stands.

In other words, the New Testament record may not be literally historical in its details regarding the chronology of the events of Easter morning or the exact words Jesus said. But that is neither the way natural memory (with its in-depth structures) operates, nor is it of real consequence for Christian theology and faith, for what is important is the *fact* that Jesus did rise on Easter (leaving the tomb empty) and the *significance* of resurrection for Christian faith and theology. And for Torrance, the fact and significance of resurrection have a quite literally unforgettable character that was indelibly impressed upon the memory of the Apostles and the early Christian community in such a way that, in spite of inaccuracies regarding the details, what is of real consequence has been faithfully and adequately preserved in the New Testament witness.[54]

Now the integration of form in biblical and theological hermeneutics Torrance advocates is profoundly *personal*, but not purely *subjective*, similar to the personal character the integration of form in Polanyi discussed in the previous chapter. The personal character of our knowledge in theological inquiry is accentuated, Torrance contends, because not only is God personal and God's self-revelation to us personal, but we are intensely personalized by God's grace in and through God's self-communication to us through Jesus Christ in the Holy Spirit.[55] The mediation of revelation cannot be separated from the mediation of reconciliation, for knowing God "requires cognitive union with him in which our whole being is affected by his love and holiness."[56] So we become more fully human and personal in our knowledge of God than ever before.

Examples of the Integration of Form in Theology

Torrance sees an example of the kind of theological activity he is suggesting in Athanasius, particularly his two-part work, *Contra Gentes/De Incarnatione*.[57] Here Torrance finds a heuristic argumentation in which Athanasius attempts to discern his way into the very center of the biblical message of God's self-revealing interaction with humanity and allow it to illumine the whole complex of intrinsic interrelations theology is concerned with.[58] Torrance finds no *a priori* arguments or attempts to derive knowledge of God abstractively from Holy Scriptures in Athanasius' work. Rather Torrance sees Athanasius attempting "through a reasoned movement of thought within the field of Christian experience and faith to penetrate into its intrinsic order and intelligibility."[59] Athanasius discloses the organic way in which creation and redemption are to be understood from the central point of reference in the incarnation of the Word or Son of God, which in turn throws light upon other theological relations and connections.[60]

I will not pursue Torrance's rather interesting and novel interpretation of *Contra Gentes*,[61] but turn to *De Incarnatione*. Here, Torrance sees Athanasius focusing on the relation between God and humanity revealed in the person and work of Jesus Christ. Torrance argues that by utilizing one probing question after another, Athanasius dispenses with unfitting or inappropriate theological conceptions so as to develop his theological interpretation in accordance with God's activity in relation to humanity. Athanasius tries to find "the appropriate kind of connection in thought which will match the inner sequence (*akolouthia*) of divine revelation," "the chain of reason (*heirmos*)" in God's gracious activity in relation to humanity, "the divine *philanthropia*" or the logic of grace incarnate in Jesus Christ.[62] Torrance sees Athanasius as attempting to uncover the "ordering force and distinctive pattern of grace (*he kat'eikona charis*)" which we find in God's self-revelation in Jesus Christ so as to conceptualize (integration of form in knowing), as far as humanly possible, the intrinsic intelligible character of and reason for (form in being)

God's redemptive activity in Christ.[63]

At the end of his discussion in *De Incarnatione*, Torrance points out that Athanasius tells his reader that within this short treatise he has offered the lover of Christ, "the basic grammar and distinctive pattern (*stoicheiosin kai charaktara*) of faith in accordance with Christ and his divine manifestation toward us."[64] Athanasius then urges his reader "to take his clue (*prophasin*) from this and go on genuinely to apply his mind to the words of the Scriptures, for in so doing he would learn more completely and clearly the exactness or precision (*akribeian*) of what has been said."[65] Thus the insights or clues that arose out of Athanasius' theological activity within the life of the Church serve to open up the intelligibility of Scripture in light of which the clues are then tested, refined, extended and unified.

An illustration of this kind of integration of form which Torrance sees arising in the history of the Church is when "the doctrine of the hypostatic union...keeps on forcing itself upon our minds and we are convinced that here we have penetrated deeply into the inner logic of the evangelical material [of the biblical witness]."[66]

A further example of the effective integration of form in theology is the *homoousion*. Here Torrance sees the Nicene fathers "examining and testing the various expressions, images and representations used of God" throughout the biblical documents and "correlating them with the objective realities and relations they were taken to serve" so that the biblical expressions and images could "be modified and corrected by relation to one another within their common frame of reference."[67] Torrance argues that through this kind of exegetical activity the Nicene theologians developed the concept of the *homoousion* so as to clarify the character of the relation between the incarnate Son and God the Father at the center of the Gospel. It also enabled them to set aside the contradictions and confusing formulations that had arisen within the Church (like Arianism) through misuse of the biblical images and the misinterpretation of the biblical witness. Thus Torrance sees the *homoousion* as "a supreme example of strict theological understanding arising out of the interpretation of Scripture."[68]

The *homoousion* sets forth the evangelical insight that in Jesus Christ, *God* is present and at work for our salvation; and in the communion of the Spirit, it is *God* who illumines our hearts and minds so that we hear the Gospel resound through the biblical witness and come to share through the same Spirit in the love of God in Christ, the love that God is as Father, Son, and Holy Spirit.[69] As Torrance states it: "What Jesus Christ does for us and to us, and what the Holy Spirit does in us, is what God himself does for us, to us, and in us."[70] The *homoousion* asserts in the strongest possible way that Jesus Christ is not some created intermediary between humanity and God, but rather God with us and for us, the very Word of God made flesh for our salvation.[71]

Torrance sees the *homoousion* as providing "compressed expression in exact and equivalent language, not so much to the biblical terms themselves but to the objective meaning or reality they were designed to point out and convey."[72] It is an accurate and highly productive integration of form that is neither deduced from the data of Scripture, nor simply imposed on the biblical witness. It is not even the result of an inductive operation in which all of the relevant texts are examined and synthesized. Rather the *homoousion* articulates the intrinsic constitutive relations in the realities to which Scripture bears witness, the revelation and redeeming acts of God through Jesus Christ in the Holy Spirit. It expresses the core of the Gospel in which the faithful know that it is *God* who has loved them to the uttermost in Jesus Christ and who unites with Christ through the Holy Spirit.

The *homoousion* is an effective, elucidatory insight which expresses and discloses the depth of truth in the gospel of Jesus Christ that every believer knows tacitly even if he cannot understand and articulate its theological categories.[73] As such, it serves as a guide to the interpretation of the biblical witness, though always in such a way that it is subordinate to the self-revelation of God mediated through the Bible and revisable in light of further interpretation of Scripture.

Furthermore, Torrance also points out that when this kind of theological activity, and the integration of form it entails, is carried a stage further, we discover a higher level of unity and simplicity which organizes the whole structure of theology: "This is the doctrine of the Holy Trinity which is forced upon our understanding as the fundamental grammar of theological thought, but in such a way that our apprehension of God is evidently grounded, in some measure at least, upon relations internal to His own eternal Being."[74]

The doctrine of the Trinity, of course, is an apprehension of God which falls exceedingly short of what God is, since Torrance notes that when we actually know God in the Gospel we always know that God is infinitely greater than we can conceive. Yet the doctrine of the Trinity represents what we must say about God in order to remain faithful to the self-revelation and self-communication of God in the Gospel as Father, Son and Holy Spirit.[75] The doctrine of the Trinity is a classic example of the kind of integration of form Torrance advocates and also of the nature of doctrine. We will examine the doctrine of the Trinity in greater detail in chapter 4.

The hypostatic union, the *homoousion*, the Trinity and several other key doctrines enable us to enter the intrinsic connections at the center of Christian faith in a way, Torrance maintains (he believes in ecumenical harmony with the classical theology of the ancient catholic Church), that discloses inner cohesion of the biblical witness so that we discern at least something of the intelligible pattern in God's *oikonomia*. These doctrines arise out of the kind of holistic integrative theological interpretation described above and these doctrines disclose the intrinsic intelligibility in God's self-revelation (form inherent in being) in a way that we could not see before they were integrated instances of form arising out of the biblical witness and the realities apprehended through that witness.[76] Such doctrinal formulations function in a disclosive manner in relation to the central realities of the Christian faith which they intend.

Axiomatic Dogmatics and Doctrine

Torrance can call the kind of scientific theology he advocates, "fluid dogmatics"[77] or "axiomatic dogmatics."[78] This kind of theology, as we have seen, does not proceed by abstraction or logical deduction on the basis of fixed premises drawn from the biblical witness or on the basis of the "data" regarding Israel or the historical Jesus uncovered by historical-critical biblical studies once it has cut away the later accretions imposed by the early Church and its theology. The theological method Torrance advocates utilizes a different and holistic integration of form that operates at deeper level. We indwell the entire biblical witness within the evangelical and doxological life of the Church until basic clues arise out of this informal process with its tacit knowing.

In this kind of scientific theological inquiry or theological science, Torrance contends that we develop these clues into a "preliminary model" (integration of form in knowing) through which we seek to disclose the intrinsic interrelations of the field of inquiry so as to grasp its intelligibility (form in being).[79] This kind of model is revisable and flexible. It is an axiomatic instrument utilized in the progressive development of theological inquiry. If successful, the model furthers our inquiry and discloses ever more fully and deeply the intrinsic interconnections and intelligibility of God's patterned self-revelation.

At this point, Torrance argues, we then go a step further and develop a higher-level *disclosure model* "through which our grasp of the inner logic of divine revelation becomes clearer and more explicit, so that the way is opened up for general clarification and simplification of the whole body of theological knowledge."[80] Here Torrance has in mind the doctrine of the Trinity and the way it unifies and simplifies our knowledge of God and the Christian faith.[81]

This is how Torrance understands doctrine. Doctrines are disclosure models. They are refined (and refineable) cognitive instruments for further theological inquiry. Or, to state it in still another way, doctrines are particular instances of the successful integration of form in theological inquiry that direct our minds in a progressively disclosive manner to the realities with which Christian faith and theology are concerned, though doctrines must remain open to, and revisable in light of, those realities. While imperfect and inadequate, doctrines bring to awareness and explicit expression something of the intelligibility, the interrelations constitutive of the realities of Christian faith that theological inquiry seeks to explore. Such doctrinal formulations function in a disclosive relation to the field of inquiry out of which they arise.

Thus doctrines, for Torrance, are not propositions corresponding to objective truths or realities as in the cognitive approach (evangelical rationalism, for example), as outlined by Lindbeck, since this is a misconceptualization and oversimplification of how thought is related to reality. It is an oversimplification that fails to take full account of the informal tacit dimension, an issue which will be more fully addressed in chapter 5. Neither are doctrines nondiscursive religious symbols that express inner supra-conceptual experiences, as is characteristic of experiential-expressivism so popular in modern theology since Schleiermacher. Doctrines are also not Lindbeck's second-order rules (the grammar) governing first-order religious discourse, though doctrine does guide the pattern of Christian discourse.

In Torrance's perspective, doctrines are disclosure-models or properly developed integrations of form arising out of the kind of theological and hermeneutical activity described above. They are theoretical formulations which can be progressively disclosive of the realities of Christian faith they signify, but always subordinate to, revisable in light of, and relativized by, those realities. Therefore for Torrance, doctrines are cognitive, but not really propositional. They are expressive or disclosive, not of pre-cognitive inner experience, but of the intrinsic and intelligible interrelations of the realities of Christian faith that are accessible only via the kind of complex participatory knowing described throughout this chapter and the previous one.

Yet doctrines are more than cognitive. They are polyvalent and serve other functions in relation to Christian faith and community. We will examine the relation of doctrine to Lindbeck's cultural-linguistic frameworks (what Torrance calls the social coefficient) in the next chapter.

The Structure of Belief

Why must Torrance's axiomatic dogmatics, with its integration of form leading to doctrine as disclosure model, be conceived the way he contends that it is? What sustains the kind of scientific theology or theological science that Torrance advocates? Daniel Hardy, in his astute essay on T. F. Torrance's theology, correctly observes that whereas others may proceed in a pragmatic manner, sustained by the fact that "it works," for Torrance, "the basis of scientific activity, whether theological or natural, is actually belief, which plays 'a normative role in the gaining and developing of all scientific knowledge.'"[82] We must examine this structure of belief and its role in Torrance's thought.

Hardy points out that there is a parallel between Torrance's understanding of the structure of belief and that of scientific activity: as human beings respond to the self-presentation of reality in the integration of form, so the object of belief grounds the human response of belief, for beliefs arise in a compulsory and personal, but non-causal or non-necessary, manner.[83] In other words, for Torrance, there is a two-way relation between the objective and subjective poles of belief, just as there is in the integration of form and all personal and rational activity.[84]

Thus Torrance defines belief as "an ontological act of recognition and assent which cannot be further analyzed, but without which there could be no rational or scientific knowledge."[85] He concludes that, "Proper belief, therefore, cannot be said to be irrational or blind, for it is a cognitive assent to some aspect of reality, a basic act of recognition in which our minds respond to a pattern or structure inherent in the world around us which imprints itself upon them."[86] Beliefs are associated with the most basic level of the relation of thought and speech to reality.[87]

Furthermore, as Hardy also points out, this means that for Torrance, belief is integral to knowledge.[88] Along with Polanyi, Torrance insists that we must recognize belief "as a source of knowledge" out of which all discovery arises, since in belief the human mind is open to the intelligibility of what we are investigating.[89] Polanyi accuses the "critical mind" of modernity of repudiating one of its two cognitive faculties–that of belief–in its quest for rational and/or empirical demonstrability.[90]

Torrance contends that no one can operate outside such a framework of belief, for it constitutes the basic convictions that orient inquiry and influence all interpretation of data.[91] To claim otherwise is, in the end, in Torrance's mind, merely a "cloak" for the will to believe whatever one wants under the false pretense of "self-critical severity."[92]

For this reason, as Hardy notes, belief for Torrance must not be placed in sharp contrast to knowledge, as in the case of Locke or Hume, as if belief requires some kind of logical demonstration. Torrance maintains that, "it is irrational to contrast faith and reason, for faith is the very mode of rationality adopted by reason in its fidelity to what it seeks to understand, and as such faith constitutes the most basic form of knowledge upon which all subsequent rational inquiry proceeds."[93] Hardy also suggests that such a view of belief or faith may appear to be similar to Locke's "maximal act of judgement" or the last resort in an attempt to sustain the possibility of knowledge.[94] However, for Torrance, belief is better described as "the resting of our minds upon objective reality ('that which really is' 'the nature and truth of things')."[95]

Thus Torrance is adamant that beliefs are not (or at least should not be) subjectively, but objectively grounded. As responses to some intelligibility or "logos" inherent in the nature of things, beliefs ought to be related to the *objective pole* of human knowledge.[96]

Furthermore, since beliefs are to be objectively grounded, they must match the distinctive nature and intrinsic intelligibility of the reality in question.[97] As Hardy points out, beliefs for Torrance "should be proportioned to the *nature of the truth* to which they are directed, to the kind of truth to which they respond."[98] This leads to a stratification of belief.[99]

Beliefs are basic convictions, Torrance maintains, that arise in our minds "compulsorily but not necessarily."[100] They are neither arbitrary conventions of the mind, nor causal and necessary impositions upon the mind. They arise as we allow our minds to be shaped by the intelligible order of that which we seek to know and which we cannot in good conscience resist.[101]

Torrance thinks that if a "necessary" relation were posited between belief and reality, as if beliefs were causally imposed upon the mind by reality, this would eliminate error, but also personal responsibility.[102] Torrance asserts that there is an irreducible personal and moral dimension involved here, as in the case of his understanding of the integration of form. A person should believe as he/she is *compelled*, though not *caused*, to believe.[103]

Proper recognition must be given to this "non-formal" or "extra-logical" relation between the mind and reality in both belief and knowledge, a relation that is non-causal and personal, yet nonetheless rational.[104] Failure to grasp this point has led to repeated misunderstanding of Torrance's epistemology and theological method, as in the case of Ronald Thiemann.[105]

This points up two more elements in Torrance's understanding of the structure of belief. The first is the essential "exclusiveness" of belief. Since belief arises in a non-causal and non-logical but nonetheless reasonable and compelling manner as a response on the basis of an inherent intelligibility of reality, it entails a judgement; a judgement that excludes alternative ways of seeing things.[106] An example of this might be the belief in a living God who interacts with the world of space and time. Such a belief excludes other ways of construing the relation between God and the world that deny the possibility of such interaction.

However, on the other hand, because belief arises under the compelling character of reality and its intelligibility, Torrance maintains that belief must remain open to modification in light of what we have yet to learn of the universe around us or of God in the case of theology, for both continually take us by surprise.[107] We only partially grasp the range of intelligibility of the universe or of God. Torrance calls this the "open range" of belief, which parallels the open character of "disclosure models" or doctrines as noted above. Belief must remain constantly open to revision in light of the reality to which belief is directed.

Together, personal beliefs form fiduciary frameworks which comprise a set of controlling convictions on which all explicit rational operations rely.[108] Torrance sees this framework of belief as quite different from Kant's regulative principles, for Kant's categories of understanding are formal *a priori* structures independent of experience, and therefore quite inert. Torrance's framework of belief is far less consciousness-centered or limited to the conscious mind, since it arises out of the tacit dimension.[109]

Such a framework of belief is informal, personal, and as such, open to revision because of its responsive, two-way relation to the depth of objective reality as that reality comes more fully into view as inquiry proceeds. This is an important point in understanding Torrance's thought, for it is this dynamic and responsive character of the human mind wherein the mind is able to expand in light of further disclosure of the fullness of reality without constricting reality to the limits of the mind's present fiduciary framework.[110] Moreover, because people indwell these fiduciary frameworks, Torrance's understanding of belief allows for deep disagreements between people's frameworks.[111]

Furthermore, frameworks of belief are embodied in communities and their traditions. Torrance asserts that it is "within the continuity of such a supporting community and the tradition it carries that the basic beliefs are transmitted from generation to generation."[112] This, of course, is just as true for the Christian community as it is for the scientific community.[113] Therefore, the Christian community plays an important role in the transmission and maintenance of the framework of belief ,which is so important in explicit theological inquiry, including doctrinal formulation.

However, since the Church interacts with the habits of thought and belief of the surrounding culture, it can come to reflect those habits, assimilating them into its presuppositional framework, which in turn can adversely influence the Church's

However, since the Church interacts with the habits of thought and belief of the surrounding culture, it can come to reflect those habits, assimilating them into its presuppositional framework, which in turn can adversely influence the Church's interpretation and appropriation of the Gospel. This brings us to the subject of the next chapter of this dissertation: the relation between this social coefficient in all knowledge and belief and the Church's theology and doctrine. Before turning to this subject, a few critical questions regarding Torrance's proposal need to be addressed.

Critical Questions About Torrance's Proposal

A repeated criticism of Thomas F. Torrance's theological position on issues in this chapter and the previous one is the frequent obscurity of his writing. Daniel Hardy indicates that, at least in part, Torrance is a victim of the intractable character of his theological subject-matter.[114] Hardy also points out that Torrance is so anxious to interconnect ideas and enable people to see important relations that he quite often lapses into "overcompressed exposition."[115]

Torrance candidly admitted this problem in his theology in an interview by Michael Bauman. When asked about the weaknesses or shortcomings of his theology, Torrance confessed that, "My weakness, I think, is my style. I do not know a way to put my theology across that makes for easy reading. Great minds...are able to combine profundity with simplicity and intelligibility."[116]

However, Daniel Hardy lodges a further criticism against Torrance's position at this point which is of significantly greater import. According to Hardy, it is not simply the difficulty of the subject-matter that creates the problem of obscurity in Torrance's theology. Rather it is the character of his position which, Hardy asserts, "verges on the private and publicly inexpressible."[117] Torrance argues for an empirico-theoretical knowledge in which the actuality of knowledge is grounded in a double-activity in which human beings *respond* to the *self-presentation* of reality. Verification, as noted toward the end of the previous chapter, requires a participatory knowing relation like that which generated the knowledge in the first place.

Thus Hardy argues that Torrance's position is one in which

way that their words and ideas are transparencies through which others can see."[119] This is not unlike helping someone see the 3-D image in the *Magic Eye*. In the end one either sees it or one does not.

The danger Hardy perceives in Torrance's position is the tendency to stay at the level of occurrence, "remaining content with the *fact* that these relations *occur*."[120] Hardy grants that Torrance's greatest contribution "lies in his careful statement, supported by evidence...of the fact that they occur in theology and the natural sciences, and occur in such a way as to have brought knowledge of the reality with which they are concerned."[121] But there are three problems that Hardy perceives with Torrance's perspective: 1.) the privileged position of those in the knowing relation; 2.) the "occasionalist" character of that position; and 3.) the "exclusivist" claims for the knowledge thus attained.[122]

Hardy's critique is direct and serious and requires thoughtful consideration. "Occasionalism" and "actualism" are standard critical responses to theologians who have been influenced by Karl Barth. How far is this a valid criticism of Torrance's epistemology?

First of all, Hardy's caricature of Torrance's position has to be qualified. For Torrance, the integration of form is not a "bare" occurrence, since it arises out of a complex process of indwelling that which one seeks to know. It does not *just* occur, for it only arises when one attends to a field of inquiry often over a long period of time. Then, and only then, do the basic insights arise, which guide further investigation. To be sure these insights or integrations develop in a non-logical or non-deductive fashion out of tacit knowing and personal participation, and therefore cannot be stated in terms of entirely explicit procedures nor displaced by analytic or abstract methods. This, of course, underscores the importance of the "occurrence" of these insights or integrations. Yet Torrance's understanding of the integration of form is not as stark as Hardy depicts it, and so not as private and publicly inexpressible as Hardy contends. In fact, as we will see in chapter 3, there is a significant communal component in this process.

A second point at which Hardy's criticism misses the mark is that the insight or integration of form does not just "occur" and then vanish. While Torrance emphasizes the significance of "reliving the event" and "ending in experience," he also maintains that, "once a thing is understood it goes on manifesting itself in the power of its own truth without having to provide further proof."[123] Notice that Torrance says "once a thing is *understood*," for this implies the process alluded to above. But also notice that once it is understood, it goes on manifesting itself. Here Torrance intends a "rational counterpart to it [knowledge of God] in our structured understanding of it, firm enough to merit philosophical analysis."[124] It is at this point that Torrance has consciously moved beyond Barth, as is clear from Torrance's question that follows the passage just quoted: "How far did Barth appreciate this and how far did he really get to grips with it?"[125]

What Torrance means by this is that an integration of form entails a cognitive counterpart to the intelligibility discovered in the field of inquiry often in the form of a concept or theory, a doctrine in theology. The Trinity or the *homoousion* are examples. Once a successful integration of form occurs, it goes on manifesting itself, not completely unlike seeing the 3-D *Magic Eye*: once you have seen it, you cannot forget that it is there and it is much easier to "relive" the occurrence of seeing it again.

A third qualification of Hardy's criticism is that Torrance and Polanyi provide formidable documentation that the detailed and intimate indwelling process leading up to the occurrence is, *due to its very nature*, not fully formalizable. This appears to be the real point of Hardy's criticism. If this is the case, then what Hardy seems to be calling for is a return to some form of foundationalism in which the conditions of knowledge are rendered completely explicit, an ideal that has been something of a "Holy Grail" for modern philosophy and theology, at least until recently when many, like the anti-foundationalists and the deconstructionists, are giving up the quest for indubitable foundations.

Torrance does not remain at the level of occurrence, but attempts to chart the integration of form as far as this is possible while acknowledging that there are limits because of the finite and historical character of human condition. Why has Torrance given his life's work to the question of method, if not to the end of pressing the inquiry concerning inquiry to its very limits?

However, even granting all of these qualifications, there is still a problem in Torrance's thought on this particular point; one that he is not wholly unaware of, even if he has not resolved it to his own satisfaction, let alone to the satisfaction of others.

Perhaps the best way to get at this issue is to return to Torrance's question as to whether Barth has really come to terms with the fact that if we human beings are to have knowledge of God it requires a rational counterpart to that knowledge in our structured understanding of it, i.e., an integration of form. Torrance argues that we cannot "leave hanging in the air, as it were, the truth of human and creaturely rationality, for on Barth's own showing it must be brought to light and fulfilled within the context of grace."[126] However, at just this point Barth seems to draw back, for fear that Christianity will be corrupted by the infusion of foreign philosophical baggage.

The result, Torrance thinks, is that Barth tends "to restrict the relation between God and man, grace and nature, to the *event* of grace without working out, at any rate in a way that satisfies his critics, the *ontology* of the creaturely structures it assumes?"[127] Thus, Barth fails to bridge the gap between theological dogmatics and our understanding of created existence, in this case, the *rational structures* which knowledge of God assumes in our knowing of it.

However–and this is the critical point, so far as Torrance's position with reference to Hardy's critique is concerned–for Torrance (and he argues, for Barth), "the *kind* of relation in question here is one that must be conceived not *statically* or *logically*, but in *dynamic* and *ontological* terms."[128] What Hardy seems to imply in his critique of Torrance's position is really a return to a static or logical relation, an epistemological foundation in which the conditions for knowledge are rendered fully explicit.

The problem, however, is that such attempts have repeatedly run aground. That is part of the reason why, in reacting against the Enlightenment's rationalistic tendency to make everything explicit in a static or logical manner (which Torrance sees as leading to skepticism), Torrance attempted to think all of this out in dynamic *and* ontological terms: the self-presentation of reality *and* the active and personal human subject responding in ways appropriate to the nature of the reality under investigation.

Let us rehearse Torrance's reconstruction of the alternatives as they developed in modernity. If one starts, like the empiricists did, with the premise that there is nothing in the mind that is not first in the senses, and that form is integrated in a static manner by deducing or abstracting it *directly* from sense data, as in the case of Newton who said he "framed no hypotheses," then one faces all the problems that Hume exposed, creating the serious impasse that they did. Causality cannot be directly deduced from sense experience.

However, if one transfers the structures in the integration of form to the human mind, conceiving them in an equally static manner in terms of necessary and legislative structures that are unchanging and imposed upon experience, as in the case of Kant, then one faces the question of whether one can ever know things-in-things or anything beyond what one constructs, something Western culture has still not recovered from. Beyond that are all the problems brought to light by the rise of historical consciousness. Kant's categories and structures themselves seem all too historically located.

Furthermore, if one posits an *inherent* isomorphism between the structures or forms already present in human reason and those found in reality, which still construes the relation in static terms, one has to account for the ground of this correlation. Fundamentalism does this through an appeal to a doctrine of verbal inspiration as the ground for an identity between the truth of statement in the biblical text and the truth of being. But the greatest difficulty for this kind of approach is again the rise of historical consciousness and all the problems in the biblical narrative uncovered by the historical-critical investigation of the Bible. The structures of the mind and the biblical text appear to be rather historically and culturally contingent.

Yet when one embraces a "cultural-linguistic" paradigm (like Lindbeck's), the structures are dynamic in that they are clearly not invariant across cultures and languages and change over time. But they can take on a certain static character in that they are sufficiently stable so as to depict a followable world adequately comprehensive to absorb the universe. Then the question is raised regarding the genesis of the cultural-linguistic matrix, as McGrath does with respect to Lindbeck, asking whether the Christian "story" arises out of human insight or revelation: is it ontological or merely conventional?

If the cultural-linguistic matrix is viewed as highly fluid, as in the case of someone like Edgar McKnight where everything seems to be in a state of flux, then the structures are clearly dynamic–in fact so dynamic that the Bible fragments into a confusing mass of incompatible, partially depicted worlds, something McKnight thinks we moderns should accept and get on with creating actualizations in line with our own "values, attitudes and responses" without getting hung up on questions of epistemic realism and ontological grounding.[129]

Yet without an ontological element, this position is subject to the critique of Feuerbach and every other hermeneutic of suspicion. This is the ground of the critique of Lindbeck's proposal (which, though quite different than McKnight's, still lacks an ontological ingredient) from the theological left that views Lindbeck's position as inculcating "ecclesiastical self-perpetuation," closing "the door to criticism," and in danger of leading "to a form of religious totalitarianism."[130] A community of hermeneutical privilege is not exempt from the hermeneutic of suspicion raised with reference to McKnight.

In contrast to all of these approaches, each of which Torrance sees as problematic,[131] Torrance calls for an integration of form which, as we have seen, "must be conceived not statically or logically, but in *dynamic* and *ontological* terms."[132] Torrance originally called attention to the problem in this regard with reference to Barth in 1970 when Torrance's article ("The Problem of Natural Theology in the Thought of Karl Barth") first appeared.[133] My suspicion is that Torrance had hoped to sift through the issues involved, move beyond Barth, and find a solution to the difficulties raised, for example, by Hardy's kind of critique, without falling back into the errors of his predecessors, as in the case of Newton, Kant and others.

However, when Torrance republished his article on natural theology in Barth's thought in 1990, he made a number of small changes, one of which is very revealing with reference to Hardy's kind of criticism. Torrance added the following passage which does not appear in the 1970 version of the article: "On the other hand, is it not rather the case that for Barth the kind of relation in question here is one that must be conceived not statically or logically, but in *dynamic* and *ontological* terms? *Yet our problem is that we do not have conceptual or linguistic tools that are sufficiently adequate for this purpose.*"[134] Here, Torrance not only appears to acknowledge the difficulty, but also seems to admit that he has not found a satisfactory solution, or at least no adequate way of conceptualizing it.[135]

Before dismissing Torrance's work on the integration of form, one would do well to ponder the difficulty of the issues involved, for it has taxed the minds of some of the greatest thinkers of the past several hundred years–Newton, Hume, Kant, Einstein and Polanyi, to mention only a few. It is to Torrance's credit that he has significantly clarified the issues involved, even if a fully satisfactory account lies beyond the purview of his own reflections.[136]

Notes

1. Torrance's critique of modern historical-critical biblical studies and theology is found particularly in Thomas F. Torrance, *Space, Time & Resurrection* (Grand Rapids: Eerdmans, 1976), pp. 1-21 and 159-93; Thomas F. Torrance, *Preaching Christ Today* (Grand Rapids: Eerdmans, 1994), pp. 1-11; and Thomas F. Torrance, "The Historical Jesus: From the Perspective of a Theologian," *The New Testament Age: Essays in Honor of Bo Reicke*, ed. William C. Weinrich (Macon, Ga.: Mercer University Press, 1984), vol. II, pp. 511-26.

2. Thomas F. Torrance, *Transformation and Convergence in the Frame of Knowledge* (Grand Rapids: Eerdmans, 1984), p. 91.

3. Torrance, *Preaching Christ*, pp. 5-8

4. Torrance, *Transformation*, p. 91.

5. Torrance, "Historical Jesus," p. 514. Torrance astutely points out that the theological viewpoint of Nicea and Chalcedon, in fact, clashed with the world-view of the times. The classical doctrines of the Christian faith (the incarnation, passion, and resurrection of Jesus Christ, the Trinity, etc.) "forced themselves upon the mind of the Christian community in sharp antithesis to what people had believed about God and in genuine conflict with...the prevailing world view; they took root in the church...only through seismic restructuring of people's religious and intellectual beliefs." Thomas F. Torrance, *Reality and Evangelical Theology* (Philadelphia: Westminster Press, 1982), p. 105.

6. Two texts crucial to the development of Nicene theology are Matthew 11:27 (Jesus says that "No one knows the Son except the Father, and no one knows the Father except the Son and anyone to whom the Son chooses to reveal him") and Matthew 28:16-20 (the Great Commission). Torrance asserts that biblical scholars "argue that Jesus could not have said that, for in accordance with their preconceptions...those reported sayings of Jesus have a theological ingredient which cannot 'scientifically' be accepted as part of the empirical data relating to the historical Jesus...they cut out theological elements from the Gospels and attribute them to the activity of the Christian Community." Torrance, *Preaching Christ*, p. 8.

7. Torrance, "Historical Jesus," p. 515.

8. Ibid.

9. Torrance, *Resurrection*, p. 3. Elsewhere Torrance points out that "ultimate beliefs" of this kind (a living God who reveals himself) constitute a framework upon which one relies in scientific activity. They operate in an informal manner as part of the "tacit" coefficient in one's inquiry. Torrance thinks that such ultimate beliefs must be dragged out into the open and put to the test. See Torrance, *Evangelical Theology*, pp. 53-55.

For Torrance, an "unbiased" approach, i.e., one operating without theological or theoretical components such as a living God who interacts with the world in the incarnation, etc., is doomed to failure because those components reflect the relations that interfuse the "Realities" to which the New Testament bears witness. The biblical witness ends as an unsolvable riddle or is transposed into a very different genre of symbol and myth generated in experiential-expressivist fashion, an orientation that has broken down under critical scrutiny.

10. Torrance, "Historical Jesus," p. 516.

11. Torrance, *Evangelical Theology*, pp. 81-82.

12. Torrance, "Historical Jesus," p. 523. This passage reveals a certain similarity between Torrance's position and Narrative theology, in that it could be said that Torrance believes that the biblical witness "depicts a followable world." See Ronald F. Thiemann's article, "Radiance and Obscurity in Biblical Narrative," in *Scriptural Authority and Narrative Interpretation*, ed. Garrett Green (Philadelphia: Fortress Press, 1987), pp. 21-23.

However, there are also significant differences, especially between Torrance and what is sometimes called the "Yale School" of Narrative theology. I believe that Torrance might accuse Lindbeck's position of being "linguistic formalism" or "conventionalism" in which the Christian Story rendered by the biblical witness is detached from, or at least left ambiguous in relation to, the control of objective reality. See Torrance, *Evangelical Theology*, p. 67.

Torrance is not primarily concerned with the "followable world" of the biblical narrative as a *literary* entity, but with the followable *Realities* to which the narratives as stories bear witness. This is rather clever on Torrance's part, for by retaining this firm distinction, Torrance is able to grant the inconsistencies in the Gospel accounts and other similar problems, for the texts point beyond themselves to the realities, and it is the realities that are of primary interest to him.

13. Torrance, "Historical Jesus," p. 523. Torrance argues that this is why theologians "find it so difficult to operate with the kind of 'established facts' or processed 'data' supplied to them by the epistemologically and scientifically deficient methods of historical criticism." Torrance, *Resurrection*, p. 10. Such "data" is torn from its relations in the biblical witness and thus loses its intrinsic intelligibility.

14. Torrance, *Evangelical Theology*, p. 83.

15. Chapter 4 below will examine Torrance's material account of God's *oikonomia* in detail.

16. For Torrance, the Bible itself is an effective integration of form in which there is a kind of isomorphism or correlation between our human modes of thought and speech and God's self-revelation. We will examine this point in detail in chapter 4.

17. Torrance's account of all of this may make him appear to be a fundamentalist, but such is not the case. In Torrance's mind Protestant fundamentalism attempts to circumvent the chasm opened up by modernity between the "realities" and the biblical witness by positing an identity between "the truth of statement" and "the truth of being" in which the Bible is construed "as a self-contained corpus of divine truths in propositional form endowed with an infallibility of statement." Torrance, *Evangelical Theology*, p. 17. But this approach, in turn, faces all the problems uncovered

by the historical-critical tradition, "the net-work of difficulties and contradictions that must be recognized, for example, in the New Testament presentation of the accounts of the resurrection." Torrance, *Resurrection*, pp. 3-4. Torrance in no way discounts many of the problems thrown up by the historical-critical method and forthrightly says that "historical-critical examination of those sources [biblical and early Christian] is certainly scientifically obligatory," even if, in the end, "the theologian knows that he cannot get very far *theologically* with historico-critical and historico-analytic methods, which can be of help to him only at comparatively superficial and formal levels of thought." Ibid., pp. 9 and 12.

18. Torrance, *Resurrection*, pp. 2-15.

19. See Thomas F. Torrance, *Reality and Scientific Theology* (Edinburgh: Scottish Academic Press, 1985), p. 81; Torrance, *Transformation*, p. 92; and Torrance, "Historical Jesus," pp. 521-22.

20. Torrance, however, never outlines all that is entailed in his approach in a systematic and comprehensive manner. In his most comprehensive treatment of hermeneutics, published under the title *Reality and Evangelical Theology*, he admits that he does not provide "a connected and constructive argument" concerning how to interpret Scripture, but rather prepares the ground by dealing with epistemological issues. See Torrance, *Evangelical Theology*, p. 53.

21. Torrance, *Scientific Theology*, pp. 83-84.

22. Torrance, *Evangelical Theology*, p. 45.

23. Torrance, *Scientific Theology*, p. 84.

24. Torrance maintains that only great theologians who were "childlike in spirit" have succeeded in coming up with this kind of basic insight that has really advanced theological understanding. Ibid.

25. See Thomas F. Torrance, *The Mediation of Christ* (Colorado Springs, Co.: Helmers & Howard, 1992), chapters 1 and 2.

26. Torrance, *Transformation*, p. 93. Elsewhere Torrance says that,

> It is there in the midst of the Church, its fellowship of love, its meditation upon God's self-revelation through the Holy Scriptures, its Eucharistic life, its worship of the Father through the Son and in the Spirit, that we become so inwardly adapted to God's interaction with us that we learn...how to think *worthily* of God, that is, in a godly way appropriate to God.

See Torrance, *Evangelical Theology*, p. 48.

Furthermore, this is not completely different from natural science, where the scientific community and its tradition also play a major role in the cultivation of the proper mind-set and skills necessary for the student to become a full-fledged scientist. See Alexander Thomson's discussion of this in his important book, *Tradition and Authority in Science and Theology* (Edinburgh: Scottish Academic Press, 1987). Thomson was one of Torrance's students.

27. Torrance, *Evangelical Theology*, p. 48. Knowing more than we can tell is what Torrance means by "theological instinct." Torrance suggests that we should become "so imbued with the mind of Christ that" we come to "think *instinctively* in a Christian way." See Thomas F. Torrance, "The Reconciliation of the Mind," *TSF Bulletin* 10, no. 30, (1987): p. 6. Torrance says that his mother and wife, though never having had any academic

training, both were imbued "with an unerring *theological instinct*, evident again and again in...[their] reaction to ideas put forward by preachers and teachers." Ibid. The importance of theological instinct in Torrance's theology is revealed in the following statement where Torrance says that, in the end, this "was the test I used to put to my students...."Has this person a genuinely theological instinct governed by the mind of Christ?" That is much more important than being able to offer a formal academic account of some doctrine or historic debate in the Church. What really counts in the end is whether a person's mind is radically transformed by Christ and...that he thinks instinctively from the depths of his mental being in a way worthy of God." Ibid.

28. Torrance, *Scientific Theology*, 118.

29. Torrance, *Evangelical Theology*, p. 49.

30. Torrance, *Transformation*, p. 93.

31. This once again reveals a parallel between Torrance's position and Narrative theology. See for example, Hans Frei, *The Eclipse of Biblical Narrative* (New Haven: Yale University Press, 1974), where Frei points out that narratives convey their meaning or depict their characters only through the complex chronological sequence and interaction of the "story." Frei's hermeneutic also entail an *integrative* mode of thought beyond that of discursive reason. This is central to Frei's critique of modern biblical hermeneutics, for in dissecting the text with its discursive modes of reason in an attempt to reach historical facticity, modern biblical scholarship destroyed the very narrative character of the biblical texts through which they depict their meaning only in light of the entire course of events of the whole narrative (whether it be a Gospel or the whole Bible).

However, Torrance's position invites a criticism of those streams of Narrative theology that depend too heavily on *literary* methods and categories in hermeneutical and theological activity. While the Bible is clearly, at least in part, narrative in character, is that all it is or claims to be? Torrance, I believe, would say no. To focus solely on the literary, in Torrance's view, is to fail once again to go far enough in hermeneutical and theological inquiry. For Torrance, the literary aspect of the biblical text is the medium through which we apprehend and think of *realities* of the Christian faith, the pattern of God's redemptive self-revelation to which the Bible bears witness. This is the subject of chapter 4 below.

For now, however, is it not Lindbeck's lack of clarity on this point–the relation between the biblical narrative and the "realities" they intend–that accounts for the ambiguity of his position regarding the "ontological" truth claims of Christian faith and theology, as noted above in chapter 1, pp. 45-46 (endnote 65), a point on which he has been repeatedly criticized? At times the Yale school of Narrative theology, with its almost exclusive emphasis on cultural-linguistic categories (as important as they are) and lack of attention to "things-in-themselves," seems to betray remnants of an underlying "Kantian" dualism, the very epistemological dualism that Torrance is at pains to overcome without falling back into positing an identity between the "truth of statement" and the "truth of being," which is also inadequate to the complexity of the subject matter of Christian faith.

One cannot help but wonder whether behind these problems there lies the age-old Lutheran darkness and *anfechtungen* of faith. It is important to remember that Kant, himself, was deeply influenced by his mother's Lutheran pietism and he never ceased to speak of that influence. He also attended the pietist "Collegium" for eight years. See Theodore Green's "Introduction" to Immanuel Kant, *Religion Within the Limits of Reason Alone*, trans. and ed. T. M. Green and H. H. Hudson (New York: Harper & Row, 1960), pp. xxii-xxiv. Is this part of the reason for the apparent Lutheran difficulty of resisting the Kantian perspective?

32. Is it not revealing that modern critical biblical scholarship has so seldom come up with the robust doctrine of the Trinity that we find in classical councilor theology?

33. Torrance, *Transformation*, p. 94.

34. Torrance, *Scientific Theology*, p. 85.

35. Torrance, *Resurrection*, p. 10.

36. Thomas F. Torrance, "The Distinctive Character of the Reformed Tradition," in *Incarnational Ministry: The Presence of Christ in Church Society, and Family*, ed. C. D. Kettler and T. H. Speidell (Colorado Springs: Helmers & Howard, 1990), pp. 13-14. Also see Torrance, *Evangelical Theology*, p. 44.

37. Torrance, *Resurrection*, p. 9.

38. Torrance, *Evangelical Theology*, pp. 100-101. This discussion is really a summary, with some further development of particular points, of an essay Torrance wrote on "The Hermeneutics of St. Athanasius" in 1970 and is reprinted in Thomas F. Torrance, *Divine Meaning: Studies in Patristic Hermeneutics* (Edinburgh: T & T Clark, 1995). In the earlier article Torrance states the guidelines this way:

> Hence interpretation is proper and correct when it does the following: 1) keeps to the scope of the divine revelation in Scripture, 2) respects the economical nature of God's acts and words, 3) keeps to the orderly connection signified by the words and sentences of Holy Scripture in order that they may yield their own interpretation, and 4) checks and proves its statements in accordance with the rule of faith that arises out of the Church's understanding of the *kerygma* as mediated to us through the apostolic writings.

See ibid., p. 234-35.

39. Torrance, *Evangelical Theology*, p. 102.

40. Ibid., p. 105. In contrast to Schleiermacher's hermeneutics, Torrance is adamant that it is through an "epistemic and not a psychological operation" that one arrives at the objective meaning that lies behind the written words, not the piety of the historical Jesus. Ibid., p. 104.

41. Torrance, *Evangelical Theology*, pp. 109-10.

42. Ibid., p. 114.

43. Ibid., pp. 114-15.

44. See ibid., pp. 118-20. Also see Torrance, "Reformed Tradition," pp. 12-14.

45. Torrance, *Evangelical Theology*, pp. 118-20. Torrance argues that, "in the last resort we have to reckon with the fact that God alone can name himself and bear witness to himself and thus prove himself to us." Ibid., p. 119. For Torrance, even with regard to the biblical witness, we have to take "into account the fact that the reports do inevitably fall short of what they indicate, for they bear witness to what is other than and beyond themselves." See Torrance, *Resurrection*, p. 6.

46. Ibid., p. 11.

47. Ibid., pp. 11-12.

48. Torrance, *Evangelical Theology*, p. 42.

49. See Torrance, *Resurrection*, p. 12. Also see Torrance, *Evangelical Theology*, pp. 13, 17-19, 64-71, 105-7, and 119-26.

50. Torrance, *Resurrection*, p. 4.

51. Ibid., pp. 12-13.

52. See Thomas F. Torrance, "My Interaction with Karl Barth," in *How Karl Barth Changed My Mind*, ed. Donald K. McKim (Grand Rapids: Eerdmans, 1986), p. 53.

53. Torrance, *Evangelical Theology*, p. 78.

54. See ibid., pp. 77-83 and Torrance, *Resurrection*, pp. 3-7.

55. Torrance, *Evangelical Theology*, pp. 45-46.

56. Torrance, *Mediation*, pp. 35-36.

57. Torrance, *Scientific Theology*, p. 86.

58. Ibid.

59. Ibid., p. 87.

60. Ibid.

61. Torrance argues that *Contra Gentes* is not a traditional form of natural theology. See ibid. Also see Torrance's essay on Athanasius' theology, including his lengthy analysis of *Contra Gentes/De Incarnatione*, in Thomas F. Torrance, *Theology in Reconciliation* (London: G. Chapman, 1975), pp. 215-66.

62. Torrance, *Scientific Theology*, p. 87-88.

63. Ibid., p. 88.

64. See Torrance, *Reconciliation*, p. 263.

65. Ibid.

66. See Thomas F. Torrance, "The Integration of Form in Natural and Theological Science," *Science, Medicine and Man* 1 (1973): p. 165.

67. Torrance, *Evangelical Theology*, p. 112.

68. Ibid. This is a very significant point and Torrance elsewhere argues that,

> Here the historical Jesus Christ and the theological Jesus Christ are found to be fused not only in a dimension of spatio-temporal depth but in a dimension of divine-human depth, for the *energeia* and the *logos* intrinsic to him are found to be intrinsic to the *being* of God itself. It is that fusion which makes the fact of Jesus Christ the creative, self-interpreting reality he is in our worshipping experience and interpreted understanding of him. Once we have come to know Jesus Christ in this way, we cannot return to the Gospels and read them in such a way as to obliterate this understanding of him from our minds, any more than, on quite a different level, we can try to fit together a second or third time the scattered pieces of a jigsaw puzzle in pretended ignorance of the picture that emerged when we completed it the first time.

Torrance, "Historical Jesus," p. 524.

69. Torrance, *Evangelical Theology*, p. 112.

70. Thomas F. Torrance, *The Christian Doctrine of God: One Being Three Persons* (Edinburgh: T & T Clark, 1996), p. 5

71. Ibid., p. 95.

72. Torrance, *Evangelical Theology*, p. 112. This, of course, is quite different than Lindbeck's notion that the meaning of *homoousion* or consubstantiality is to be thought of "not as a first-order proposition with ontological reference, but as second-order rule of speech," which Lindbeck thinks was the intent of Athanasius, a point that will be taken up later in this book. See George Lindbeck, *The Nature of Doctrine: Religion and Theology in a Postliberal Age* (Philadelphia: Westminster Press, 1984), p. 94.

73. Torrance, *Christian Doctrine*, p. 98

74. Torrance, *Transformation*, p. 95.

75. Ibid. For an in depth discussion of how the doctrine of the Trinity arises in Torrance's theology, see Elmer M. Colyer, *How To Read T. F. Torrance: Understanding His Trinitarian & Scientific Theology* (Downers Grove, Ill.: InterVarsity Press, 2001), pp. 285-301.

76. Torrance, *Transformation*, p. 95.

77. See Torrance, *Evangelical Theology*, pp. 49-51.

78. See Torrance, *Scientific Theology*, p. 93.

79. Ibid., p. 85.

80. Ibid., p. 86.

81. See Colyer, *How To Read*, chapter 8, pp. 285-321.

82. See Daniel W. Hardy, "Thomas F. Torrance," in *The Modern Theologians: An Introduction to Christian Theology in the Twentieth Century*, ed. David F. Ford (New York: Basil Blackwell Inc., 1989), I:79.

83. Ibid.

84. See Torrance, *Evangelical Theology*, p. 60 and Torrance's article, "The Framework of Belief," in *Belief in Science and in Christian Life: The Relevance of Michael Polanyi's Thought for Christian Faith and Life*, ed. Thomas F. Torrance (Edinburgh: Handsel Press, 1980), pp . 9-10.

85. Torrance, *Evangelical Theology*, p. 53.

86. Torrance, "Framework of Belief," pp. 11-12. Also see Thomas F. Torrance, "Ultimate Beliefs and the Scientific Revolution," *Cross Currents* 30, no. 2 (Summer, 1980): pp. 136-37.

87. Beliefs, in Torrance's words, "are to be understood as expressing the fundamental commitment of the mind to reality...on which the reason relies in any authentic thrust toward the truth." See Torrance, "Ultimate Beliefs," p. 131.

88. Hardy, "Torrance," p. 80.

89. Torrance, "Framework of Belief," p. 9.

90. See ibid., p. 8. In contrast, Polanyi and Torrance insist upon recognition and restoration of belief as a source of knowledge.

91. Ibid., p. 10. Beliefs form a basic framework on which we "rely in performing explicit operations in inquiry and reasoning...[and] fulfill their function in an informal way." See Torrance, "Ultimate Beliefs," p. 136. They are part of the "tacit dimension" of rational knowledge. This is similar to Lindbeck's cultural-linguistic *a priori*, except that for Torrance the framework of belief is much more interactive with what we seek to know and therefore, as we shall see, open to criticism and modification, even if its relation to the objective pole cannot be made fully explicit.

92. Torrance, "Framework of Belief," p. 19.

93. Torrance, "Ultimate Beliefs," p. 132. Torrance appeals to Patristic theology with its repeated reference to Isaiah 9:7: "If you will not believe, you will not understand." Thus Torrance maintains that belief or faith is integral not only to theological science, but to natural science as well. Ibid.

Natural science operates with certain "ultimate beliefs" without which there would be no science–beliefs like, "there is order in the universe," which science cannot prove because they have to be assumed in any attempt at proof or disproof, but beliefs which are nonetheless rational.

94. See Hardy, "Torrance," p. 80.

95. Torrance, "Ultimate Beliefs," p. 132.

96. Torrance, "Framework of Belief," p. 12.

97. Torrance, *Evangelical Theology*, p. 57.

98. Hardy, "Torrance," p. 80.

99. Torrance also distinguishes between "ultimate beliefs" that we cannot reasonably avoid, such as "there is order in the universe," and "penultimate beliefs," which involve a judgement between conflicting alternatives. An example of a penultimate belief might be the "contingent" character of the universe. See Torrance, "Ultimate Beliefs," pp. 139-42. Torrance also distinguishes between "explicit" and "implicit" beliefs and discusses "working" beliefs and "dependent" beliefs. See ibid. and Torrance, "Framework of Belief," pp. 18-20.

100. Torrance, "Framework of Belief," p. 13.

101. Ibid., pp. 13-14.

102. Ibid., p. 14.

103. Ibid., pp. 13-14.

104. See Torrance, "Framework of Belief," p. 10 and Thomas F. Torrance, *Christian Theology and Scientific Culture* (New York: Oxford University Press, 1981), p. 63.

105. See endnote 109, pp. 50-51 above.

106. See Torrance, "Framework of Belief," p. 14.

107. Ibid., p. 15.

108. Torrance, "Ultimate Beliefs," p. 133.

109. See Hardy, "Torrance," p. 81.

110. Ibid.

111. See ibid., p. 82.

112. Torrance, "Framework of Belief," p. 21.

113. See again Thomson, *Tradition*, pp. 24-30.

114. Hardy, "Torrance," p. 86.

115. Ibid.

116. See Michael Bauman, *Roundtable: Conversations with European Theologians* (Grand Rapids: Baker House Press, 1990), pp. 117-18. One of my goals in these first two chapters has been to overcome this problem inherent in Torrance's writings by attempting to outline his basic epistemic orientation with a degree of clarity as it bears upon the nature of doctrine.

117. Hardy, "Torrance," p. 86.

118. Ibid., p.87.

119. Ibid.

120. Ibid.

121. Ibid.

122. Ibid., pp. 87-88.

123. Torrance, *Scientific Theology*, p. xi.

124. Thomas F. Torrance, *Karl Barth: Biblical and Evangelical Theologian* (Edinburgh: T & T Clark, 1990), p. 154-55.

125. Ibid.

126. Ibid., pp. 155-56.

127. Ibid., p. 156.

128. Ibid.

129. This is an example of what Ernest Fortin calls "easy-going nihilism."

130. See Mark Corner and Gordon Kaufman's reviews of Lindbeck's book in the following journals: *Modern Theology* 3 (October 1986): pp. 110-12 and *Theology Today* 42 (July 1986): pp. 240-42. Herwi Rikhof also warns against some forms of Narrative theology ending in a form of ideology. See Herwi Rikhof, *The Concept of Church* (London: Palmos Press, 1981), p. 148.

131. It is highly possible that there may be other positions beyond those Torrance considers that are not subject to the problems raised by his discussions of the positions of various thinkers on these issues. This is a question beyond the scope of the present monograph.

132. Torrance, *Karl Barth*, p. 156. Elsewhere Torrance speaks of conceiving reason as "not something substantial but verbal, not so much a state as an act...so that reason is described as the capacity to behave consciously in terms of the nature of the object." See Thomas F. Torrance, "Faith and Philosophy," *The Hibbert Journal* 45 (1948-49): p. 243. Torrance also acknowledges his indebtedness to his former teacher, John Macmurray, for this. See ibid.

133. See Thomas F. Torrance, "The Problem of Natural Theology in the Thought of Karl Barth," in *Religious Studies* 6 (1970): pp. 121-35.

134. Torrance, *Karl Barth*, p. 156.

135. I agree with Torrance, that the answer to this problem is not to be found in an epistemology of the Third Person of the Trinity. See Thomas F. Torrance, *God and Rationality* (London: Oxford University Press, 1971; reprint Eugene, Ore.: Wipf & Stock, 1997), pp. 165-92.

136. Maybe Hardy can point the way, even if he provides us with few clues in his discussion of Torrance's position.

Chapter 3
Doctrine and Community

Introduction

This chapter deals with the relation between doctrine and Christian community in Thomas F. Torrance's theology. As noted above in chapter 2, it is within the Church, the worshiping community of the people of God, in prayer, meditating upon the message of Scripture, and learning from others that we develop what Torrance calls "theological instinct" out of which arises the basic clues or insights into the intelligibility or order inherent in God's self-revelation in Israel and in Jesus Christ and the saving events associated with that self-revelation.[1]

Furthermore, all scientific pursuits, according to Torrance, are related to the structures and paradigms of the communities in which we think and express ourselves.[2] Those structures and paradigms embodied in group habits of life and thought in the Church and in society influence theological inquiry and doctrine. There is a personal and social coefficient in all knowledge, including knowledge of God and doctrine.

This is simply an implication of Torrance's contention that we are already within the knowing relation, that there are no final categories in the Kantian sense, and that we do not apprehend anything without a conceptual framework or theoretical component, for the communities in which we are raised form the conceptualities and cognitive activities we bring to the knowing relation. This means that the social coefficient in knowledge and the role of the Church in theological inquiry is of critical importance for Torrance's theology and his understanding of doctrine. This is also one of the fascinating elements of Torrance's theology and his understanding of doctrine, for he concedes not a little to sociology of knowledge (as do Lindbeck and McGrath), yet he consistently argues for a critical, epistemic realism.

Doctrine, for Torrance, cannot (and should not) be abstracted from forms of life in social-conceptual fields.[3] This coefficient can aid, but also impede, knowledge of God and the development of doctrine. Sorting out the various interrelations between doctrine and community in Torrance's theology is the task of this chapter.

This presents several difficulties for interpreting Torrance's thought in this area. While the subject of the personal and social coefficient in theology and doctrine appears in many of Torrance's writings, the focus is often on the negative aspect of the social coefficient–the way in which the Church, in its interaction with the world, becomes assimilated to the psychological and social patterns of surrounding culture, which, in turn, often adversely affect theology and doctrine.[4] Thus it is difficult to gain a clear and complete understanding of the nature and role of this social coefficient in Torrance's theology.

Furthermore, virtually all of Torrance's discussions of the social coefficient in knowledge of God and doctrine occur within the matrix of other subject matter. Only once in all of his writings does Torrance devote an entire chapter or essay to the subject. This is in chapter 4, of his important book, *Reality and Scientific Theology*, which we will examine in some detail.[5] One wishes that Torrance would have provided further elaboration of this significant theme in his theology.

The result is that what Torrance has written is highly suggestive, but could be more fully developed. This chapter will seek to cope with these difficulties by following the basic trajectory of Torrance's discussion of "The Social Coefficient of Knowledge," in his book, *Reality and Scientific Theology*, supplementing it with a wide range of references from Torrance's treatment of this theme in other places in his writings and relating it to the nature of doctrine. This chapter will outline 1.) the social coefficient in knowledge, including how it should develop and function, 2.) the Church as the social coefficient in knowledge of God and doctrine, and 3.) problems posed by the social coefficient. Through the course of this discussion the relation of doctrine and Christian community in Torrance's theology will come into view.

The order of these sections does *not* reflect methodological or other priorities in Torrance's thought, as though he first developed theory concerning the social coefficient of knowledge in general and then applied it to the Church and theology.

It is simply one of the easiest ways to enter the horizon of Torrance's understanding of the social coefficient of knowledge and its implications for the relation between doctrine and Christian community.

The Social Coefficient in Knowledge

The Semantic Intentionality of Art-form

Torrance begins his treatment of "The Social Coefficient of Knowledge" with a revealing discussion of art-form and its relation to reality.[6] I discussed Torrance's understanding of the integration of form at some length in the first two chapters of this monograph. But the form that arises in ordinary knowing and scientific inquiry is not the only type of form operative in human life and thought. Art constitutes an additional kind of form that Torrance calls "suggestive form."[7]

Art is partially the outcome of human imagination and creativity, but it is also related to objective features and properties of the world around us.[8] Torrance argues that art has to be (or at least should be) related to that "profound aspect of reality in its ultimate harmony, unity and simplicity, which outruns the explicit and formalized forms..."[9] like the concepts and theories developed in science. Art, whether painting, music or literature, is the universal human mode for expressing this kind of subtle form, though Torrance notes that art also constitutes a basic element in all rational activity, which we perceive in the beauty of a concept theory, in the elegance of mathematical proof, or even in "the beauty of holiness."[10]

Thus, in Torrance's perspective, art is not (or should not be) purely constructive, or even simply expressive of inner states of human consciousness, but disclosive of the inarticulate harmony, unity, simplicity, etc. of some aspect of reality. Torrance's concern here is not with art-form as such, but rather with the kind of *semantic intentionality* it embodies, an intentionality in which human consciousness is directed in this delicate manner to the depth of reality.[11]

Torrance sees semantic intentionality, the orientation of openness of human consciousness to the intelligible ground of reality, as of great significance not only in art but in other spheres as well. It is "semantic intentionality that gives meaning to the whole framework of human life so that without it every culture slips away into meaninglessness."[12]

This is precisely the problem that Torrance sees developing in the romantic period of modern art in which there is a shift in orientation away from an intentionality toward the ultimate ground of reality to a view of art as predominately subjective and personal. The meaning of art comes to be lodged in the human subject and dominated by self-expression or self-fulfillment.[13]

Torrance grants that the romantic perspective is a reaction against the kind of art conceived as mimetic congruence with reality, but he argues that much of "modern" art still reflects a world in which humanity is out of touch with the universe of which humanity is a constitutive part.[14] Modern art, in Torrance's mind, tries to construct its own meaning. Yet by imposing constructed meaning, real meaning eludes modern art form.[15] Here Torrance's critique of modern art parallels his analysis and critique of the shift in the integration of form in the modern period in philosophy/science and in biblical studies as developed in the previous two chapters.

Art, by its very nature, requires an artificiality or estrangement from reality, Torrance grants, in the kind of relation to reality it embodies.[16] Thus he argues that a work of art should free human imagination from "imprisonment in the mimetic forms" and enable us to transcend the limitations of our place in history/culture.[17] Art ought to be a sensitive kind of form in touch with ultimate reality, the "unformalisable *forma formans*." Art should embody open textured patterns of beauty and meaning that "reverberate...in the human spirit" keeping it open to the subtle symmetries and ultimate harmony of nature.[18]

Yet when completely detached from reality, art becomes "merely a dream."[19] For Torrance, genuine artistic expression has to be in touch with the reality and intelligibility of the universe without reducing it to precise explicit formalization. Thus art ought to indicate far more than it explicitly depicts.[20] Such a work of art is so full of meaning that it engenders universal appreciation across space and time, because the human mind becomes open "to a level of reality that is invariant for each and every generation."[21] A work of art ought to set the human imagination free from its imprisonment in the limitations of various modes of explicit form.[22]

The issue at stake here, in Torrance's mind, is the relation of art-form to reality, "for it is in this extremely sensitive area that we have to do with these informal, creative, and spontaneous movements of thought which are so basic and all-important in every area of knowledge."[23] For Torrance, art plays (or should play) a role in shaping the "tacit dimension" (integral for the development of explicit knowledge), helping give it a positive correlation with the universe of space and time within which we live. Art form illustrates the role a cultural-linguistic framework (in Torrance's words, "a social coefficient") should play in development of the tacit dimension.

The Semantic Intentionality of the Social Coefficient

As art-form can embody a "semantic intentionality," orienting human imagination toward the fullness and depth of reality, providing what Polanyi calls "heuristic vision," so a society or community provides a frame of life and thought, including the full gamut of all that this entails (institutions, language, tradition, education, etc.), within which meaning emerges and the knowing relation is established and maintained. These social patterns are what Torrance means by the "social coefficient of knowledge." In fact, it is clear from what Torrance says about art, that art itself has a role to play in the social coefficient, even in theology, as will become clear later in this chapter. It is within this "correlation between our personal and social structures and the intelligible grounds of reality" that new thoughts and fresh glimpses of reality are born.[24]

Thus Torrance maintains that, "Regarded in this way the social coefficient of knowledge constitutes from generation to generation the sensitive matrix within which our all-important informal relations with reality are evoked, and thus constitutes the medium in which those relations while not formally communicable are nevertheless communicated through the common participation in the affected modification of social consciousness."[25] As a child comes to know more than she can tell about the world around her by the age of five, so very early we develop the capacity to identify and understand the significant manifestations in the world around through the social coefficient in which we grow up.[26] Only as we are "nursed and trained" in this social coefficient of knowledge latent in society or a particular community do we gain skills in judgement through which we relate experience to patterns of meaning and move from initial recognition through the process of inquiry to deeper and, in some cases, totally new knowledge.[27]

Now such a social coefficient of knowledge can only be analyzed *a posteriori*, after it has developed.[28] The reason is that it arises (or should arise) within the interaction between a community and the world around it or between a particular community and a field of inquiry (scientific or religious).[29] According to Torrance, a genuine social coefficient of knowledge has no validity or meaning if it is cut off from what is known. The reason is that it has no independent existence, nor does it contribute knowledge as if it were an *a priori* cognitive structure that did not arise in symbiotic relation to what is known.[30] Thus the social coefficient or "the cognitional structure of our social consciousness" does not generate knowledge of reality in and of itself, but rather predisposes us toward explicit apprehension of the intelligible order of reality.[31] This is a critical point in understanding Torrance's theology and the relation of community and doctrine. It is also the point at which the similarity, yet radical difference, between Torrance's position and that of George Lindbeck becomes perhaps most evident.

According to Torrance, it must be granted that nothing is apprehended without the synthesizing and conceptualizing activity of human reason, which he sees as the root idea and element of truth behind Kant's synthetic *a priori*. Yet there are no final categories in the Kantian sense, as was noted in the discussion of the integration of form in chapter 1 above, for these categories arise (or should arise) dynamically out of the ongoing knowing relation in such a way that they are correlated with the intelligibility inherent in reality. Thus Torrance argues that neither can the social coefficient of knowledge be viewed as a corporate form of the synthetic *a priori*, a constructive social structure lodged in communal consciousness, and therefore open to analysis in itself cut off from actual experience and knowledge.[32] What Torrance is arguing against at this point seems to be very near to Lindbeck's own position.[33]

In contrast to Lindbeck, Torrance maintains that the *subjective* coefficient of knowledge is "the capacity of the subject to be affected and modified by what it knows independent of itself."[34] In similar vein, the *social* coefficient of knowledge is "the capacity of a society or a community to be affected and modified through its advance in knowledge of what is independently real."[35] There is (or should be) a real relation between the social coefficient and the intelligible order of objective reality.

It is this element of epistemic realism, which conditions (or should condition) the social coefficient, that distinguishes Torrance's position from Lindbeck's and enables Torrance to escape the relativistic tendencies of sociology of knowledge, while at the same time acknowledging the undeniable role of the social coefficient in all knowledge.[36] Where in Lindbeck's proposal is there this kind of interactive element found in Torrance's understanding of the subjective and social coefficients of knowledge?

Now one must remember that for Torrance the subjective and social coefficient of knowledge has "to do with an *affect*, not an *effect*," with reference to its capacity to be modified by what it knows.[37] The knowing relation and the forms that arise cannot be construed in causal or logical terms, which is what distinguishes Torrance's position from the kind of foundationalism attributed to Torrance by Ronald Thiemann, as noted in chapter 1 above.[38] Torrance maintains that the social coefficient of knowledge is an affected adaptation of social consciousness and we cannot develop specifiable cognitive content from it when it is isolated from the known and treated in itself.[39]

However, it is because of its capacity to be affected and modified in its orientation toward objective being that the social coefficient of knowledge embodied in a society or community can provide the matrix within which meaning and knowledge emerge and are sustained.[40] But for Torrance the social coefficient does this as a "suggestive reference" similar to art-form, rather than in explicit reference as in the case mathematical or logical form.[41]

Thus, while in one sense the social coefficient plays a quasi-transcendental role (similar to that outlined by Lindbeck) in shaping the development of a member of the society or particular community and orienting him toward the significant manifestations of reality, once it has served that purpose, there is (or should be) an inversion in the knowing relation in which the manifestation of reality once again affects and modifies the subjective coefficient, leading to correction or even reconstruction of the social coefficient in which the individual has been nurtured. Where in Lindbeck's theory does one find this kind of epistemic inversion? Is it not this lack of a critical principle, an epistemic inversion, or a critical realist element which has elicited the criticism that Lindbeck's position fosters "ecclesiastical self-perpetuation" by theologians like Gordon Kaufman, as mentioned above?[42]

This process of epistemic inversion is also what happens (or should happen) in the forward advance of inquiry in any field. Einstein's training in Newtonian science helped prepare him for his subsequent radical questioning of some of Newton's fundamental notions as Einstein engaged in his ongoing inquiry and was forced to think himself beyond Newtonian and Kantian categories.

Christianity, Marxism & The Structure of Social Existence

Torrance further differentiates his own "Christian" understanding of the social structure of human beings by comparing it to Marxism. According to Marx, "The mode of production of material life conditions the general process of social, political and intellectual life. It is not the consciousness of men that determines their existence, but their social existence that determines their consciousness."[43] Torrance sees this as giving rise to a disturbing correlation between human society and technological rationality in which people's social and personal existence is determined by the interrelations of material production and economic processes in technological society.[44]

The Christian Church, in Torrance's mind, is not a human-made institution, but one of divine origin. The Church develops within human socio-historical life as "social correlate of an intelligible realm" that we discover rather than create and to which we attempt to be faithful in all aspects of our thought and life.[45] Here Torrance sees a human community related to an infinite intelligibility giving "rise to open structures of life and thought" in correlation with that indeterminate intelligibility stretching out beyond ourselves.[46]

Thus while Marxism and Christianity both maintain that human knowledge is interconnected with the socio-historical structure of human life, the way they conceptualize how communal beliefs arise and develop is radically different.[47] For Marxism the structure of intellectual life is rooted in an economic determinism of the material processes of history.

For the Christian community, the structure of its beliefs and life, Torrance argues, is an organization that develops under the influence of a spiritual reality to which we respond in progressive transformation of our socio-historical existence. Our understanding and our life should progressively adapt to the intrinsic intelligibility of this spiritual reality through our free and open inquiry into it.[48] This kind of social pattern is true not only of Christianity and theological science in correlation with the transcendent Reality and intelligibility of God; Torrance contends that it ought also mark human society in general and the whole range of natural sciences in relation to the reality and intelligibility of the created universe of which humanity is a constitutive part.

In Torrance's mind this generates a concept of a free society of persons with open structures of thought and life correlated to the depth and range of the intrinsic intelligibility of reality, contingent and divine–an intelligibility only partially grasped and therefore pursued unfettered by closed ideologies, yielding a notion of science and society both open to transformation in light of further disclosures of reality.[49]

We will not retrace the trajectory of Torrance's understanding of the "personal" character of the epistemic process as outlined in chapters 1 and 2 above which underlies this whole discussion, but rather go on to draw out its implications for social existence and the social coefficient of knowledge.

According to Torrance, "personal" knowledge is not "subjective" in the negative sense of the word, for we come to know something only insofar as we pass beyond ourselves, indwell the field of inquiry, discern something of its intelligibility, and openly assent to it and allow thought (and life) to be reconstructed in light of it.[50] While this implies "intensely personal acts of relation, discernment and judgement," in any genuine knowledge, this demands that we distinguish our knowing from what we seek to know, and allow these personal acts to be challenged and shaped by what we seek to know.[51]

All knowledge has a personal and social coefficient, which, if eliminated, would render the human mind simply a complex mechanical brain.[52] Only through this kind of complex interaction between the knower and the known does knowledge come about. This implies that "Personal subjective-mode of being" is in fact "the bearer of objectivity."[53] An orientation beyond oneself, Torrance contends, is part of what it means to be a personal being.[54]

Furthermore, it is within the interpersonal structure of our social existence, our openness as persons to one another, that we experience reality and together develop communal convictions concerning what we seek to know, for that which is objective is in some sense shareable for it transcends each of us and all of us.[55] It is in inter-subjective social existence, in interaction with other rational agents, that we transcend our individual limits and can participate in the experience and understanding of others.[56] Thus human understanding ought to be repeatedly stretched beyond what we already know and lead to the reconstruction of our previous knowledge.[57]

Inter-personal relations, then, ought to also have a transcendent quality in which we are genuinely open to one another and to the claims of objective reality.[58] When a community proceeds in genuine openness to the transcendent intelligibility of objective reality and in openness to one another, there can be a deepening correlation between the structures of our social consciousness and the harmonious structures in the universal nature of things. In this way an appropriate social coefficient of knowledge develops, one responsive to objective reality, nurturing proper semantic intentionality.[59]

This social sub-structure of knowledge is crucial, Torrance argues, for it provides us with an inarticulate grasp of reality or the tacit dimension upon which the openness of a community toward reality relies (for the Christian community, openness to God).[60] On this point Torrance's social coefficient and Lindbeck's cultural-linguistic framework are extremely close. But for Torrance, a proper social coefficient arises out of intimate experience of the reality with which it is (or should be) correlated, the point where Lindbeck's position in ambiguous.[61]

This inarticulate grasp of reality is the indispensable basis or condition of all explicit knowledge.[62] As such it plays a pivotal role, undergirding and guiding formalized knowledge. It functions heuristically, enabling us to come to new discoveries, but also generates a particular kind of culture or community.[63] It enables (or should enable) us to live at home in our relationship with God and one another (in the Christian community) or at home in the universe (if it is a more general social coefficient).[64]

Here Torrance emphasizes the importance of language which is basic to the social coefficient of knowledge and where the web of meaning is lodged, for he sees language as the "house of being" (Heidegger) through which we come to know reality,[65] a subject we will take up is some detail in chapter 5.

The Difficulty of Genuine Knowledge

While there is an inevitable correlation between the frame of our social consciousness and all human knowledge and life, this does not mean that it is necessarily a correct or effective correlation. There is always the possibility of error or distortion. A properly formed social coefficient of knowledge provides the sensitive matrix within which appropriate knowing can develop, but an improper social coefficient can grow in upon itself and lose its openness to the intelligibility of reality.[66] A social coefficient can become deformed and impede our relationship with objective reality and with one another. This demands a critical element with reference to the social coefficient in which we test those structures and convictions in light of their creative ground.[67]

Thus, when we enter the knowing relation with a structure of meaning or frame of knowledge that has been conditioned by factors or concepts incommensurate with, or of little relevance to, the reality in question, then distortion can easily take place. Torrance argues that distortion is a particular danger when the social coefficient becomes ingrown and primarily self-expressive/assertive rather than oriented beyond itself.[68] Once again, it is also important to remember that for Torrance, the social coefficient of knowledge, or the cognitional structure of our social consciousness, should not be the source of our conceptualizations, but only formative of openness and readiness for apprehending what is beyond it.[69] It does not generate concepts or provide informational content, but should rather "predispose us toward explicit apprehension" of the intrinsic intelligibly of nature or of God's self-revelation.[70]

All of this becomes immensely complex when one considers Torrance's admission that there is not *a* social coefficient of knowledge, rather multiple social coefficients that arise in symbiosis not simply between society and the world of intelligible reality, but in particular communities (scientific, religious, etc.) and their individual fields of interest, coefficients which are not sharply cut off from one another,[71] a problem that we will take up in a later section of this chapter.

However, at this juncture, it is important to note that Torrance grants the difficulty of genuine knowledge and the fact that our social environments often adversely affect our ability to perceive so that we become nearly incapable of seeing things as they are. Only by transcending the boundaries of our inherited frameworks of thought and life are we freed for real knowledge and for life.[72] Furthermore, since these frameworks of thought are rooted in the substructure of our social existence, that social existence must itself change if we are to advance beyond the current horizon.[73] The radical character of Torrance's proposal becomes evident at this point in that not only must our frameworks of thought suffer change as inquiry advances, but also our personal and social existence.

Still, Torrance acknowledges that this transcending of our present horizon cannot be accomplished simply by destroying old frameworks of thought and beginning anew (Torrance here names nihilists, anarchists, and Marcusans of the new left).[74] Torrance views this with disdain as a rather irrational hope, for we cannot advance into the new without at least some guidance from the old, though he agrees that this can only come about through a struggle with the social structures in which we are implicated.[75]

Once again, it is at this point that Torrance finds Michael Polanyi's emphasis on dedication to the claims of genuinely transcendent reality (that is independent of our knowing of it and that can only be known out of itself) to be an important corrective to the social coefficient of knowledge turned in upon itself, for continually breaking through the limits of our conceptions demands a reciprocal continuous openness on our part. It is in the acknowledgement of this moral obligation to transcendent reality that Torrance finds "our freedom as rational beings," both as individuals and also as members of a society or community.[76] A social coefficient of knowledge so grounded is in a position to serve the positive role which Torrance contends that it should.

The Church as the Social Coefficient

The Character of Church as the Social Coefficient

In this section we will discuss Torrance's understanding of the Christian Church as the social correlate of God's self-revelation and its implications for theology and the nature of doctrine. According to Torrance, the Church is "the inter-personal community of ongoing symbiosis" between God and the world.[77]

In developing his notion of the Church as the social coefficient in knowledge of God, Torrance argues that the Church is called into existence by the Word of God and sustained in mission and life in the world by an ongoing covenant relation to God. Thus the Christian community is correlated with the hidden infinite reality of God (partially accessible), which no individual can ever fully grasp so that the whole Christian community throughout history is a more adequate correlate.[78] As the social correlate of God's self-revelation, the Church should be continually and unrestrictedly open to the astonishing infinity and eternity of God which the Church only grasps in a partial way, for even in self-revelation God always remains transcendent over all our knowledge of God.[79]

It is through this kind of unbounded openness that the Church's various forms of life and thought in history ought to develop and reflect at the contingent creaturely level something of the transcendent reality of God and therein also the true meaning of humanity and the creaturely universe God created.[80] For Torrance, openness to, and worship of, the majesty of God who is greater than we can conceive is part of the appropriate orientation of the human mind in response to God's self-revelation.[81] Since it is an openness to the infinite reality of God, it is an openness that has a "distinctly indefinite, inarticulate character."[82]

Part of the Church's role in this very openness correlated with the ineffable transcendence of God even in self-revelation is thus to lift the horizon of humanity and human culture beyond the creaturely to the transcendent majesty and reality of God. In this way the Church embodies the all-important social coefficient of knowledge of God, providing "the semantic focus within which faith and intuitive contact with God may spring up and yield ever-deepening understanding of him."[83] Here the Church as the social coefficient in knowledge of God should function somewhat like the kind of art that Torrance advocates or the general socio-cultural frame of knowledge in society, providing a distinctive milieu (beyond that of other social coefficients), which establishes and maintains people's relations with God. In the case of the Church, openness to unlimited reality of God who is greater than we can conceive.[84]

Now Torrance is adamant that this is not an independent openness or readiness traceable to something immanent and autonomous in human or social beings apart from a relation to the living God, a crucial point in Torrance's theology. Rather this personal and social coefficient embodied in the Church arises in reciprocity with God's self-revelation so that its source as well as its particular texture or shape lies in that self-revelation. God's self-revelation progressively shapes the corporate response and utilizes it in service of God's continuing self-communication to all of humanity.[85]

Torrance argues for a "realist" understanding of the Church as the community of reciprocity called forth by God's self-revelation. This is part of Torrance's answer to the charge of revelational "actualism" or "occasionalism," for the Church is the Body of Christ in history, the creaturely correlate of God's self-revelation, the community sustained throughout its life and activity in space and time in covenanted relation to God.[86] Torrance's view of God's relation to humanity is not that of a "mathematical point" or simply an "event," but rather a community of reciprocity in relation to God moving through time.[87] For Torrance, God's self-revelation always incorporates a human personal/social coefficient involving the totality of the human response and every aspect of human life.[88]

Furthermore, Torrance notes that this coefficient cannot be abstracted out of that relation of reciprocity and treated as an autonomous structure or epistemological *a priori*, anymore than there are final categories in the Kantian sense, or treated as an *a priori* general social coefficient regarded as a corporate counterpart to Kant's synthetic *a priori*.[89] Rather Torrance characterizes the social coefficient of knowledge of God embodied in Israel and the Church as an "affected modification" within the relationship between God and humanity.[90]

In other words the proper social coefficient is not innate in humanity, but is elicited in humanity by God, though not without the full active participation of humanity. It is an adaptation of humanity by the Spirit of God which includes full human agency throughout: The Holy Spirit is God in God's "royal freedom" as God "to be present to the creature to realize and bring to completion the creative purpose of God" for the creature.[91] As such it may not be abstracted out of the relation of reciprocity with God and treated as an autonomous structure.

Nevertheless, Torrance admits that the social coefficient of theological knowledge cannot be cut off from the social coefficients of other fields of inquiry, for knowledge of God is always by human beings in community (or rather communities) who are always involved in other rational and personal pursuits.[92] This can and often does create an ongoing tension between an adequate coefficient of knowledge of God arising out of the relation of reciprocity established in correlation to God's self-revelation and a coefficient refracted or distorted under the conditioning of elements deriving from various aspects of the surrounding culture, a problem we will take up in the next section of this chapter.

Theology and Doctrine in the Church

Now for Torrance, it is in this community of reciprocity called into being by the Word of God, sustained in covenanted partnership with God and openness to God, that theology and doctrinal formulation and clarification must take place as theology seeks to serve the self-revelation of God and to articulate knowledge of God in creaturely forms of thought and speech correlated with that self-revelation. According to Torrance, as outlined in chapter 2 above, it is in the context of worship, thanksgiving and wonder within the fellowship of the Church in contact with God that the theologian's mind is formed for apprehension of God.[93] Theology and doctrinal statement and development cannot be abstracted from its appropriate matrix within the Church, which provides the initial and ongoing orientation for theology and doctrine.

Torrance argues that,

> It is thus through the common tradition of shared spiritual experience and insight in the Church that the theologian makes cognitive contact with the hidden realities of God....By developing appropriate intellectual instruments with which to lay bare the underlying epistemological pattern of thought, and by tracing the chains of connection throughout the coherent body of theological knowledge, he feels his way forward to a more precise understanding of the ways and works of God in the hope of deepening the Church's grasp of divine Reality.[94]

Torrance maintains that, "theology and the life of the Church are inseparable, and theological activity belongs to the strenuous work and daily living of the Church."[95] These are in no way set in sharp contrast in Torrance's thought.[96] Within the Christian community, prayerful meditation upon Scripture and the discipline of hard mental activity like that which occurs in intense hermeneutical activity must be interwoven in theological inquiry and doctrinal formulation.[97]

Torrance sees both a vertical and horizontal dimension to

the Church as the social coefficient in knowledge of God which the writers of the New Testament speak of as *koinonia*. It refers to our fellowship with God through Christ in Spirit, but also to our fellowship with one another as members of the Body of Christ.[98] This is something which Torrance believes evangelical churches have missed, for "in the general development of the Evangelical Churches...there has been a failure to appreciate adequately the living embodiment of faith and truth in the corporate life and structure of the Church."[99]

At this juncture it is also helpful to point out that Torrance distinguishes between different levels of thought and reality, a subject that will be discussed in some depth in chapter 5. Here we will simply note Torrance's distinction between the evangelical and doxological level of Christian experience (hearing the Word of God and participating in worship) and the theological level where explicit theological formulation takes place.[100]

While these levels can be distinguished, they should not be separated. Rather the two must be coordinated: "That theological concepts and statements [doctrines]...must be correlated with empirical concepts and statements grounded in our actual day-by-day knowledge of God is inescapably implied by the interaction of God with us in the universe of space and time which he has created."[101] What Torrance means is that while theology must develop technical vocabulary and other tools of a highly abstract character in its inquiry and doctrinal formulation (*homoousios*, for example), this kind of precise activity must not be abstracted or detached from the evangelical and doxological level of the ongoing Christian life within the worshiping Christian community. Both levels are of critical importance and they should not become detached.

Thus the Christian community plays a pivotal role in theology and doctrine. By its very nature doctrine is rooted in the Church and in the life of the Church, for theological inquiry and doctrinal formulation is a refinement and extension of the knowledge of God that arises out of the Church's evangelical and doxological experience of the divine events and realities of God's self-revelation in Israel and in Jesus Christ.[102] Cut off from those realities and that experience, knowledge of God and doctrine would be empty.[103]

Torrance also contends that it was in this manner, within the matrix of the Church as the social coefficient in knowledge of God, that classical patristic theology (as in the Niceno-Constantinopolitan Creed and the conciliar theology which grew out of it) actually developed and laid the foundation for subsequent Christian theology.[104] Out of such theological activity, examining the biblical witness within the evangelical and doxological life of the early Church, the doctrine of *homoousion* developed so that in and through its formulation, in Torrance's words, "the inner logic of grace in the economic condescension of God in Jesus Christ and the inherent intelligibility of divine Reality in the immanent relations within the Godhead came to expression in a disciplined theological way."[105] This, in turn, has had a decisive impact on subsequent formulation of Christian doctrine and interpretation of Scripture.[106] The same is true of the doctrines of the hypostatic union and the holy Trinity.

These doctrines also influenced the patterns of life and liturgy in the Church. Theology and doctrinal formulation are not purely intellectual exercises because knowledge of God is soteriological and participatory. All of human existence and life in history is implicated. Therefore doctrine cannot but serve multiple functions in the Church, defining the Church's identity, shaping its worship, interpreting and expressing its experience, serving as the grammar of its language, as well as making truth-claims about God and the Gospel.

Doctrine is related to the realities and events of the Christian faith through the Church's experience of them within its evangelical and doxological life, so that Christian community plays a significant role in theological inquiry and doctrinal formulation. Yet for Torrance, the relation between doctrine and the Christian community is complex so that doctrine also contributes to the life of the Church in multiple ways, clarifying and deepening its understanding of the realities and events of God's self-revelation, helping the people of God rightly refer their thought, worship and life beyond themselves to the Gospel and through the Gospel to God, giving the Church a particular identity, etc. This complexity is due to the fact that theology and doctrine are embedded in the matrix of the Church as the social coefficient in relation to God so that doctrine and community mutually influence one another. It is this complexity and mutual influence that leads Torrance to a more sophisticated understanding of the nature of doctrine than we find in Lindbeck's cultural-linguistic proposal, one that integrates the cognitive and communal characteristics of doctrine more fully than Lindbeck does.

Chapter 3

Problems Posed by the Social Coefficient

As mentioned above, the knowledge of God coming to articulation in doctrinal formulation with which Torrance is concerned is knowledge by persons whose existence is socially, culturally and historically conditioned.[107] The fluidity of human life and thought allows social coefficients from different fields of inquiry to influence one another, creating the potential for prior structures of meaning or systems of ideas conditioned by concepts that have arisen elsewhere to deform the social coefficient in our knowledge of God, leading to distortion.[108]

An example of this kind of distortion and the problems and tensions that can result from an inadequate social coefficient or general frame of knowledge is seen in Einstein's struggle with the framework of scientific knowledge informed by rationalistic empiricism. Einstein had to reject the notion that ideas are deduced from experience in a positivist or empiricist manner and develop relativity theory on a holistic basis in which empirical and theoretical factors inhere in one another in reality and in our knowledge of it.[109] In so doing, Einstein was forced to reconstruct the foundations of physics, leading to a different account of how form is integrated, as we saw in chapter 1 above, all of which is quite different from the general frame of knowledge from Descartes and Newton through Hume and Kant.[110]

Our concern here, however, is with the Church's understanding of God, which can also be refracted through its involvement in the world of human culture, especially when society's general frame of knowledge becomes self-contained and loses its openness to the intelligibility of the created universe. Thus the corporate relation toward God in and through the Church and its tradition can become distorted by the influence of non-theological factors with their source in some transient phase of human culture. The result is often interpretations of revelation and divergent patterns of Church order in conflict with one another.[111]

Here Torrance sees one of the causes of Church division, for instead of serving as a reconciling force in human society, overcoming the divisions that arise in a world impacted by sin, the Church has all too often allowed the tensions in the world to cut back into its own life with schismatic results.[112] Torrance finds this particularly troubling today because of the pluralistic fragmentation that he sees infecting Western culture, which the

Church has come to reflect.[113]

One of the reasons for this problem is that the Church must communicate the message of the reconciling love of God in Jesus Christ in the idiom of the culture. This can lead to the temptation to adapt the interpretation of that message to prevailing paradigms of the social consciousness of secular life.[114]

Torrance identifies further influences that contribute to distortion of the social coefficient in knowledge of God and doctrinal formulation: the struggle is not only with the structures of secular life, but with "popular religion," and with sin, which often infects the Christian community in subtle and profound ways.[115]

Examples of the Intrusion of Non-theological Factors

This conditioning by non-theological factors can adversely impact doctrine. An example of the way in which doctrine can be influenced by the intrusion of inappropriate factors from the cultural milieu is seen in Torrance's discussion of the difficulty facing Christian faith and thought as it came into contact with the Greco-Roman world and its dualisms between the eternal world of being and the mutable world of becoming or the realm of the intelligible and the realm of the sensible.[116]

As Torrance sees it, the Church (and its theology) was faced with the problem of how to avoid the dualisms that were destructive to the integrity of the message of the Gospel and yet how to allow that message to take root and realize itself within the Greco-Roman world. Torrance maintains that, "Either it [the Church] had to re-create the foundations of the culture in which it took root, or it had to effect some sort of synthesis with it while leaving it basically intact."[117] Torrance argues that theologically at least the Church embraced the first alternative.[118] This was a struggle for the Church, as is evident in the Arian controversy, which Torrance sees as a clash between these two alternatives.

The Arians, in Torrance's mind, were deeply influenced by the dualism mentioned above and drew a deep separation (*chorismos*) between God and creation, which deeply influenced their understanding of the Son or Word of God. This led to a deep divide between "the eternal unknowable Being of God the Father and the Logos or the Son."[119] The Arians argued that

God originally created the Logos or the Son and the Logos then became the agent by which God created everything else.[120] Thus in the end, for the Arians, the Son or Logos belongs to the created side of the *chorismos* between God and the world (the Word does not inhere in the Being of God) and "in the last analysis is a detached and therefore only a changeable image of God."[121] Torrance points out that Athanasius saw this as implying the ultimate unknowability of God, which he denounced as a form of atheism.[122]

The controversy and the final results are well-known. What is of interest here is the way in which Torrance sees inappropriate elements from the surrounding culture impacting the formulation and development of doctrine in the Church.

The controversy also reveals the way that doctrine played a crucial role in the "social demarcation" of the Church from other religious groups, defining what is "Christian," as Alister McGrath astutely observes, something Torrance also affirms.[123] This is an interesting point in relation to Nicene theology, for it indicates the fact that the Nicene theologians did not impose Greek philosophy upon the biblical witness, as some scholars contend. In fact, just the opposite is closer to the truth: Nicene theology drew upon the biblical view of the relation between God and the created universe (coming to expression in the doctrines of creation and incarnation) and challenged the dualisms latent in much of Greek thought down to their very roots. Torrance sees the early Church, with its theology and doctrine, transforming the prevailing general framework of thought of Greco-Roman culture so that the Gospel could take root within it.

Another example of the way in which doctrine can be influenced by the intrusion of inappropriate factors from the cultural milieu is evident in Torrance's discussion of the way in which a receptacle notion of space influenced the development of doctrine. Torrance deals with this subject at great length in his important book, *Space, Time and Incarnation*, and also in several other places.[124]

According to Torrance, the early Church was forced to deal with the problem of space when the Gospel began to be expounded in Greek culture, for in that culture some form of the receptacle notion of space predominated.[125] Since the Church's doctrine of creation out of nothing implied that space and time arise in and with creation, and since the doctrine of the incarnation meant that the Son of God entered our world of space and time, Patristic theology had to come to terms with the fact that God interacts with the universe of space and time of which humanity is a part in such a way as to "assert the reality of space and time for God in His relations with us."[126]

Torrance argues that while Patristic theology rejected the notion of space as a container or vessel and developed a "relational and differential concept of space" with reference to the interaction between God and world, Western thought generally took over a receptacle notion of space that, when integrated into theological reflection, created a host of difficulties, including divisions in the Church, right up to the present day.[127] Here we will briefly examine only one example of what Torrance intends.

Lutheran theology took over a receptacle notion of space, Torrance maintains, and built it into its doctrine of the "real presence" of Christ in the Eucharist and into its Christology.[128] Torrance asserts that, "The receptacle notion of space was extremely important for Luther for it was his way of asserting the reality and actuality of the Son of God in our human and earthly existence, and he concentrated with a furious intensity upon the fact that the whole Son or Word of God is contained in the infant of Bethlehem and communicated to us in the sacrament of the Lord's Supper."[129]

However, when Reformed theologians attempted to reclaim the Patristic understanding of the Son of God descending from heaven in the Incarnation (which Torrance suggests was understood not in *spatial* terms, but rather in *theological* terms in accordance with the other prior statements of the Niceno-Constantinopolitan Creed that the Son is "God from God, Light from Light") without abandoning his government of the universe, Lutherans operating with a receptacle notion of space interpreted this to mean that something of the Son of God was left "outside" (extra) of the Incarnation, resulting in the "*extra Calvinisticum*."[130] A similar tension was at stake with reference to the ascension, for the Lutherans read the Reformed statements concerning the location of the body of Christ to mean confined there as in a container, which, in turn, had negative implications for the presence of Christ in the Eucharist.[131]

Now Torrance grants that there was significant confusion and terminological imprecision on both sides of this complicated debate. But the root problem is a concept of space developed outside the field of theology and imported into theological reflection, impacting how doctrine was formulated.

Here Torrance thinks that Patristic theology, in its rejection of a receptacle notion of space and in its development of a "relational and differential concept of space as the seat of relations or the place of meeting and activity in the interaction between God and the world," is better, for it is "a distinctively theological understanding of space not tied down to any particular cosmology."[132] Torrance thinks that we ought to work out today a kind of relational and differential theological structure or doctrine similar to that of the early Church.[133]

What is important to note in this discussion is the way non-theological factors influence the social coefficient of knowledge of God and impact doctrinal formulation and debate in profound ways. The receptacle notion of space profoundly shaped the way certain doctrines were understood and precipitated deep tensions between different Christian groups in the process.[134] Torrance discusses other examples of the way in which non-theological factors influence doctrine as well.[135]

Theology Pursued in Space and Time

However, one of the fascinating things about Torrance's position is that while he is concerned with the intrusion of non-theological factors into doctrinal formulation and with developing a strictly *theological* notion of space and time in light of God's interaction with this world, he is unwilling to restrict theology to a God/humanity relationship in which theological concepts are only correlated with the "inner spiritual world of the religious subject." The reason is that this all too easily detaches faith in Jesus Christ "from all empirical correlates in space and time" in an effort to shield Christian faith from critical attack by an objectivist natural science.[136] If human beings are to have knowledge of God, it must be knowledge within the world of space and time, whatever problems that creates for theology and doctrine.

This means that theology–and the way the nature of doctrine is conceived–is forced into the field of God's creative interaction with the world of space and time. This field, for Torrance, is the events and realities of God's self-revelation, preeminently the incarnation of the Word or Son of God within the matrix of Israel where "spatio-temporally conditioned knowledge" of God in Jesus Christ arises.[137]

This is also why Torrance is adamant that theology must not

resolve away its "empirical correlates" in space and time, like the empty tomb with reference to the resurrection, even if we can understand and appreciate the empty tomb only in light of theoretical or theological elements that cannot be directly deduced from it.[138] And since the Truth of God is mediated to us through the medium of the objectivities and intelligibilities of creation, as is preeminently evident in the incarnation, this contingent intelligibility and objectivity cannot be overlooked in theology or doctrine.[139]

Thus Torrance argues that the kind of theology and doctrinal formulation that he advocates, "will not allow us to resolve away spatial and temporal relations or escape from the rational structures that the creation of space and time import, nor will it allow us to elaborate notions of space and time *in abstracto* and then to use them as fixed forms within which to interpret the work of God, forcing our understanding of His grace into their rigid mold."[140] Here we see that, despite the critical posture Torrance adopts toward the way in which human culture can negatively influence the Church, theology and doctrinal formulation, this does not mean that Torrance sees human culture and the knowledge achieved in that culture in solely negative terms.[141]

Doctrinal Criticism

In light of this discussion of the fact that theology (and doctrine) is a fully human enterprise and that non-theological factors often deform doctrinal formulation, Torrance contends that theology must be a critical science that questions the Church's interpretation of Holy Scripture and doctrine. Theology must identify and root out the preconceptions that adversely influence the Church's thought and life.[142] Thus while the kind of theological science (and doctrinal formulation) that Torrance advocates arises within the life of the Christian community, it must also lead that community forward in the repentant rethinking of all aspects of its preaching, teaching, outreach, and life.[143] This demand for repentance (*metanoia*) in which the Church is progressively liberated from the ideological twist of the prevailing social consciousness is scientifically obligatory and it inevitably entails a renewal of the Church's whole interpersonal life and mission, since doctrine and life are not sharply separated in Torrance's theology.[144]

This leads Torrance toward the kind of doctrinal criticism of McGrath.[145] For Torrance, scientific theology "is obliged to examine historical doctrines with a view to distinguishing in them what is proper to the authentic substance of the faith and what is foreign to it but which has understandably been merged with it from the paradigms of contemporary society."[146]

Along similar lines, in speaking of the role of theology and doctrine in overcoming the divisions in the Church due to the assimilation of divergent cultural traditions, Torrance maintains that theology, in its critical mode, needs

> to dig into the foundations and re-examine the connections between historical theology and the cultural environment of the Church, in order to lay bare the core of basic beliefs and doctrines at the centre of the Church's faith and distinguish it from the body of secondary concepts and relations which may well have served an important purpose in the past at some critical juncture in the history of the Church but which in the last analysis have only a peripheral significance so far as the substance of the faith is concerned.[147]

It is at just this point that doctrinal criticism and reformulation can play a significant ecumenical role, for Torrance suggests that it is possible to confront differences between churches from behind by removing the intrusive non-theological factors that generated the divisions in the first place.[148] For this reason, Torrance argues that the scientific theology he advocates, with its criticism and reformulation of doctrine, "thus becomes the *sine qua non* of ecumenism in which we come to grips with the psychological and sociological conditioning even of our most profound theological concepts."[149]

This is not simply the task of individual theologians, but rather of the whole Christian community. In fact, Torrance maintains that the more ecumenical theological statements or doctrines are, "i.e., the more they are formulated within the openness of the members of the whole Community to one another before God, the more likely they are to escape distortion through false in-turned subjectivity and to be properly open toward God."[150] In this way not only does the Christian community play a role in doctrinal formulation, but doctrinal criticism, with its resulting reformulation and affirmation of doctrine, also plays a crucial role in the Christian community.

Yet Torrance is not content with doctrinal criticism in which the Church, through the aid of theology, repentantly rethinks its interpretation of Scripture, its preaching, its mission, and its life, for theology ought to attempt to lift the mind of the Church above that of the current socio-cultural milieu so that the Christian community can exert a similar influence upon the surrounding culture.[151] One of Torrance's personal agendas in his life as a Christian scholar has been "to evangelize the foundations, so to speak, of scientific culture, so that a dogmatics can take root in that kind of structure."[152]

Torrance acknowledges that, "That is a big task, I know, but it's a task which I've learned from Greek patristic theology above all and to which in some measure I would like to contribute in our own day."[153] One could view Torrance's dialogue with natural science and his work in developing a rigorous theological science and philosophy of theological science as an attempt to speak the Gospel within contemporary culture and its idiom, and to transform that culture without allowing it to distort the Gospel in the process.[154]

There is not space here to discuss the details of this further, but what is important to note is that, for Torrance, doctrine should play a role not only in the Church, but also in the surrounding human culture, as it did in the early Church.[155] But why is this kind of reconstruction needed? Because, as discussed earlier, the "received frame of thought" or social coefficient of knowledge affects the habits of mind or the subjective and mental components in knowing.

This brings us back to where we began this chapter: the fact that the social coefficient plays an undeniable role in the knowing relation, for it is there that our understanding is nourished, our informal relations with reality are evoked, and intimations or clues arise that initiate and carry forward proper scientific inquiry, and thus advance explicit knowledge.[156]

Yet when the social coefficient is inappropriate, as Torrance believes is the case with the received frame of knowledge in Western culture, what is demanded is a reconstruction or transformation in that fundamental frame of knowledge. This is a transformation in which doctrine should play a role, as it did in the early Church and the "masterful ideas" it injected into the culture of that day.[157] For Torrance, "instead of suppressing the personal and social coefficients of human knowledge, theology is evangelically concerned for their conversion and regeneration in accordance with the Truth of God as it is in Christ Jesus."[158]

Chapter 3

Notes

1. This process is not unlike Lindbeck's notion of catechesis, though Torrance's strong critical realism differentiates his position from Lindbeck's cultural-linguistic approach, as will become clear later in this chapter and especially in chapters 4 and 5. See George Lindbeck, *The Nature of Doctrine: Religion and Theology in a Postliberal Age* (Philadelphia: Westminster Press, 1984), pp. 132-33.

2. Thomas F. Torrance, *Reality and Scientific Theology* (Edinburgh: Scottish Academic Press, 1985), p. xv.

3. See Thomas F. Torrance, *God and Rationality* (New York: Oxford University Press, 1971), p. 17. Also see Thomas F. Torrance, *Theological Science* (London: Oxford University Press, 1969), pp. 210-11.

4. See Thomas F. Torrance, *Theology in Reconstruction* (London: SCM, 1965), pp. 19-23, 117-22, 146-49, 182-85, and 264-67, for example.

5. See Torrance, *Scientific Theology*, pp. 98-130.

6. Ibid., pp. 98-102.

7. Ibid., p. 98.

8. Ibid.

9. Ibid.

10. Ibid.

11. Ibid., p. 99.

12. Ibid.

13. Ibid., p. 100.

14. Ibid., pp. 100-101.

15. Ibid., p. 101.

16. Ibid.

17. Ibid.

18. Ibid., pp. 98-99.

19. Ibid.

20. Ibid.

21. Ibid.

22. Ibid., p. 101.

23. Ibid.

24. Ibid., p. 102. But the question is, in Torrance's mind, as reflected in his discussion of art, is the cultural-linguistic framework of personal and social existence "semantic as a whole," or positively correlated with the world of space and time? Ibid. If it is not, then how can it provide the matrix for one's basic relation to reality which nourishes meaning and is the source of the essential clues that are of critical importance, even the "*sine qua non*," for all scientific and rational inquiry? Ibid.

25. Ibid., p. 104.

26. Ibid.

27. Ibid.

28. Ibid., p. 102.

29. Ibid.

30. Ibid.

31. Ibid., p. 114.
32. Ibid., p. 103.
33. See Lindbeck, *Doctrine*, pp. 32-41.
34. Torrance, *Scientific Theology*, p. 103.
35. Ibid.
36. Torrance can say that "Through human language thinking is inescapably bound up with the institutions, patterns, and traditions of the communities in which we live–that is why even the most refined scientific concepts are psychologically conditioned." Torrance, *Rationality*, p. 117. Also see Torrance, *Theological Science*, p. 210.

However, while our thinking is implicitly shaped by the tradition of our culture, etc., Torrance argues that,

> This does not imply that we must operate uncritically within the knowledge or wisdom accumulated in our cultural tradition, just because we are unable to extricate ourselves from involvement in it. On the contrary, it is because our thought is so powerfully influenced by culture that we must bring its latent assumptions out into the open and put them to the test....Hence if theology is not to be swamped by cultural relativism but is to retain its integrity, it must put all cultural assumptions rigorously to the test before the compelling claims of its own proper subject-matter and its objective evidential grounds.

Thomas F. Torrance, *Christian Theology and Scientific Culture* (New York: Oxford University Press, 1980), pp. 13-14.

37. Torrance, *Scientific Theology*, p. 103.
38. See pp. 50-51, endnote 109.
39. Torrance, *Scientific Theology*, p. 103.
40. Ibid.
41. Ibid.
42. See p. 91, endnote 130 above.
43. Karl Marx, *A Contribution to a Critique of Political Economy*, trans. S.W. Ryazanskaya (New York: , 1970), p. 20. Also see Torrance, *Scientific Theology*, p. 107.
44. Torrance, *Scientific Theology*, pp. 107-8.
45. Ibid., p. 108.
46. Ibid.
47. Ibid.
48. Ibid., pp. 108-9.
49. Ibid. Torrance notes in regard to Michael Polanyi that,

> In wrestling with the problem of pure science in face of the Marxist rejection of it, he became convinced that no pure... science is possible except on the ground of the acknowledgement of a truth independent of ourselves which we are unable to manipulate for our own ideological ends, or on the ground of a recognition of natural law as a real feature of nature which, as such, exists beyond our control. Pure science involves the unfettered freedom of inquiry and thought, but it is freedom that is possible only on the ground of unconditional obligation to the 'truth of truth'–i.e., to a 'transcendent reality' over which we have no control....What kind of society emerges as the correlate of pure science, and the unbounded, intrinsic

> intelligibility of the universe to which it is dedicated? To the *open universe* disclosed by the advance of pure science, there ought to arise something like the *free society.*

Thomas F. Torrance, *Transformation and Convergence in the Frame of Knowledge: Explorations in the Interrelations of Scientific and Theological Enterprise* (Grand Rapids: Eerdmans, 1984), p. 179. Here we see the political over-tones of Torrance's thought.

50. Torrance, *Scientific Theology,* p. 111.

51. Ibid.

52. Torrance, *Theological Science*, p. 303.

53. Torrance, *Scientific Theology*, p. 109. This point of a human (personal and social) coefficient in all knowledge, in Torrance's perspective, must be frankly admitted and then controlled, not arbitrarily, but correctly under the claims of the intrinsic intelligibility of reality that transcends our knowing and in community and openness to the conjoint correction of others. See Torrance, *Transformation*, pp. 132-35.

54. Torrance, *Scientific Theology*, p. 110.

55. Ibid., p. 112. This is a crucial point in Torrance's epistemology that Hardy has not fully grasped in his analysis of Torrance's position, as noted at the end of the previous chapter.

56. Ibid., pp. 110-11.

57. Ibid., p. 111.

58. Ibid.

59. Ibid., pp. 112-13.

60. Ibid., p. 112.

61. Ibid.

62. Ibid.

63. Ibid., pp. 112-13.

64. Ibid.

65. Ibid., p. 114.

66. Ibid., p. 104.

67. Ibid., p. 113.

68. Ibid.

69. Ibid., pp. 115-16.

70. Ibid., p. 114.

71. See ibid., pp. 102 and 105.

72. Ibid., p. 115.

73. Ibid. Elsewhere Torrance notes that, "whenever natural science engages in heuristic acts which require the formation of new concepts and terms it is forced to struggle with the patterns and rigidities of the community mind in order to free its thinking for the really new." See Torrance, *Rationality*, p. 118.

74. Torrance, *Scientific Theology*, p. 116.

75. Ibid.

76. Ibid., pp. 116-17.

77. Ibid. Torrance sees a deep correlation between Christian faith, pure science and free society on this point for all are dedicated to transcendent reality (contingent and divine). Ibid.

78. Ibid., pp. 117-18.

79. Ibid., pp. 106 and 118.

80. Ibid.

81. Ibid., p. 106.
82. Ibid.
83. Ibid.
84. Ibid.
85. Ibid., p. 105.
86. See Torrance, *Theological Science*, p. 212. For an interesting discussion of Torrance's criticism of Barth on this point, see Thomas F. Torrance, *Karl Barth: Biblical and Evangelical Theologian* (Edinburgh: T & T Clark, 1990), pp. 133-135. Here Torrance recounts his final conversation with Barth in which he pointed out that some of Barth's former students had moved in the direction of a docetic view of the resurrection and that toward the end of the *Church Dogmatics* it seemed as if the "humanity of God" had somewhat displaced the humanity of the risen Jesus, with a resultant loss of the priestly ministry of the ascended Jesus on the basis of Jesus' vicarious humanity, which is what provides the grounding of Torrance's realist doctrine of the Church. Torrance went on point out Barth's distinction between *Wassertaufe* and *Geisttaufe*, "already rejected by Irenaeus in the second century as a form of Gnostic dualism," which could be construed as an example of Barth's "actualism" in his doctrine of the Church and sacraments. Torrance's high view of the sacraments ought to be a caution to those who are quick to label him a "Barthian."
87. See Torrance, *Karl Barth*, pp. 37-38 and 152-59.
88. Torrance, *Scientific Theology*, p. 105. The material side of Torrance's understanding of the social coefficient of knowledge of God embodied in the people of God (Israel and the Church) will be discussed at length in chapter 4 below.
89. See ibid., pp. 102-7.
90. Ibid., p. 106. Underlying this whole discussion is Torrance's understanding of the "contingent" nature of humanity in relation to God that entails both dependence, yet utter difference. See Torrance, *Theological Science*, pp. 55-105 and Thomas F. Torrance, *Divine and Contingent Order* (Oxford: Oxford University Press, 1981; reprint, Edinburgh: T & T Clark, 1998). Also see Elmer M. Colyer, *How to Read T. F. Torrance: Understanding His Trinitarian and Scientific Theology* (Downers Grove, Ill.: InterVarsity Press, 2001), pp. 169-207.
91. Torrance, *Reconstruction*, p. 221. Torrance, *Scientific Theology*, pp. 106-7. On Torrance's understanding of the relation between divine and human agency, see Colyer, *How to Read*, pp. 117-23.
92. Torrance, *Scientific Theology*, p. 105.
93. Ibid., p. 118.
94. Ibid. Torrance maintains that, "The object of theological knowledge is engaged in *purposive* action–God fulfilling His creative and redeeming purposes. He is not known except within these purposes....We cannot know God against His will...nor can we know Him...apart from His claim upon... our existence....In other words, we cannot truly know God without being reconciled and renewed in Jesus Christ. Thus the objectivity of our theological knowledge is immutably soteriological in nature" Torrance, *Theological Science*, p. 41. Also see Thomas F. Torrance, *The Mediation of Christ* (Colorado Springs, Co.: Helmers & Howard, 1992), pp. 35-36.
95. See Thomas F. Torrance, "Our Witness Through Doctrine," in *Conflict and Agreement in the Church*, vol. 1 (London: Lutterworth Press, 1959), p. 94.

Torrance further states that, "the Reformed Church sought from the very beginning to allow the dogmatic and ecclesiastical forms of the Church's life and ministry to interpenetrate each other in obedience to the Word of God....Liturgy and theology go hand in hand....Such is the integration of doctrine and discipline, of faith and order, of worship and theology so characteristic of the Calvinistic Reformation." Ibid.

96. Thomas Langford has criticized Torrance as having "an extremely rationalistic or intellectualistic understanding of faith." See Thomas Langford, "T. F. Torrance's Theological Science: A Reaction," *Scottish Journal of Theology* 25 (May 1972): p. 158. But this criticism is difficult to sustain when one considers the role of Christian life and community in Torrance's theology. Torrance responds to the criticism that his understanding of "the task of Christian theology" seems to be "a severely intellectualistic enterprise" by saying that, "we cannot undertake these tasks [theology and doctrinal formulation] without a living, personal experience of the Truth, and without constant prayer that we may be given illumination to understand and ability to speak of the Truth which by its very nature is utterly beyond us." Thomas F. Torrance, *Reality and Evangelical Theology* (Philadelphia: Westminster Press, 1982), p. 136.

Langford was responding to Torrance's book, *Theological Science*, published long before *Reality and Evangelical Theology*. However, similar statements are found in *Theological Science*: theological statements "are at their very root statements of inquiry, prayer and praise to God made in the Name of Jesus." See Torrance, *Theological Science*, p. 160. Also see pp. 39, 41, 135, 158, 163, 200, 210, 212-14 and 282.

97. Torrance, *Scientific Theology*, pp. 118-19.

98. Ibid., p. 119. Also see Torrance, *Theological Science*, pp. 135, 163-65, & 210-12.

99. Thomas F. Torrance, *Theological Dialogue between Orthodox and Reformed Churches* (Edinburgh: Scottish Academic Press, 1985), p. 107.

100. Thomas F. Torrance, "The Framework of Belief," in *Belief in Science and in Christian Life: The Relevance of Michael Polanyi's Thought for Christian Life and Faith*, ed. Thomas F. Torrance (Edinburgh: Handsel Press, 1980), p. 24. Also see Torrance, *Evangelical Theology*, pp. 35-36.

101. Torrance, *Evangelical Theology*, p. 36.

102. See Torrance, *Scientific Theology*, p. 85.

103. Ibid.

104. Torrance, *Evangelical Theology*. p. 49.

105. Ibid., p. 113. See pp. 107-13 for Torrance's full discussion of this.

106. Ibid.

107. Torrance, *Scientific Theology*, p. 105. Torrance acknowledges that "Theology can never operate outside the historical situation and therefore cannot but be conditioned by the notions and tools which it uses from age to age." See Torrance, *Rationality*, p. 4.

108. See Torrance, *Theological Science*, pp. 221 and 231. It is the flexibility of human thought and life that allows it to expand and enter new horizons of experience and knowledge. Yet that same fluidity also allows for the kind of transfer and/or imposition of form that leads to distortion.

Torrance notes that, "It is not easy to disengage scientific thinking from popular thinking in any field of knowledge. This becomes evident, as Thomas Kuhn has shown us once again, whenever we begin making some notable scientific advance, for the struggle to break free from preconceptions reveals how deeply conditioned even our scientific concepts can be by psychological and sociological factors at work in the community in which we live and work." Torrance, *Rationality*, p. 46.

109. Torrance, *Transformation*, pp. xi-xii.

110. See Torrance, *Rationality*, p. 118.

111. Torrance, *Scientific Theology*, pp. 119-20 and 151.

112. Ibid., p. 120. Torrance maintains that,

> Many of our theological and ecclesiological divisions appear to have their roots there: not in any real divergence as to the fundamental datum of divine revelation or in the permanent substance of apostolic faith, but to differences resulting from the assimilation of the Christian faith and the Christian way of life to alien frameworks of thought and behavior in the worldly environment of the Church....Looked at in this way, the Orthodox, Roman Catholic and Evangelical Churches are seen to differ, not in their essential relation to Christ, but in the measure they have expressed their faith and life in divergent cultural traditions.

Thomas F. Torrance, *Theology in Reconciliation: Essays towards Evangelical and Catholic Unity in East and West* (London: Geoffrey Chapman, 1975; reprint, Eugene, Ore.: Wipf & Stock, 1997), p. 8.

113. Torrance, *Scientific Theology*, p. 120. Also see pp. 151-52.

114. Ibid.

115. Ibid., p. 120. Also see Torrance, *Rationality*, pp. 118-19, and Torrance, *Theological Science*, p. 277-79.

116. See Torrance, *Reconciliation*, pp. 27-40 (especially 29-33) and 215-26.

117. Ibid., p. 29.

118. Ibid.

119. Ibid., p. 224.

120. Ibid., pp. 224-25.

121. Ibid., p. 225.

122. Ibid.

123. See Alister E. McGrath, *The Genesis of Doctrine: A Study in the Foundations of Doctrinal Criticism* (Cambridge, Mass.: Basil Blackwell, 1990), pp. 37-52.

124. Torrance discusses the various problems that a receptacle notion of space created in the development of doctrine at different points in the history of the Church in Thomas F. Torrance, *Space, Time and Incarnation* (London: Oxford University Press, 1969). Also see Thomas F. Torrance, "The Relation of the Incarnation to Space in Nicene Theology," in *The Ecumenical World of Orthodox Civilization*, ed. A. Blane (The Hague: Mouton, 1973), pp. 43-70 and Torrance, *Rationality*, pp. 123-134.

125. Torrance, *Rationality*, p. 123. See Torrance, *Incarnation*, pp. 4-11 for a discussion of Greek ideas of space.

126. Torrance, *Rationality*, pp. 123-4.

127. Ibid., p. 124. Also see Torrance, *Incarnation*, pp. 22-51.

128. Torrance, *Rationality*, p. 126.

129. Ibid.

130. Ibid.

131. Ibid., pp. 126-27. Also see Torrance, *Incarnation*, pp. 131-35.

132. Torrance, *Rationality*, p. 124. Also see Torrance, *Incarnation*, pp. 15-21 and Torrance, "The Relation of the Incarnation," pp. 61-70. Torrance sees such a notion of space in relation to God as developed in accordance with the nature of the reality of God who transcends space-time that arises in and with creation.

Of course, Torrance also points out that relativity theory has dealt a crushing blow to the receptacle conception of space and time as independent of what goes on within them. Yet, Torrance forthrightly asserts–and this is an important point for those who think that he is building theology on post-Einsteinian science–that, "this does not mean that Christian theology must give up the old scientific notions of space in order to adopt a more modern one, but that dialogue with natural science in its struggle to under-stand space and time in the natural processes of this world, theology...must strive to develop a strictly *theological* under-standing of space and time in the light of God's interaction with this world as revealed in the incarnation...in space-time." Torrance, *Rationality*, p. 131. Torrance also asserts that,

> This does not mean that Christian theology can or should ever be grounded on natural science, but it does mean that as we allow ourselves to be questioned by rigorous scientific analysis we are helped to discriminate what is truly theological, arising on the ground of God's self-revelation, from distorting foreign structures that have so often been grafted on to it but which turn out to be no more that obsolete deposits in the Christian consciousness from some passing phase of human culture.

Torrance, *Reconciliation*, p. 275.

133. Torrance, *Rationality*, p. 128.

134. Torrance even indicates that, "As we look back upon these questions it seems very evident that the essential intention of Roman, Lutheran, and Reformed accounts of the real presence of Christ was the same, and indeed that the pure theological content of their statements was pretty much uniform, but what divided them so sharply was the alien concept of the receptacle and the dubious theological structures to which it gave rise in its advocates and also in its opponents." Ibid., p. 128.

135. See for example Torrance's discussion of Church order in ibid., pp. 128-31 or his discussion of other points at which the receptacle notion of space influenced various Christological doctrines in the history of the Church in Torrance, *Incarnation*.

136. See Torrance, *Evangelical Theology*, p. 29. This can also be seen as one of Torrance's damaging critiques of the experiential-expressivist tradition, which often did attempt to shield Christianity from the critical questions and implications raised by the results of natural science by moving the ground of the Christian faith to a realm beyond that implicated by natural science. This expressivist perspective, of course, implies an underlying dualism, often between a materialist universe governed by a rigid cause and effect and a realm of spirit or human freedom. This seems to lead almost inevitably to a dualist anthropology, in which humanity somehow lives on both sides of the divide, with the ground of religion, of course, residing in the transcendental realm. The problem then, however, is what this does to the relationship between Christian faith and the space-time structures of the universe.

Torrance is quite unwilling to restrict Christian faith and theology to a God/human transcendental relation, even if transcendentality is communicated and deposited in concrete forms in space and time. Torrance sees such a restriction as a perennial temptation for theology, of which experiential-expressivism is but one example. The temptation is that once the truths and doctrines of faith are detached from their ground in God's self-revelation, they cannot remain as mere ideas, and so they are regrafted onto something else, such as the inner world of human being, the Church, culture, etc. See Torrance, *Theological Science*, p. 213.

137. See Torrance, *Evangelical Theology* pp. 29-39.

138. See ibid., pp. 35-38. Also see Thomas F. Torrance, *Space, Time and Resurrection* (Edinburgh: Handsel Press, 1976), pp. 21-26, where he states that, "theological formulations which are concerned with the creative and redeeming acts of God in space and time cannot be without their empirical correlates, in respect to which they are open to critical questioning and testing from the natural (including the human) sciences" (p. 23). Here we see a point where Torrance differs from those who rely on narrative as a literary category, construing the Christian faith in exclusively cultural-linguistic categories to avoid having to deal with just the kind of "empirical correlates" that Torrance demands and that are open to the questioning and testing by science. The historical Jesus and his life and death in physical space and time, and the empty tomb are correlates of the Incarnation. Ibid., pp. 36-37. Also see ibid., pp. 23-26.

139. Torrance, *Evangelical Theology*, pp. 26-39 and 152-56.

140. Torrance, *Rationality*, p. 130. Also see Torrance, *Evangelical Theology*, chapter 1, "The Bounds of Christian Theology," pp. 21-51, for an important discussion of a cluster of related issues.

141. His positive estimation of the tremendous advances of natural science and the positive role that a proper social coefficient can play, combined with his emphasis on God's involvement in the objectivities and intelligibilities of the space-time universe and the fact that the truth of creation is brought to light and fulfilled by revelation, should put such a notion to rest. Torrance has thought out the relationship between theological science and natural science, and Christian faith and non-Christian culture with great care.

142. Torrance, *Evangelical Theology*, p. 47.

143. Ibid.

144. See Torrance, *Rationality*, pp. 116-20 and Torrance, *Scientific Theology*, pp. 40-48.

145. McGrath describes doctrinal criticism as a discipline that "seeks to evaluate the reliability and adequacy of the doctrinal formulations of the Christian tradition, by identifying what they purport to represent, clarifying pressures and influences which lead to their genesis, and suggesting criteria–historical and theological–by which they may be evaluated and, if necessary, restated. See McGrath, *Doctrine*, pp. vii-viii.

146. See Torrance, *Reconciliation*, p. 273. Here Torrance also notes that "Sociologists tell us that the theology of every generation is conditioned by the culture through which it passes–and of course they are right. But whereas the sociologists are professedly indifferent to whether such a state of affairs is right or wrong, a scientific theology cannot remain indifferent." Ibid.

147. Ibid., pp. 8-9.

148. Ibid., p. 9. Here, I believe, is part of Torrance's motivation for beginning with the doctrine of the holy Trinity in his involvement in the dialogue between the Reformed and Orthodox Churches. See Torrance, ed., *Theological Dialogue*, p. xi.

149. See Torrance, *Rationality*, p. 118. Torrance, drawing on a passage from one of the Church Fathers, even argues that through the reformation of its life and doctrine, the Church should be viewed not as growing older, but as getting younger and younger. See Torrance, "Our Witness", p. 96.

150. Torrance, *Rationality*, p. 190.

151. Torrance, *Scientific Theology*, p. 120.

152. See John I. Hesselink, "A Pilgrimage in the School of Faith: An Interview with T. F. Torrance," *Reformed Review* 38, no. 1 (1984): p. 60. Torrance also notes that throughout his career, "My main intent has been to clear the ground for a dogmatics in the modern era, because the kind of dogmatics we learned from Calvin and Barth needs to be thought out and expressed more succinctly within the rigorous scientific context in which we work and which will undoubtedly dominate the whole future." Ibid.

Torrance's concern extends beyond theology and the life of the Church to society and its institutions. In this same interview, Torrance indicated that he was working on a project in the area of ethics and law and its bearing upon the politico-social sphere, now published as, Thomas F. Torrance, *Juridical Law and Physical Law: Toward a Realist Foundation for Human Law* (Edinburgh: Scottish Academic Press, 1982). As post-Einsteinian science has had to move beyond a positivist notion of natural law to one that is in harmony with the reality of the universe, so Torrance thinks that Western Culture must move beyond conventionalism and positivism in ethics and law. Torrance asserts, "I believe that theologians MUST contribute to the foundations of society, and this involves rethinking the basis of law, not simply natural law but also juridical law." See Hesselink, "Pilgrimage," p. 63.

153. See ibid., p.60. Torrance see the early Church injecting into European thought several crucial ideas which later were crucial to the development of modern science. Ibid. Elsewhere Torrance argues that in reconstructing the foundations of ancient philosophy, science and culture, early Christian theology developed three "masterful ideas" which arose "out of careful thinking together of the doctrines of the incarnation of the eternal 'Logos' and of the creation of the world out of nothing." See Thomas F. Torrance, *The Ground and Grammar of Theology* (Charlottesville: The University of Virginia Press, 1980), p. 52. The three "masterful ideas" are, 1.) the rational unity of the universe; 2.) the contingent rationality or intelligibility of the universe; and 3.) the contingent freedom of the universe. See ibid., pp. 52-74.

154. It is this intent that propelled Torrance to edit a series of books, under the aegis of the Templeton Foundation, called *Theology and Science at the Frontiers of Knowledge*, which envisages nothing less than "a reconstruction of the very foundations of modern thought and culture, similar to that which took place in the early centuries of the Christian era, when the unitary outlook of Judaeo-Christian thought transformed that of the ancient world, and made possible the eventual rise of modern empirico-theoretical science." See Torrance, *Scientific Theology*, p. ix, the "General Forward" to this series of books. Torrance, and others who are contributing to the series (twenty to twenty-five volumes were projected), are concerned

with healing the "disintegrated form and fragmented culture" of the Western world. Ibid.

155. Thus while Torrance sees Karl Barth's theology as a tremendous "advance far ahead of his contemporaries," it did not lead to this kind of reconstruction of surrounding culture and "the socio-cultural frame of thought, within which theology continues to function, remains largely unchanged." See Torrance, *Transformation,* p. viii.

156. See ibid., p. x and Torrance, *Scientific Theology*, pp. 101-4 and 112-14.

157. Here we see a difference between Torrance and Lindbeck, for Lindbeck (and others who operate out of similar kinds of Narrative theology, like Stanley Hauerwas) seems to view the Church as an island in the vast sea of "decontexualized" pseudo-Christianity that only serves to immunize against the kind of "catechesis" that is really needed; a Church that only with great difficulty attracts "assiduous catechumens." See Lindbeck, *Doctrine*, pp. 132-34. But what is missing is a strong emphasis on the "Christ Transforming Culture" motif that is evident in Torrance at this point.

At any rate, there is a significant difference between Torrance and Lindbeck on this point and their respective views of doctrine. For Lindbeck doctrines are second-order rules governing first-order discussion, which seem to have very little, if any, implication beyond the Christian community. For Torrance the doctrines of creation and incarnation have ontological implications of such a magnitude that they have a contribution to make in the transformation of culture and in natural science. Torrance even asserts, "not that theology today must be grounded upon the new science, but rather that this science, in point of fact, rests upon foundational ideas that science did not and could not have produced on its own, ideas that derive from the Christian understanding of the relation of God to the universe." See Torrance, *Ground and Grammar*, p. 73.

158. Torrance, *Theological Science*, p. 278.

Chapter 4
Doctrine and a Realist Revelation

Introduction

McGrath on the Genesis of Doctrine

In the last chapter we saw how Torrance contends that it is within the Christian community, the social coefficient of knowledge of God, that we find the appropriate matrix within which our semantic relations in knowledge of God are established and maintained, for it is here that our basic informal relations are evoked and our anticipatory grasp of Christian faith (that initiates and guides inquiry) is gained and sustained, leading in due course to doctrinal formulation. The Church and its tradition constitute a living embodiment of faith and truth. Doctrine and the nature of doctrine are rooted in the Church and the life of the Church.

However, since the Church is in the world and called to speak the Gospel to the world in the idiom of the culture, it cannot avoid the influence of inarticulate social coefficients and articulate frameworks of thought arising out of other fields of inquiry or the general frame of knowledge that has established itself within the society. Thus the Church has to reckon with the distortion that can and does occur in its life and doctrine due to the conditioning of factors deriving from various passing phases of the surrounding culture.

In light of this, Torrance, like Alister McGrath, calls for doctrinal criticism in which we come to terms with the psychological and social conditioning of doctrine to the end of distinguishing what is proper to the authentic substance of the faith and what is, in fact, cultural.

McGrath traces the "genesis of doctrine" and doctrinal criticism back to the historical Jesus and the tradition(s) about him embodied in the biblical narratives: "without prejudice to the question of what the *ultimate* external referent of doctrinal formulations might be, I wish to suggest that the proximate external referent is the history of Jesus of Nazareth. This history, mediated by a tradition and a *Lebensform*, generates and regulates doctrine."[1] For McGrath, the attempt to "demarcate the significance of Jesus" constitutes the origin of Christian doctrine and it is in reference to Jesus that doctrine is regulated through the discipline of doctrinal criticism.[2]

McGrath criticizes Lindbeck on this point because of Lindbeck's "studied evasion of the central question of revelation...whether the Christian idiom...originates from accumulated human insight, or from the self-disclosure of God in the Christ event."[3] Furthermore, McGrath complains of Lindbeck's "hesitation over the claims of epistemological realism."[4]

However, McGrath himself does not really develop the conversation beyond the historical Jesus, the biblical narratives about him, and McGrath's own attempt at "a precise understanding...of the factors which stimulate and govern doctrinal formulations, in all their historical and systematic complexity."[5] Thus, McGrath's approach to defining the nature of doctrine ends up being primarily historical: the "development of doctrine as a historical phenomenon must underlie any theory of the nature of doctrine."[6]

I regard McGrath's treatment of doctrine as a historical phenomenon as quite brilliant, but I am equally troubled by his failure to follow up his initial comments concerning revelation and epistemic realism with substantive discussion of what this means for the historical Jesus, the narratives about him, the genesis of doctrine, and the nature of doctrine. I agree that the development of doctrine as a historical phenomenon has something important to contribute to a theory concerning the nature of doctrine. Yet is this a sufficient grounding for a theory of doctrine? McGrath seems to admit that it is not.

McGrath grants that doctrinal criticism cannot rest entirely upon historical analysis and that there must be a "creative dialectic" between the historical and descriptive and the theological and prescriptive (Torrance would undoubtedly accept this, at least to a point). McGrath also grants that a "full analysis" of this dialectic lies beyond the scope of his book, though he hopes that some clarification will result.[7]

Nevertheless, McGrath still erects an artificial boundary in his discussion of doctrine at doctrine's "proximate external referent," the "history of Jesus of Nazareth" and the subsequent tradition about him, leaving the "question of what the *ultimate* external referent of doctrinal formulations might be" without "prejudice" to be sure, but rather undifferentiated.[8] Yet how can doctrine, the genesis of doctrine and the nature of doctrine be bracketed in this manner? If there is an "ultimate external referent" of doctrine (God's *oikonomia*, the Trinity), must this not in fact condition doctrine, the genesis of doctrine and the nature of doctrine?

One cannot rest content with a theory of doctrine that does not address this level. The Jesus of history and the history of Jesus (narratives about Jesus) did not just happen. In Torrance's view, they are bound up with the intelligible realities and events of God's self-revelation, and only understandable in light of them.

Furthermore, while McGrath correctly criticizes Lindbeck for failing to discuss the relation between the Christian idiom (biblical narrative and its narrated world) and revelation, McGrath himself does not explain that relation satisfactorily, speaking only of God's self-disclosure in the "Christ-event." Nor does McGrath explain what bearing this might have on doctrine and the nature of doctrine. But can one develop a theory of doctrine without also entering into a theological/historical treatment of revelation, its relation to Israel, to Jesus Christ, to the Bible, and the relations between doctrine and all of these various elements? How do the characteristics of God's self-revelation condition doctrine and the nature of doctrine?[9]

Torrance's Contribution

It is at this point, where McGrath's study is the weakest, that Torrance has a real contribution to make to the discussion of the nature of doctrine, for Torrance's understanding of the nature of doctrine is grounded in, and integrated with, his "Realist Interpretation of God's Self-Revelation."[10] Here Torrance's position is sharply differentiated from propositionalism, experiential-expressivism and Lindbeck's cultural-linguistic theory of doctrine. Torrance's contribution carries the discussion of the nature of doctrine considerably beyond McGrath's work, which stops short of the depth of Torrance's reflection in this area. Whether one agrees with the details of Torrance's discussion or not, Torrance's penetrating analysis in developing his realist interpretation of God's self-revelation reveals the artificiality of bracketing the discussion of doctrine and the nature of doctrine at 1.) the formal level as with Lindbeck's cultural-linguistic theory, and 2.) the historical level of the Jesus of history and the history of Jesus.

As will become clear in the course of this chapter, Torrance's rigorous scientific predilection will not let him remain content with any kind of separation between form and content or artificial restriction of inquiry to the level of history. From the beginning of his career, Torrance has attempted to probe "into the essential connections embodied in the material content of our knowledge of God and his relation to us in creation and redemption, and...to develop a coherent and consistent account of Christian theology as an organic whole in a rigorously scientific way in terms of its objective truth and inner logic...pursued on its own ground and in its own right."[11] Torrance's understanding of the nature of doctrine arises out of doctrine's relation to the realities, events and relations embodied in God's self-revelation to humanity through God's historical dialogue with Israel and in the incarnation of the Word and Truth, God in Jesus Christ, which gave rise to the Old and New Testaments of Scripture.[12]

Without entering into a discussion of Torrance's realist interpretation of God's self-revelation one will not properly understand his conception of the nature of doctrine. Furthermore, it is doubtful whether any theory of the nature of doctrine will prove satisfactory without a similar rigorous delineation of the material content and fundamental structure of the realities that are constitutive of the Christian faith.[13]

This chapter will outline Torrance's account of those realities, events, and relations that form and inform the biblical narrative and generate doctrine. This will further clarify Torrance's understanding of the nature of doctrine, since for Torrance the nature of doctrine cannot be separated from those realities and events.

It should be noted that Torrance's material account of the realities, events and relations of God's self-revelation is an example of his hermeneutics and realist integration of form in which he attempts to penetrate through the biblical text to those realities and events witnessed to and embodied in Scripture, and then in light of those realities to clarify the character of Scripture, its interpretation, the character of theological inquiry, and the nature of doctrine. Here we see the concrete and rigorous correlation of method and content in Torrance's conception of theological science discussed in chapters 1 and 2 above. This chapter outlines the place of Israel in the mediation of revelation, the vicarious humanity of Jesus Christ, the Apostolic foundation of the Church and the New Testament, the role of the Holy Spirit, the character of Scripture, and Torrance's realist interpretation of God's self-revelation and doctrine.

A Realist Interpretation of God's Self-Revelation

In beginning this discussion of Torrance's realist interpretation of God's self-revelation it is imperative that we remember that for Torrance there is no *inherent isomorphism* between the created and contingent rationality of the universe and the uncreated rationality of God that could serve as a logical bridge from knowledge of the world to knowledge of God.[14] Nor is there a dualism or deistic disjunction between God and the world that excludes any real Word from God to the world God has created.[15] Rather Torrance's position can be characterized as "interactionist" for "God is thought of as interacting closely with the world of nature and history without being confused with it."[16]

Furthermore, as noted in the last chapter, since human beings are creatures of space and time, human knowledge of God must be knowledge within the world of space and time. Thus in focusing on the self-revelation of God to humanity through God's dialogue with Israel and in the incarnation in Jesus Christ that gave rise to Scripture, Torrance argues that, "By revelation is meant, then, not some vague, inarticulate awareness of God projected out of human consciousness, but an intelligible, articulate revealing of God by God whom we are enabled to apprehend through the creative power of his Word addressed to us, yet a revealing of God by God which is actualized within the conditions of our creaturely existence and therefore within the medium of our human thought and speech."[17] For Torrance, this is a revelation which "posits and sustains" humanity and full human agency throughout the movement of revelation from God to humanity and humanity to God.[18]

Such a profound reciprocity is created between God and humanity that in assuming creaturely human form this divine revelation "summons an answering movement" from humanity toward God "which is taken up into the movement of revelation as a constitutive ingredient" in God's self-revelation to humanity.[19] This happens in such a way that God's Word to humanity becomes at the same time the obedient response of humanity in life, thought and speech (a cultural-linguistic framework) so that God's revelation is realized within our human creaturely conditions as well as rooted in God's own divine Reality and Life.[20] Doctrine (and the nature of doctrine), for Torrance, has to be related to that reciprocity, a reciprocity that is not of an experiential-expressivist or a strictly propositionalist character, as will become clear as we proceed.

Furthermore, Torrance is adamant that it is in and through this revelation of God, which is actualized in our creaturely humanity, first in Israel and then fully in Jesus Christ, that we come to know anything about God's self-revelation and the human response to it that revelation elicits.[21] Our knowledge of it does not arise out of phenomenological analysis of ancient Israel or the early Church.[22] It is preeminently in Jesus Christ that we find this two-way connection between God and humanity, where the Word of God in truly present and the human response is faithful and true, so that Christ himself is simultaneously the Word of God to humanity and that same Word acknowledged, articulated and lived out within our own humanity.[23]

Thus, what we find in Torrance's theology is not a timeless and spaceless revelation conceived exclusively in terms of an "event," provoking the charge of "occasionalism," but rather a pattern of continued interaction between God and the time-space structures of this world in God's historical dialogue with Israel and in the incarnation of the Word of God, a revelation that includes and sustains the human response first in Israel, and then in Jesus Christ and in the Apostolic foundation of the Church and Scripture. Torrance describes this as "an orderly continuum of successive patterns of change and coherent structures within which God may reflect and fulfil His own creative and redemptive intentionality...not a movement that passes over these structures [of this world] or gets stuck in them, for it continues to operate livingly and creatively in space-time...fulfilling the divine purpose within it and pressing that fulfillment to its consummation in the new creation."[24]

This means that Torrance has a conception of revelation which is *dynamic* and *ontological* on both the divine and human poles: it is something that "happens" in space-time through God's interaction (divine agency) and includes an active human response (full human agency); and it entails real disclosure on the part of God, yet assumes (and transforms in the process) real creaturely structures in space and time.[25]

Thus if we are to know God, we must know God within the field of relations that God has actually set up in Israel and in the incarnation and apostolic foundation of the Church. This is the material basis (the actual realities, events and relations constitutive of Christian faith) upon which doctrine arises and which cannot but condition the nature of doctrine.

Israel and the Mediation of Revelation

The reciprocity that God's self-revelation creates as it is actualized within the conditions of our creaturely existence takes a corporate form. Torrance argues that for revelation to be intelligible and communicable for human beings, it has to be embodied with the interpersonal and communal structure of humanity.[26] In other words, God's self-revelation to humanity includes a social coefficient as part of its embodiment with our creaturely human reality. This reciprocity, which is called into correlation by and with the movement of God's self-revelation, involves "a community of reciprocity" between God and humanity established in human history, which under the influence of that self-revelation "becomes the appropriate medium of its continuing communications" to humanity.[27]

Torrance maintains that this is, in fact, what took place in God's dealings with the people of Israel, for as we saw above, Torrance's view of revelation is not simply an event operating only tangentially to human existence and history. Knowledge of God requires a personal and social integration of form that involves not only forms of thought, but also forms of life (a cultural-linguistic framework) for its apprehension and articulation. God indwelt Israel through the Word in such an intimate, personal, distinctive, covenanted manner over time that Israel was progressively molded and shaped in obedience or disobedience to be an appropriate community for the continuation of God's self-revelation in history.[28]

It is important to remember that for Torrance we do not apprehend anything without the synthesizing and conceptualizing activity of human reason.[29] Since, as noted above in pointing to Torrance's understanding of the *contingent* relation that exists between the created universe and God, there is no inherent isomorphism between human life and thought and knowledge of God, God elicits an isomorphism by electing Israel out of the mass of humanity and subjecting Israel to intense interaction and dialogue, generating the appropriate forms of life and thought to serve God's self-revelation.[30]

Thus, in Torrance's mind, Israel has an indispensable role to play in the mediation of revelation, for God took Israel into his hands in this singular manner in order to provide the appropriate cultural-linguistic framework, the forms of understanding, worship and expression, through which apprehension of God could be made accessible to human beings and knowledge of God could take root in the soil of humanity.[31]

This process in the life of Israel was not a painless one, for Torrance points out that the mediation of divine revelation through the life and thought of Israel not only included a disclosure of God's nature, but also entailed an uncovering of the sinful offence to God deep in the human heart.[32] In fact, Torrance maintains that God's dealings with Israel served often to intensify this enmity toward God.[33]

However, through it all the Word of God came to Israel in such a creative and compelling manner that it adapted Israel's responses at every level in service of God's continuing self-communication to humanity.[34] This shaping process included not simply the moral and religious consciousness of Israel, but impacted its very life and culture at all levels so that we cannot abstract some religious concept of Israel, Torrance argues, from the physical particularity of Israel.[35]

For Torrance this means that the Old Testament Scriptures, which arose within the ongoing reciprocity, which God etched out in Israel's life and thought, can not be treated as "free-floating divine oracles with an independent existence of their own, in spite of their written form, for they cannot properly be detached from their embodiment in the whole historical fact of Israel and its vicarious role in the reception and communication of the Word of God to the human race, not least in the incarnate form of Jesus Christ."[36] Thus Torrance maintains, only through the medium of Israel has God's self-revelation provided humanity with permanent structures of thought and speech for the apprehension and articulation of that revelation.[37]

The Old Testament Scriptures are "assumed within the orbit of the New Testament" where they provide the basic structures utilized in articulating the Gospel, though Torrance notes that these structures are ultimately deepened and transformed in relation to Christ.[38] Torrance gives a number of examples of the permanent structures he has in mind, including the Word and Name of God, revelation, mercy, truth, holiness, messiah, prophet, priest, covenant, sacrifice, forgiveness, reconciliation, redemption, atonement, etc., and those basic patterns of worship found in Israel's ancient liturgy or in the psalms.[39]

Thus nearly all the basic concepts appropriated by Christianity were formed through the course of God's dealings with Israel in history.[40] In this way, Torrance maintains that God formed Israel to be the womb for the incarnation, the appropriate matrix of thought, speech and life for the definitive reception of revelation in Christ.[41] Apart from Israel's mediation of revelation, the incarnation of the Word of God in Jesus Christ would have been an absolute enigma.[42] Only within the matrix of patterns embodied in Israel's life and thought could Christ be "recognized as Son of God and Saviour and his crucifixion could be interpreted as an atoning sacrifice for sin."[43]

For Torrance, the mediation of revelation that occurred in the course of God's covenanted interaction with Israel entailed a progressive movement of revelation and a progressively shaped human response deposited in the Old Testament Scriptures, a response that is of more than transient value even though it pointed ahead to its fulfillment in Jesus Christ.[44] This means that the Old Testament, understood out of this continuum of orderly successive patterns of change embodied within the life of Israel, cannot but condition doctrine and the nature of doctrine, for doctrine arises out of the medium of relations and structures established and embodied in Israel and the Old Testament as they point ahead and provide the matrix for God's ultimate self-revelation in the incarnation of the Word and Truth of God in Jesus Christ.[45] It is in Jesus Christ, Torrance points out, that this whole prehistory of the mediation of God's self-revelation in Israel is gathered up, fulfilled and reshaped into the cultural-linguistic framework within which God's final revelation in Christ becomes intelligible and communicable to humanity through history.[46]

Incarnation: Christ's Vicarious Humanity

In the fullness of time, in the incarnation of the Word and Son of God, Jesus Christ was born of Mary within the matrix of Israel where there had been a progressive and organic correlation of God's revelation and a response forged in the corporate medium of the covenanted community. God's ultimate self-revelation entered humanity in such a way that it was heard, understood, and actualized in the grace and truth of a completely faithful human response to God the Father.[47] Thus in the life and mission of the Word made flesh in Jesus, mediating and reconciling God and humanity in and through his person, a correlation or isomorphism is established between God's self-communication and human reception of communication within which God's self-revelation is not only embodied in humanity, but also a true and faithful response is forged by humanity to God.[48]

This brings us to Torrance's understanding of the vicarious humanity of Christ in which the Word of God assimilated human rationality, language, and life as constitutive ingredients in God's final self-revelation to humanity.[49] According to Torrance, in Jesus Christ, God's articulate self-communication speaks to humanity through human language from one human being to another, for in Jesus Christ, God appropriates human speech and thus forms a full and final human creaturely expression of the divine Word in the words of Jesus of Nazareth.[50]

Furthermore, Torrance argues that in the incarnation, God came to us in the depth of our *fallen* and *depraved* humanity: "The Incarnation is to be understood as the coming of God to take upon himself our fallen human nature, our actual human existence laden with sin and guilt, our humanity diseased in mind and soul in its estrangement or alienation from the Creator."[51] However, Torrance notes that this does not mean that Christ sinned or became contaminated by the sinful nature he appropriated from us, for Christ overcame the destructive evil entrenched in our human condition through his own perfect obedience throughout his life so as to condemn sin and deliver humanity from it.[52] From his birth to his resurrection, Jesus Christ united himself to humanity in such a way as to reconcile, heal, sanctify, and recreate it.[53]

Torrance is adamant that this includes Christ assuming the alienated *mind* of sinful humanity so as to redeem, heal and sanctify human rationality and speech from deep within the rational core of humanity.[54] Here again we see the interrelation in Torrance's theology not only between the incarnation and the atonement, but also between revelation and reconciliation, for it is here in the human mind of Christ that humanity recovers true knowledge of God.[55] Thus Torrance argues that the *prophetic* office of Christ cannot be separated from Christ's *priestly* office: Jesus' teachings found in the Gospels are essential to his saving work.[56]

Torrance concludes that Jesus Christ "is the hearing and speaking" human being assumed by the Word of God in the incarnation.[57] Here we have neither a Word of God and a response of humanity only loosely related in a Nestorian dualism, nor an Apollinarianism in which the human word is displaced, but rather "the indivisible, all-significant middle term," the full and vicarious humanity of Christ involving genuine human agency and human word in response to and *enhypostatic* in the Word of God.[58]

Torrance also indicates that in Jesus Christ word and event, speech and event, are inextricably bound together throughout Christ's revealing and reconciling action on our behalf.[59] Here in Jesus Christ full reciprocity between God and humanity and humanity and God in all aspects of human life has been established within our human and creaturely life so that we can hear God's Word and meet God "face to face."[60] As such, Torrance argues, "*the real text* of New Testament revelation is *the humanity of Jesus*."[61]

This reciprocity which has been established in Jesus Christ within the matrix of Israel, Torrance argues, is corporate in nature in such a way that it generates a community of reciprocity in the apostolic foundation of the Church so that God's self-communication can be actualized and become communicable throughout human history.[62] Here Torrance develops two points: 1.) the correlation between the uncreated Word and Rationality of God and the created word and rationality of humanity, and 2.) the movement from God's self-revelation in Jesus to its universal form through Pentecost in the apostolic foundation of the Church as the Body of Christ.[63] We will deal with the first point within the present section and take up the second in the next section on "The Apostolic Foundation of the Church."

Torrance points out that the Word of God incarnate in Jesus Christ is the same Word through whom the creaturely universe was created, the Word who unceasingly sustains the universe and its order.[64] Once again, it is important to note the *contingent* relation Torrance sees between the Word of God and creation in which the Word called the created universe into being out of nothing, giving it a contingent order of its own that God respects and sustains.

This means that in creating the universe, including humanity, out of nothing, God "confers upon it a created rationality different from, yet dependent on, His own transcendent rationality, and thus gives it an inner law of its own which is not self-explanatory, to be sure, but which endures before God as the truth and goodness of created reality upheld by His eternal Word."[65] It was into this universe and this humanity that the Word of God came in the incarnation, assimilating this created rationality (*logos*) to the Rationality and Word (*Logos*) of God in order to provide from the side of humanity the appropriate response to God, as we have already noted.[66]

By this eternal Word of God becoming incarnate as a human being within the contingent existence and rationality of this universe, sharing in the "full conditions" of human life, thought and speech, the Word of God became intelligible and communicable in and through human thought and speech to all people.[67] Thus Torrance concludes that within the incarnation and the hypostatic union between the divine and human nature, there is a union between uncreated Rationality and created rationality, so that in and through this creaturely human word within the vicarious humanity of Jesus Christ, God's Word is mediated to all humanity.[68] Even though the contingent human modes of thought and speech in themselves are inadequate to speak about God or articulate divine Truth, yet they have nevertheless been assumed by God in Jesus Christ, transformed and utilized by God's self-revelation in such a way that they mediate divine Truth beyond their creaturely capacity.[69]

The character of God's self-revelation in Jesus Christ within the matrix of Israel and the correlation between the divine Word and human words in Christ's vicarious humanity condition doctrine and the nature of doctrine. For Torrance, doctrines are "responses to the Truth as it is in Jesus,"[70] for it is most fully in Jesus Christ that we find an isomorphism between God's self-revelation and our appropriate human response to that revelation in life, thought and speech. Doctrine is not concerned with developing a logical system of our knowledge of God, nor with religious self-consciousness and developing it into systematic form, nor even with the historical consciousness of the Church.[71] Rather doctrine is concerned with the "Word of God made flesh in Jesus Christ, and with the revelation of the Word fulfilled in the apostolic testimony and tradition...[and with] the disciplined articulation of the Church's understanding of the Word."[72] While doctrine cannot to be reduced to Christology, doctrine for Torrance has a Christological center which conditions the nature of doctrine, as will become clearer as this chapter continues to unfold.[73]

The Apostolic Foundation of the Church

The Apostolic Nucleus

The corporate nature of the reciprocity established in Jesus Christ entails a second point of great significance for understanding Torrance's realist interpretation of God's self-revelation. This is the movement from the particularized form which that revelation took in Jesus Christ to its universalized outworking through Pentecost in the Apostolic foundation of the Church as the Body of Christ and in the formation of the New Testament.[74] In the union of the eternal divine Word and the creaturely human word in the incarnation, Jesus Christ is not only God's Word to humanity, not only humanity's word (response) to God, but also human word communicable in interpersonal human discourse.[75]

In order for this universal outworking of God's self-revelation to be accomplished, God's self-communication to humanity in and through Jesus Christ had to enter the interpersonal reciprocities of human community and form the appropriate structures of thought, speech and life for the ongoing prolongation of that revelation in human history.[76] Torrance argues that Christ formed "a nucleus within the speaker-hearer relations" of his disciples, a social coefficient rooted in and in correlation with the reciprocity between God and humanity in Jesus himself described in the previous section.

This social coefficient thus became "the controlling basis for the folding out of the self-witness of Christ into witness to Christ informed, empowered, and used by Christ's self-witness so that it could take the field as the communicable form of his self-witness in history, i.e., as the specific form intended by Christ for the proclamation of God's Word" to all humanity.[77] Christ's indwelling of the contingent created structures constitutive of humanity included the onto-relational, interpersonal reciprocities of human persons in their social relations.[78]

Torrance maintains that this is, in fact, what took place in the Apostolic foundation of the Church and in the Apostolic formulation of the kerygma, a Church and a kerygma formed by Christ's self-witness.[79] As the apostles were caught up in the revealing and reconciling mediation of Christ and formed to be the nucleus of Christ's Church, their proclamation answered and extended the Word that is Christ "in such a way that it became the controlled unfolding of his own revelation within the mind and language of the apostolic foundation," and therefore the authoritative expression of Christ's own kerygma.[80]

The fact that God did not simply come into humanity, Torrance argues, but has actually become fully human and encounters and addresses us *as a human being* (Jesus of Nazareth), "means that God has veiled his revelation in creaturely flesh."[81] This is part of the fact that God does not remain aloof from our creaturely and historical existence, but meets us within the objectivities and intelligibilities of the created world of space and time (Torrance's interactionist God-world relation).[82]

However, since God's revelation is veiled in its unveiling, there must take place an unveiling of what was thus veiled in the incarnation of the Word.[83] Following Barth, Torrance suggests that this unveiling begins with the resurrection of Jesus Christ from the dead, for it was there that the disciples began to really understand who Jesus was and is.[84] In fact, Torrance maintains, the disciples "allowed the majestic **I am** of the risen Lord...to provide the revealing enlightenment and objective depth to their report of the words and deeds of Jesus in such a way that their account of his life and mission provided the Gospels with a unifying intra-structure."[85] Torrance can say that "The resurrection imposes upon all that has taken place hitherto an entirely different aspect, so that things begin to fall into place and steadily to take on a depth of meaning and consistency impossible to conceive before."[86] Here finally "is the key to the...enigma of Jesus, for it provides it with a structure consistent with the whole sequence of events leading up to and beyond the crucifixion."[87] Thus the significance embedded in God's whole *oikonomia* (the pattern of God's revealing and saving activity, form in being) back through Jesus to God's dealings with Israel and forward through the ascension and Pentecost to the Apostolic Church is disclosed (integration of form in knowing).

Elsewhere Torrance likens this whole process in the Apostolic foundation of the Church to the solving of a jig-saw puzzle in which a basic insight or clue leads progressively to the coming into view of the full pattern of the puzzle:

> When the crucified Jesus rose from the dead and poured out his Spirit on Pentecost, the intrinsic significance of his Person and all he had said and done broke forth in its self-evidencing power and seized hold of the Church as the very Word or Logos of God. Looking back we can say that the Apostles and Fathers came upon a basic insight in the light of which the whole saving Event of Jesus Christ came to be understood out of its intrinsic intelligibility and within the framework of objective meaning which it created for itself in the context of Israel.[88]

Under the continuing influence of the risen Christ through the outpouring of the Spirit at Pentecost, the Apostolic Church was so reconciled and joined to the Mind of Christ that it came to reflect that Mind in its own witness to Christ.[89]

The Deposit of Faith

In light of this discussion, Torrance's understanding of "The Deposit of Faith" becomes clear.[90] Torrance maintains that the deposit of faith must be understood as

> the whole living Fact of Christ and his saving Acts in the indivisible unity of his Person, Word and Life, as through the Resurrection and Pentecost he fulfilled and unfolded the content of his self-revelation as Saviour and Lord within his Church.[91]

While the deposit of faith is not to be identified with or resolved into the Apostolic word, since it continues to be identical with God's revelation in Christ, it does mean that from the formation of the Apostolic foundation of the Church onward people can only access the deposit of faith in its Apostolic articulation configured by the Apostolic encounter with the risen Christ and the outpouring of the Spirit at Pentecost. Only through the Apostolic interpretation and proclamation of the Gospel mediated through the New Testament does Christ continue to make himself known, reconciling humanity to God in the power of the Holy Spirit.[92]

Thus Torrance maintains that the deposit of faith spans two levels.[93] At the first and deepest level, "it is identical with the whole saving Event of the incarnate, crucified and risen Son of God."[94] Yet on the other level "it is identical with the faithful reception and interpretation of the Gospel as it took authoritative shape in the Apostolic Foundation of the Church and thus in the NT Scriptures."[95]

The Genesis of the New Testament

It is here that Torrance finds the genesis of the New Testament Scriptures, which gives them their ontological grounding and distinctive quality.[96] It is out of this complex interaction between God and humanity in history through Jesus Christ (within the matrix of Israel) in the Holy Spirit that the New Testament came into being and developed its distinctive character within the early Church. The New Testament, according to Torrance, therefore is the "divinely inspired linguistic medium" for the continuing self-communication of the Gospel through history and authoritative for both Christian faith and practice.[97] The New Testament writers maintained that their proclamation about Christ had its genesis and authorization in Jesus Christ himself.[98] We will have more to say about the genesis of the New Testament and its relation to the Apostolic foundation and doctrine in a later section of this chapter.

Here, however, it is important to note that the purpose of the inspired biblical witness in its written form is to enable us to "stand with the original witnesses," hear the living Word of God, Jesus Christ himself, participate in the reconciling activity of the Word, and like the first witnesses, repent, believe and live in communion with the Triune God of grace.[99] In so doing, the New Testament writers do not point to themselves and their spirituality, but rather direct us to Christ's vicarious humanity as both the source and distinctive pattern for all of our responses to God.[100]

Torrance further notes that with the incarnation of the Word of God in Christ and the community of reciprocity we have been discussing, we have a situation in which the forms of thought and speech developed in God's creative dialogue with Israel in history are fulfilled. Yet those forms are also relativized, reconfigured and transcended by the final and permanent forms which the Word of God has assumed in Jesus Christ and his life, teaching, death and resurrection.[101] However, it is always "Jesus Christ in Israel and not apart from Israel, so that Israel the servant of the Lord is nevertheless included by God for ever within his elected way of mediating knowledge of himself to the world."[102]

For Torrance, it is critical that the forms of thought and speech in which God's self-revelation is mediated to us in the New Testament should never become detached from their historical connection and actual reference to Jesus Christ himself so that the New Testament becomes an isolated object of independent investigation in itself cut off from God's *oikonomia* out of which the NT documents arose.[103] This means that the biblical witness must be ever understood, not simply out of the social or religious history of Israel or the Church, but in light of that *oikonomia.*[104] This hermeneutical principle is simply Torrance's rigorous development of the fact that God's self-revelation is veiled even in its unveiling by its very character as a *Self*-revelation of God *within* the creaturely structures of *our* humanity.

Embodied Truth

Throughout this entire discussion it is clear that Torrance operates with a notion of "embodied truth," in which in "Christ Jesus, event and message, fact and meaning, the Word and the word, the Truth and truths, are all intrinsically integrated and cannot be torn apart without serious dismemberment and distortion of the Faith."[105] This is true of both levels of the deposit of faith and it reveals a crucial point where Torrance has moved beyond Karl Barth, a point missed by Torrance's critics.

In Torrance perspective, the Word and the words are intrinsically integrated (but it is a *created*, not *inherent*, isomorphism), but not identical. They should be distinguished, but must never be separated. This cannot but have hermeneutical implications for theology and theological method (an application of Torrance's basic axiom that the nature of the object under investigation must determine every aspect of scientific inquiry).

The significance of this for doctrine and the nature of

doctrine is evident in Torrance's discussion of the early Church in its clarification of the doctrinal substance of the Faith. The doctrines or credal formulae developing within the Church are not propositions logically deduced from the original Deposit of Faith but were coherent convictions in process of taking form in the mind of the Church through a general consensus arising spontaneously out of the Apostolic Deposit of Faith and controlled by the implicit structure embodied in it.[106] As such, they are not to be abstracted from the "objective substance of the whole coherent structure of the Faith, for they are what they are only through their conjoint embodiment in it...ordered and integrated from beyond themselves by their common ground in the Apostolic Deposit of Faith."[107] Their truth lies not in themselves but in being rightly related to the Truth out of which they have arisen.[108] It is at precisely this point that Torrance has taken the discussion of the nature of doctrine significantly beyond Lindbeck and McGrath, who both prematurely delimit their discussions of the nature of doctrine.

The Role of the Holy Spirit

Here we need to examine what Torrance speaks of as "another moment" in knowledge of God or revelation in which the objective action of God in the incarnation "becomes a subjective reality in our actual knowledge."[109] Torrance points out that this is not an "additional" moment that adds any content to our knowledge of God in Jesus Christ, but a moment in the sense that what was objectively revealed in Jesus Christ is subjectively realized in us.[110] Torrance, of course, is speaking of the Spirit of God who is free to meet us and to be the presence within us and open us subjectively for knowledge of and communion with God.[111]

There is no way that we can attempt a full and balanced treatment of the role of the Holy Spirit in Torrance's realist interpretation of God's self-revelation in relation to doctrine and the nature of doctrine. Rather the emphasis will be on several points crucial to the present discussion.[112]

The Holy Spirit as the Utter Godness of God

In Torrance's mind, in the coming of the Holy Spirit at Pentecost something new and unique took place.[113] However, Torrance sees the Spirit already continuously active in creation and preservation. Following Basil, Torrance maintains that, "The Holy Spirit is God himself who is inconceivably able, without ceasing to be God, to be present to the creature in a very real way, and in virtue of that presence to realize the relation of the creature toward himself which it needs in order to live."[114] Yet in this creative and preserving activity the Spirit does not overwhelm the creature or undermine its creaturely reality, but rather is continuously active from within the creature, granting the creature freedom to realize its creatureliness in the presence of God.[115]

Torrance also maintains that this relation between the Creator and the creature, which is constantly yet contingently maintained by the Spirit, is both presupposed in divine revelation and brought to light and fulfilled in that revelation.[116] This is true not only of revelation, but also of reconciliation, redemption and all of God's interaction with humanity.[117]

At Pentecost, Torrance sees the Spirit at work in a distinctive manner in addition to the Spirit's original and sustaining work of creation. This distinctively new mode of activity on the part of the Holy Spirit is conditioned and determined "by the great evangelical facts that lie behind it [the incarnation and atonement], for they made possible this new mode of the Spirit's activity."[118]

When Torrance speaks of the new coming of the Holy Spirit at Pentecost as a coming in the utter Godness of God, his concern is to affirm a diastasis in which the Holy Spirit is not confused with humanity's inward moral or religious states.[119] Torrance notes that because the Spirit in not cognoscible in accordance with the Spirit's nature and mode of being as *Spirit*, there is a danger that "we lapse into the error of confounding him either with the Church within whose sphere we meet the Spirit or with the human heart, for it is within us that the Spirit is sent by Christ to bear witness."[120]

Torrance is also similarly concerned to reject any notion of a created medium between God and humanity by affirming the direct creative activity of the Holy Spirit as God and Lord, and to restore what the Greek fathers called *theosis* (deification), though understood in terms of humanity being made free for God by God (including knowledge of God that cannot be separated from soteriology) and not in terms of the divinization of humanity.[121]

Thus Torrance asserts that in the coming of the Spirit, God "resists, and objects to, every attempt on our part to subdue or redact the possibility of knowledge grounded in His divine freedom to an immanent and latent possibility which we deem ourselves to possess apart from him in virtue of our own being."[122] In fact, it is only in and through the reconciliation accomplished in Christ "that the Spirit of God may be poured upon his creatures without consuming them in judgement."[123] This brings us to the second heading in discussing Torrance's view of the role of the Spirit in revelation in relation to doctrine.

The Spirit and Christ Mediate One Another

It is critical to note that while it is proper to distinguish between the missions of the first and second Persons of the holy Trinity in Torrance's theology, they should not be sharply separated.[124] According to Torrance, the co-activity and co-essentiality of the Spirit and the Son mean that "the doctrine of the Spirit must be allowed to interpenetrate the doctrine of Christ and his revealing and reconciling work, for it is the Spirit who mediates the Son as it is the Son who mediates the Spirit."[125] Failure to take note of this can lead to serious misunderstanding of Torrance's position.

This relation between the Spirit and the Son is especially evident in the birth of Christ, but also in all his life and work.[126] Torrance appeals to Basil who said that "all things done in the economy of the coming of our Lord in the flesh–all is through the Spirit."[127] Torrance develops this idea at some length with reference to Christ's baptism, temptation, prayer and offering of himself as a sacrifice for sin.[128]

Yet while the Spirit was actively involved in realizing all things done in the economy of the Son, it is through Christ in his divine and human natures that the Spirit is mediated to us. Torrance argues that,

> Since he is himself both the God who gives and the Man who receives in one Person he is in a position to transfer in a profound and intimate way what belongs to us in our human nature to himself and to transfer what is his to our human nature in him. That applies above all to the gift of the Holy Spirit whom

> he received fully and completely in his human nature for us. Hence in the union of divine and human natures in the Son the Eternal Spirit of...God has composed himself...to dwell in human nature, and human nature has been adapted...receive and bear that same Holy Spirit.[129]

Torrance emphasizes the agony that it cost Jesus Christ to mediate the Holy Spirit to us in receiving the consuming holiness of the Spirit into the human nature which Christ took from our fallen and alienated condition.[130] Thus, for Torrance, it is not an "isolated" or "naked" Spirit who is mediated to us, but the "Spirit charged with all the experience of Jesus."[131]

Yet the Spirit could not be mediated to others through Christ while they were yet in their sins or received until atonement for sin was complete, but only after Christ had sanctified himself through the Spirit and perfected in our human nature his one offering for all humanity.[132] Only when the vicarious humanity of Christ was taken up into union with the Triune God in the ascension, could the Holy Spirit come to dwell in and with humanity and mediate the revealing, reconciling and renewing of Christ to us.[133]

Thus the Spirit goes forth from God and returns to God, answering and extending the twofold work of the Son when he came down for us and for our salvation and ascended again to God the Father, presenting to the Father the humanity which he assumed from us and redeemed and sanctified.[134]

For Torrance, when we speak of the coming of the Spirit at Pentecost, and all that means for the Church, including the Church's theology and doctrine, and how the nature of doctrine is to be conceived, we must think of the Spirit's activity "in strict correlativity" to Jesus Christ and his substitutionary life, death and resurrection. The Spirit not only actualizes within us what Jesus Christ has done for us, but also open us up for Christ in a radical manner so that "we find our life *not in ourselves but out of ourselves, objectively in him*."[135] Through the Spirit we are united with Christ in his total identification with us. The Spirit comes forth from God, unites us to the response, obedience, faith and worship of Jesus Christ himself, and returns to God, raising us up with Christ in response, obedience, faith and worship.[136]

Here we see the implication and the outworking of Torrance's understanding of the vicarious humanity of Jesus Christ, including the important *anhypostasia/enhypostasia* couplet, in which human nature and human rationality are fully respected and maintained throughout the co-activity of the Spirit and the co-activity of the Son.[137] At every point in Torrance's *ordo salutis* (order of salvation) there is full divine and full human agency so that all of grace includes all of humanity, including human rationality and language (doctrine).

The Holy Spirit Focuses Attention on Jesus Christ

Torrance emphasizes that while the vicarious life and mediatorial work of Christ led to the gift of the Spirit, the function of the Holy Spirit was (and is) not to bear witness to Himself, but rather to Christ as God and Savior.[138] In fact, the Holy Spirit is not cognoscible in his own *hypostasis* or personal mode of being.[139] Here Torrance draws upon the teaching of Athanasius, arguing that we take our knowledge of the Spirit from the Son.[140]

Furthermore, only Jesus Christ the incarnate Son is the *logos*, the *eidos* of the Triune God.[141] This is of considerable importance in understanding Torrance's doctrine of the Spirit in relation to the nature of doctrine, for it means that the Holy Spirit brings us no new knowledge, nor any content other than or independent of the Word of God mediated to us through Jesus Christ. Rather, Torrance asserts that "in and through the Spirit divine revelation is actualized subjectively within human experience and understanding in a way without which its intention as revelation of God would not be fulfilled."[142] Nevertheless, Torrance also affirms that only *in the Spirit* do we really know the Son.[143] Only God can know God and only God can make God known to humanity.[144]

Thus Torrance sees the Spirit as hiding Himself from us in His mode of activity as Spirit, "throwing his eternal Light on the Father through the Son and upon the Son in the Father."[145] So long as the Spirit was not yet sent in this new way, the disciples did not understand the significance of all that Jesus Christ said and did.[146] But when the Spirit of Truth came upon the Church at Pentecost, what Christ said and did was not lost, but gathered up and understood in the light of both Christ's resurrection from the dead and the activity of the Spirit enlightening the disciples to the Truth of God incarnate in Jesus Christ.[147]

Here is the Apostolic foundation of the Church and the New Testament Scriptures, for when the Holy Spirit was poured out at Pentecost, the Spirit bore witness to Christ and led the disciples to become the eye and ear witnesses of Christ in a new way so that they became the sphere within which Christ is proclaimed and the Gospel is heard and believed. Torrance asserts that, "Thus through the coming of the Spirit God brings his self-revelation to its fulfillment, for the Spirit is the creative Subject of God's revelation to us and the creative Subject in our reception and understanding of that revelation."[148]

Yet, the Spirit does not fulfill His role by *continuing* a work begun by Christ, as if there was passage from the economy of the Son to that of the Spirit. On the contrary, Torrance maintains that, in and through the Spirit, Jesus Christ himself returns to be with us, making the Church the Body of Christ where Christ continues to live and speak for the salvation of the world.[149] The Spirit calls attention to Christ, opens up the Church for Christ, mediating the reconciliation, sanctification, regeneration and revelation effected in Christ's vicarious humanity to the Church, so that the Church finds its life and its thought in Jesus Christ himself. In so doing, Torrance asserts that Christ so reconciled the disciples to himself that Christ assumed their witness "into oneness with his own Word, so that the Apostolic word is Word of Christ."[150] We will return to this subject in the next section.

Here, however, it also is important to note that for Torrance, the Church, in all its life and thought, including its doctrine, must be related to Christ through the Apostolic witness *in* the Spirit. Torrance is adamant that God's self-revelation and self-communication in the incarnation are not understandable apart from God's self-giving to us in the Spirit, for it is in and through the Holy Spirit that "we are united to Christ the incarnate Son of the Father, and are made through this union with him in the Spirit to participate, human creations though we are, in the Communion which the Father, the Son and the Holy Spirit...are in themselves."[151] Part of the reason for this is that revelation and reconciliation are inseparable for Torrance, as noted at several places above.[152] We cannot know the Truth without becoming at one with the Truth. This cannot but include atonement, forgiveness and conversion, for Jesus repeatedly told the disciples that they had to take up the Cross in order to follow him.[153] This comes about through the Holy Spirit and it is the reason why Torrance says that his understanding of the nature of doctrine cannot be separated either from the events and realities of God's self-revelation or from an *evangelical and doxological experience of those realities and events*.

God always remains the transcendent Subject and Lord in self-revelation and self-communication so that it is only as the Spirit and Christ mutually mediate one another in the way described throughout this section that our knowledge is of *God* and not just of the forms of thought and speech in which that knowledge comes to us.[154] Through the Spirit, we come to share in the incarnate Son's knowledge of the God the Father realized in Christ's vicarious humanity.[155] In the incarnation God adapts knowledge of God to our creaturely structures of knowledge and adapts those structures to knowledge of God. In the Holy Spirit God utilizes those creaturely structures as the means by which we apprehend God and know God in God's divine reality as Triune.[156]

This is what makes knowledge of God *sui generis*. Thus doctrine and the nature of doctrine are conditioned by the way in which they are related to Christ through the Apostolic foundation of the Church and the Scriptures *in* the Spirit. The next section will pick up this theme and develop it in relation to the character of Scripture and its interpretation, while the final section will discuss all of this in relation to doctrine, including the Trinity as a concrete example of doctrine and the nature of doctrine.

Character of Scripture and Interpretation

The reason for this extended discussion of God's ongoing interaction with the created order in the covenanted relationship God established with Israel and fulfilled in the incarnation in Jesus Christ and the outpouring of the Holy Spirit before discussing the character of Scripture, its interpretation, and the implications of all of this for the nature of doctrine, is that if one fails to see the relationship between the realities and events of God's self-revelation in God's *oikonomia* in history and the Old and New Testaments of Scripture which these realities and events generate and ground, it is easy to misunderstand Torrance's views of Scripture and nature of doctrine as they are related to the realities and events of God's self-revelation and our experience of them. Such misunderstanding, in turn, leads to the charge of "actualism" and "occasionalism," for when Scripture is abstracted from the concrete space-time track that God's self-revelation has taken (including the creaturely structures it has assumed) it easily seems as if the relation between God and humanity is reduced simply to the event of grace or revelation. The Bible appears to serve as little more than an occasion for God "speaking" a Word by the Holy Spirit that is only tangentially related to the text or words of the biblical witness.[157] But this is, in fact, a misunderstanding at least of Torrance's mature position, as I hope is evident from the preceding discussion.

This section will draw out some of the implications of the preceding discussion for Torrance's understanding of the character of Scripture and its interpretation, and then turn to the subject of the relation between Torrance's realist interpretation of God's self-revelation and doctrinal formulation and the nature of doctrine, for doctrine in Torrance's mind cannot but be conditioned by the economic lines of God's interaction in space-time with Israel and in God's ultimate self-revelation through the Son and in the Spirit and the concrete structures that revelation has assumed.[158]

Thus, it should be clear by now that for Torrance, a "realist" interpretation of God's self-revelation is a revelation integrally related to the Bible, for the biblical witness is the creaturely form (cultural-linguistic structure) which that revelation has assumed in space and time and through which God continues to reveal Himself to humanity.[159] The Bible should be approached and read with reverence for it is the appointed place where God addresses us.[160]

This does not mean that there is a direct identity between the words of Scripture and the revealed Word of God, for Torrance maintains that the relation between God's self-revelation and the Scriptures is fundamentally asymmetrical.[161] The "Bible itself is not to be thought of as an incarnate transcript of the ineffable speech inherent in the being of God" for there is no hypostatic union between the Word of God and the human creaturely words of the Bible.[162] The Word of God cannot be read directly off its pages.

Yet for Torrance, revelation cannot be detached from the Bible, for in the concrete course that God's self-revelation has taken in God's dialogue with Israel and in the incarnation of the Word of God, God "has uniquely and sovereignly coordinated the biblical word with his eternal Word, and adapted the written form and contents of the Bible to his Word, in such a way that the living Voice of God is made to resound through the Bible to all who have ears to hear."[163] The Bible is the written Word of God, the communicable form God's self-revelation has taken.[164]

Torrance affirms the inspiration of Scripture, but not an inspiration cut off from the realities and events of God's self-revelation as outlined above, especially the mediation between the Word of God and the word of humanity actualized in Jesus Christ.[165] When the inspiration of Scripture is cut off from the realities and events of God's self-revelation, the Bible often comes to be viewed as essentially oracular in character: revelation is conceived of as fundamentally propositional and doctrine is deduced directly from the text and related directly to the Truth of God through verbal inspiration by the Holy Spirit, while the surface of the text is abstracted from its in-depth relation to God through God's *oikonomia* in Israel and Jesus Christ.

In contrast, Torrance upholds the concrete, historical character of revelation in the Bible, for the Bible reflects the history of God's self-revelation and self-communication through "the specific space-time track" of the covenant interaction with Israel so as to shape Israel into the appropriate social coefficient for the actualization of God's final self-revelation in Jesus Christ.[166] Scripture came into being within that interaction and embodies and reflects it.

Thus for Torrance the bond between the Bible and the Word of God is not "a static or necessary one," but a dynamic one, wrought in the concrete situations of space and time, established by God and unceasingly sustained through the presence and activity of the Word in the Spirit.[167]

Here Torrance conceives of the relation between God's self-revelation and the Holy Scriptures as dynamic and ontological not only in origin but also in ongoing relation, for it is a relation that God continuously sustains, for God's self-communication continues to resound in and through the Scriptures brought into being for this purpose through God's interaction in history.[168] Furthermore, for Torrance, we hear this Word that resounds through the Bible in a corollary dynamic and ontological manner only through the presence and activity of the Holy Spirit, for the Holy Spirit is God in God's sovereign freedom to be present in these creaturely structures through the mutual mediation of the Word and Spirit discussed in the previous section.[169]

However, while God has brought this relation between revelation and Scripture into being and maintains it by freely and purposely making Himself present in Scripture, realizing his revelation to us in and through it, God remains transcendent over Scripture and Lord of Scripture in such a way that while the Bible is constituted as the "external basis" for God's continuing self-revelation, that self-revelation takes place anew through the biblical witness via the Word and Spirit.[170]

In other words, Torrance is arguing that since God's activity inheres in God's being (God's speech is God's act of *self*-revelation), and vice versa, the Bible "cannot be what it is inspired by the Holy Spirit to be, if its continuing link with God acting and speaking in Person is broken or disregarded."[171] The Bible is the written form of the Word of God, and it continues to be "the Word of God communicated to us in virtue of the fact that God continuously coordinates it with the active presence of his Word and Spirit and thereby affirms, activates, and substantiates it as his Word."[172] It is this kind of divine Presence that makes the Bible what it is, for although God transcends the creaturely forms of our thought and speech, God has bound God's self-revelation to them so that we are ever dependent on the Scriptures for our knowledge of God.[173]

What is at stake here, in Torrance's mind, is the oneness between God and the content of God's self-revelation: "we must think of the nature and the reality of the Biblical content of revelation as deriving from and as ever grounded in the continuous self-revealing and self-giving of God through the Son and in the Spirit, for what God reveals of himself and his actual self-revealing are one and the same."[174] God is eternally in God's own trinitarian life the personal living and loving Father, Son and Holy Spirit that God is in God's relations with us in God's self-revelation through the Gospel in history.[175] Thus for Torrance, there is an "unbroken consubstantial relation between the free continuous act of God's self-communication and the living content of what he communicates by divine revelation to us in and through the Holy Scriptures."[176]

For this reason, God's self-revelation, which comes to us in and through the written words of the Bible, must be continuously given and received in a living relation to God where it is substantiated as God's own transcendent reality.[177] This, of course, is where some will still object and see this as nevertheless dangerously close to "actualism" or "occasionalism." I have purposely attempted to draw out the relation between Torrance's dynamic and ontological understanding of God's self-revelation in its concrete coordination with the creaturely structures that revelation has assumed through the events and realities of God's interaction with the world in Israel and supremely in the incarnation of the Word of God in Jesus Christ, for it is at precisely this point that Torrance's critics (and Barth's critics[178]) often understand his position, and it serves at least as a caution for those who invoke the charge of occasionalism.

However, in Torrance's own mind, the identity of God with the content of God's saving revelation leads not to occasionalism, but to an astonishing deepening of the character of the Bible that impacts how Scripture is read and interpreted. We begin to read and interpret the biblical witness in light of the realities and events of God's *oikonomia* out of which it arose, expecting to encounter the very Reality of God through the Word in the Spirit.[179]

This understanding of the character of Scripture means that for Torrance, the Bible is properly understood only as we focus both on the text and the *realities* to which it bears witness.[180] We do not attempt to penetrate into the subjective states of biblical writers (or even Jesus), rather we share with the writers their orientation away from themselves in the Spirit through Jesus Christ to the living God.[181] Torrance sees this as involving a "cross-level movement of thought" in which we understand the text and the realities to which it bears witness at the same time.[182] Elsewhere Torrance calls this a "bi-polarity" between "the words and the Word, the worldly form of revelation and its divine content" that requires us to acknowledge Bible function as a *witness* to the self-revelation of God.[183]

Thus Torrance sees here "an elliptical movement...in which his [God's] Word breaks into the movement of our human thought and fills it with the content of his self-revelation,"[184] though not apart from the movement of human thought in an exegetico-theological interpretation of Scripture described in chapter 2 above. We do not leave the biblical word behind, for we are not able to know God except on the basis of the biblical witness.[185] Torrance's concern is that while we cannot attain knowledge of God apart from the Bible, when we focus just on the text it can lose its in-depth significance in its grounding in the realities and events of God's self-revelation and its semantic function of directing us to them.[186]

Furthermore, Torrance sees this as fully consistent with a realist understanding of the semantic relation between language and reality which we will discuss in more detail in chapter 5.[187] Biblical statements do not possess the Truth in themselves, but rather refer to the Truth by being grounded in it and controlled by it, yet in such a way that the biblical statements are distinguished from it. There is an element of inadequacy in the biblical witness.[188] Yet it is an inadequacy that is proper to the Bible's semantic function as a witness to God.

We carefully attend to (indwell) what the text of Scripture says in order to understand the Word of God that sounds through it, while at the same time, as our minds come under the compelling claims of the realities and events to which the text refers, we allow those realities to clarify what the text says, though the ontological priority always remains with the realities and not the text itself.[189] This is not an easy or painless process, because revelation does not achieve its end apart from reconciliation.[190]

Now the implication of this for Torrance, as noted in another context, is that we rightly know God and interpret God's self-revelation through Scripture only within the Church in an attitude of worship, "where to the godly reason God is more to be adored than expressed."[191] Only as we steep ourselves in the Bible, so that the truth of God's self-revelation permeates our minds, are we able to understand that truth and gain insight into it.[192]

This, of course, is equally true of the articulation of these insights in the formulation of doctrine and it indicates something of the nature of doctrine with reference to the Bible and the realities and events of God's self-revelation to which Scripture is related. Since I have already discussed Torrance's hermeneutics at some length in chapter 2, we will not pursue this further here. The issue now is to draw out the implications of the preceding discussion for Torrance's understanding of the nature of doctrine.

Realist Revelation and Doctrine

By now it should be quite clear that doctrines, for Torrance, are not theological propositions deduced from biblical statements treated like fixed premises. The reason for this is that biblical statements are not related to the realities and events of God's self-revelation in that manner. The Bible is not a self-contained statement of divine truth in propositional form.[193] Nor is it simply a sacred text moving through history, anchored only in a cultural/linguistic tradition, even one linked to the historical Jesus. For Torrance, one cannot interpret Scripture properly without treating it in accordance with its character in relation to the realities it intends and in accordance with our evangelical and doxological experience of those realities through the biblical witness.

In Torrance's perspective, the human forms of thought and speech found in Scripture are grounded and structured through God's *oikonomia,* the orderly pattern of God's activity in history in fulfilling of God's saving purpose, as discussed throughout this chapter.[194] As such, the Bible is the indispensable and authoritative medium through which God's self-revelation continues to be heard in the Church and comes to expression in doctrine. Torrance maintains that Holy Scripture is the source and norm for all our theological statements, but in accordance with the dynamic and ontological way he understands Scripture and its interpretation, as discussed above.[195]

Thus doctrine, for Torrance, arises out of the biblical witness as we indwell the semantic focus of biblical statements and "learn to trace back their objective reference beyond what is written to their source in the infinite depth of Truth in the Being of God, and if we are to do that we must follow the economic line of divine action that gave rise to them in space and time and continues to govern their meaning."[196] This undoubtedly involves rigorous exegetico-theological activity on the part of the interpreter, but only through the ineffable role of the Holy Spirit does the Word of God resound through Scripture.

Doctrines are not the result of organizing biblical quotations and working this content into a systematic order, though doctrinal formulation requires strenuous intellectual activity.[197] For Torrance, doctrines are more like "coherent convictions in the process of taking explicit form in the mind of the Church through a general consensus arising spontaneously out of the Apostolic Deposit of Faith controlled by the implicit structure embodied in it."[198] Doctrine cannot be abstracted from its relationship to the embodied form that God's self-revelation has taken in Jesus Christ and its out-folding in the Apostolic foundation of the Church.[199]

We must not forget the corporate nature of doctrinal

formulation in Torrance's theology discussed at length in the last chapter. For Torrance, doctrines are "corporate recognition statements of the Church...reached only after catholic consideration and synodical formulation."[200] Thus, as far as doctrine is concerned, it is not just the Bible that is the source of doctrinal reflection, but God's self-revelation through the Bible in the midst of the Church in the complex and embodied manner outlined throughout this chapter.

The Old Testament is important in this regard, for it is here in the matrix of Israel that the incarnation of the Word of God took place. In Torrance's mind, when the Church abstracts the Gospel from Israel and the Old Testament, the Gospel and doctrine suffer deformation. The Old Testament, and the historical mediation of revelation reflected in it, is indispensable for the interpretation of the New Testament and therefore for doctrinal formulation, even if the Old Testament itself is not only fulfilled but transcended and relativized by the final and permanent forms which the Word of God has taken in the incarnation and its embodiment in the Apostolic church.

Torrance is adamant that doctrine is not to be understood in "experiential/expressivist" fashion either, for doctrine is not "concerned with the religious consciousness and with working it out into a systematic form according to its own immanent laws."[201] Torrance will have nothing to do with "the transmutation of revelation into the subjectivity of religious consciousness or Christian experience or faith."[202] Rather, Torrance is concerned that doctrine be grounded *through* a subject/object relation between the interpreter and the text, and *through* a subject/object relation between the biblical witness and that to which it bears witness, *in* "'object/object' relations, that is, *intelligible relations inherent in the objective realities* to which the Holy Scriptures bear witness."[203] Torrance can even say that in pointing beyond themselves to the events and realities of God's self-revelation, the "biblical statements are so grounded in and controlled by a basic pattern of truth in those objective realities that it is imprinted upon them,"[204] but in the dynamic and ontological manner discussed in the previous section on the character of Scripture.

From these last statements it should also be clear that doctrine in Torrance's theology is not to be understood as simply related to the historical Jesus and the narratives about him, for doctrine is, at least in part, concerned with intelligible relations inherent in God's economy (from God's historical dialogue with Israel through the sending of the Holy Spirit at Pentecost), relations without which, in Torrance's mind, the historical Jesus is not fully intelligible. To bracket doctrine and the nature of doctrine at the historical Jesus and the narratives about him, even temporarily, is in Torrance's perspective to cut them off from the very relations in God's *oikonomia* which give meaning and depth to all that the biblical witness has to say about Jesus.

Furthermore, in light of this, we see that doctrines in Torrance's theology are also not second-order rules governing first-order discourse, as in Lindbeck's new cultural/linguistic paradigm, though like Lindbeck, Torrance does affirm a notion of embodied truth and the importance of the social coefficient in knowledge.

Torrance's rejection of Lindbeck's "rule-theory" view of the nature of doctrine is evident with reference to *homoousion* which Lindbeck sees as "not a first-order proposition, but as a second-order rule of speech."[205] For Torrance, "The *homoousion*, however, expresses not just a conceptual coherence with which we operate in organizing our own notions, but an objective coherence in the ontic relatedness of divine and human reality of Jesus Christ and indeed in the intelligible communion of the Triune God in himself as well as in his relations toward us through Christ and in his Spirit."[206] *Homoousios* is a paradigmatic instance of doctrine in Torrance's theology that serves to display the nature of doctrine, as we saw in chapter 2 above.

Another paradigmatic instance of doctrine for Torrance which helps to disclose the nature of doctrine in relation to the realities and events of God's self-revelation is the doctrine of the holy Trinity, for here in the "trinitarian ground of our actual knowledge of God mediated through Holy Scripture" the "discernment of the objective meaning of biblical revelation and understanding of God's self-revelation as Father, Son and Holy Spirit coincide."[207] Our concern here is not primarily with the content of the doctrine of the Trinity, but with the way in which it is related through Scripture to the realities and events of God's self-revelation and the way the doctrine of the Trinity arises out of that self-revelation.[208]

For Torrance, the doctrine of the Trinity is not built up "through adducing explicit biblical statements...but in an in-depth examination of the inherent structure of biblical revelation imposed upon it through the three-fold act of God's self-revelation as Father, Son and Holy Spirit."[209] Furthermore, this trinitarian structure in our knowledge of God is also not something we can deduce or infer from previous knowledge, for the *doctrine* of the Trinity is an integration of form in which our creaturely rationality takes on the imprint of Trinity through a process of indwelling (as described in chapter 2).

The *doctrine* of the Trinity answers and discloses the intrinsic interrelations constitutive of God's trinitarian self-revelation.[210] There is no inherent isomorphism (no vestiges of the Trinity) between human cognitional structure and God's trinitarian self-revelation. That isomorphism has to be created. Knowledge of God requires an appropriate rational structure in our knowing of God for, as we have seen, there is no knowledge without form. For Torrance, revelation is not restricted to the event of grace.

Yet this must not be an autonomous rational structure developed independent of actual knowledge of God.[211] Rather it must arise in relation to the intelligible content of God's self-revelation so that our doctrine (rational structure) discloses the intrinsic relations of that revelation.[212] This occurs through the kind of inquiry described at length in chapter 2.[213]

What Torrance is concerned to do in this discussion of the trinitarian structure of our knowledge of God is to express the way in which our knowledge of God is trinitarian from the very beginning, even if we are not explicitly aware of it.[214] The doctrine of the Trinity is a modification in our rational (and personal) being (involving full human agency) that comes about through the creative and transforming character of the divine object (Subject) of knowledge (full divine Agency).[215]

Torrance is convinced that our knowledge of God is trinitarian right from the outset, though in an implicit manner. The informal, undefined trinitarian pattern of God's self-revelation is embedded in the deposit of faith described above and imprinted upon New Testament, for the *oikonomia* of God's redemptive activity through Jesus Christ and in the outpouring of the Holy Spirit at Pentecost in inherently trinitarian.[216] Thus as the Church indwells the Scriptures, encounters the Gospel (the love of God through the grace of Christ in the communion of the Gospel) and responds in faith, worship and service (in the Spirit through Christ to God the Father), the Church's life and thinking begin to take on the imprint of the these trinitarian relations, in a spontaneous, holistic and tacit manner.

This implicit trinitarian pattern, which arises at the evangelical and doxological level within the day to day life of the Church, came to explicit articulation in the early Church as the Christian community was forced to ask and answer basic questions about Jesus Christ and the precise nature of the relation of being and agency between God the Father and Christ the Son.[217] The Church, in reflecting upon its encounter with God in the Gospel, found that it had to affirm that in Jesus Christ God's self-revelation and self-communication was not just a mode, face or aspect of God, but a communication of God's very *Self.* They were compelled to affirm in the strongest possible way that what Jesus Christ is and what he accomplishes in life, death and resurrection for our salvation, *God* accomplishes for us. There is a *oneness in being and activity* between the Son and God the Father.[218] The *homoousion* signifies that Jesus Christ is no created intermediary between God and humanity, but God come into our midst for our salvation.

Yet the Church soon found that it had to ask and answer the same kind of question in relation to the Holy Spirit, since it is in and through the Spirit that God unites us with Christ and through Christ with the Father so that we come to share in the Love and Life that God is in God's own eternal Being-in-communion.[219] Once again the Church found itself compelled to affirm the *oneness in being* not only between the God the Father and God the Son, but also with reference to God the Holy Spirit. In Torrance's own words: "What Jesus Christ does for us and to us, and what the Holy Spirit does in us, is what God himself does for us, to us, and in us."[220]

Yet in distinguishing between God's self-giving through Christ and God's self-giving in the Spirit, the Church could not but also recognize ineffable differentiations within the one Being of God, and not simply at the level of their exegetical activity, but in the Church's evangelical and doxological encounter with God in and through the message of the Gospel.[221] Thus for Torrance, the formulation of the doctrine of the Trinity is no speculative movement of thought, but rather an articulation of what is already implicit in actual evangelical and doxological day to day life of the Church. The doctrine of the Trinity discloses the depth of divine reality and truth implicit in the Gospel itself that every Christian knows even if she does not fully understand it and cannot articulate it in explicit terms.

The Church was compelled to affirm that despite the fact

that the mystery of God is more to be adored than explored (that it is a mystery that stretches out beyond what we can begin to fathom and articulate), God is not ultimately different in God's own being and life than the love of God the Father which we know through the grace of Jesus Christ in the communion of the Holy Spirit. In the Holy Spirit who unites us with Christ and through Christ with the Father, we are, in fact, in touch with *God*, and "with trinitarian relations of love immanent in God,"[222] intrinsic and intelligible relations embodied in God's *oikonomia* as a *Self*-communication of God. This is part of the absolutely astonishing character of the Gospel: God loves us with the very love that God is.[223]

We cannot develop the content of Torrance's doctrine of the Trinity, including his intensely personalized concept of God's being (*ousia*), his use of *perichoresis* to articulate the mutual indwelling and coinhering of the three divine persons and their coactivity in the one being of God and in God's *oikonomia*, and his onto-relational concept of divine person.[224] What is important here is what the doctrine of the Trinity reveals about the nature of doctrine in the way that doctrine arises as an integration of form in relation to the actual relations intrinsic to God's trinitarian self-revelation.

Torrance summarizes his understanding of the character of the *doctrine* of the Trinity by asserting that it is

> a refined model comprising a minimum of basic concepts immediately derived from divine revelation and our intuitive apprehension of God in his saving activity in history, together with a minimum of secondary concepts or relations of thought which are connected together in such a way that through this doctrinal model we allow our understanding to come under the articulate revelation and power of God's own Reality and seek to grasp in our thought as much as we may what God communicates to us of his own unity and simplicity.[225]

Torrance's concern in doctrinal formulation is not with a conceptual system, but with relations that are revealed to be immanent in God as Father, Son and Holy Spirit in the communion of love and knowledge God establishes with us in the Gospel.[226] Doctrine arises as an integration of form and functions in a disclosive manner in relation to God's trinitarian self-revelation. Torrance is also adamant that we must never allow our doctrinal formulations of the Trinity to be cut off from the constitutive elements in God's self-revelation and in our evangelical and doxological experience and apprehension of God that gave rise to those concepts.[227] Doctrine is cognitive, but also so much more.

Furthermore, Torrance argues that the creaturely concepts and expressions we utilize in doctrinal formulation can be of "genuine theological significance" only when they direct our attention away from themselves as doctrines to the ineffable relations constitutive of God's self-revelation and what it discloses to us of God who is greater than we can ever conceive.[228] Doctrines properly fulfill their function when they disclose these relations and enable us to grasp and articulate something of "the inner relations of God which are the fundamental relations in and behind our experience of" God, relations which are the source of our knowledge of God.[229]

Doctrines are never complete in themselves, for they only arise out of, and must remain ever responsive to, the Truth of God in the Gospel that exceeds their ability to express.[230] While they come into being in response to God's self-revelation and are sustained by that revelation, they nevertheless have an open range in keeping with the fact that though God condescends in the incarnation to make Himself known within our objectivities and intelligibilities of space and time, God still transcends the range of human thought and speech.[231]

Thus Torrance maintains that "the inadequacy of our formulation of the Trinity of God is an essential element in its truth and precision" for it is "*not a picturing model* with some kind of point to point correspondence between it and God, but *a disclosure model* through which God's self-revelation impresses itself upon us."[232] The next chapter will develop the precise relationship between doctrine and truth in Torrance's theology.

Of course, for Torrance, all of this depends upon whether we understand "the 'economic condescension' of God in the incarnation in a realist way or not, i.e., whether we believe that in Jesus Christ we are in direct contact with the ultimate Reality and Truth of God in our spatiotemporal existence or not."[233] If not, Torrance thinks that we cannot suppose any objective relationship between what the New Testament tells us about God and what God is in God's own life.[234]

Ultimate beliefs are at stake here: Torrance affirms a living God who creatively interacts with humanity in space and time.[235] The genesis of doctrine and the nature of doctrine in Torrance's theology are ultimately conditioned not simply by doctrine's proximate referent, the Jesus of history and the history of Jesus, but rather by the *Self*-revealing God we come to know through Jesus Christ and in the Holy Spirit. Torrance contends that if one operates with a framework of thought that will not allow one to take seriously the Bible's claim to speak of such a God, then one will not be able engage in the kind of theological inquiry that he advocates. The result will be a very different understanding of doctrine and the nature of doctrine than that of Thomas F. Torrance discussed in this chapter.

Notes

1. Alister E. McGrath, *The Genesis of Doctrine: A Study in the Foundations of Doctrinal Criticism* (Cambridge, Mass.: Basil Blackwell, 1990), p. 32. Also see pp. 1-6. McGrath further identifies three elements that precipitate doctrinal reflection and formulation: 1.) the "transmission of conflict through the biblical source material upon which theological reflection is...based"; 2.) "the narrative nature of the scriptural material itself" (that requires interpretation); and 3.) "the need to interact with a language and a conceptual framework not designed with the specific needs of Christian theology in mind." See ibid., p. 4.

2. Ibid., p. 2.

3. Ibid., p. 28.

4. Ibid., p. 31.

5. Ibid., p. 33.

6. Ibid., p. 34.

7. Ibid., p. ix.

8. Ibid., p. 32.

9. McGrath's construal of doctrine and the nature of doctrine, as developed in *The Genesis of Doctrine*, ends with the "Christ-event" associated with the historical Jesus, traditions (interpretations embodied in the Biblical documents) about him, and further interpretations (doctrines) of the initial interpretations. Now, to be sure, it is clear that McGrath thinks that the Church believes a whole lot more about the Christ-event than this, as does McGrath himself. But that is not the point.

What is of critical significance is the *methodology* by which McGrath develops his *theory* of the genesis and nature of doctrine, not what the Church (or McGrath) believes about revelation, Jesus Christ, the Bible, etc. Despite his admission that there must be a "creative dialectic between the historical and theological," it appears that McGrath has, in some real sense, methodologically bracketed his discussion at a rather undifferentiated "historical phenomenon," the Christ-event associated with the historical Jesus, *in developing his theory of doctrine*.

Yet from Torrance's perspective, is this not already a compromise of the fundamental axiom that it is the nature of the reality that must determine both the methodology and the conceptuality employed in discovering and articulating that nature as it comes into view through advancing inquiry? If there is an intelligible divine reality embodied in the "Christ-event," then must this not condition all of the elements mentioned above, including doctrine and the nature of doctrine? As brilliant and helpful as McGrath's treatment is, does he take us very far in developing this aspect of an adequate theory of the nature of doctrine?

In order to be fair to McGrath, it must be pointed out that he describes his book as "tentative and provisional" and hopes it will "stimulate discussion." He plans "a more substantial subsequent engagement" of the doctrinal criticism in the future, at which time he may address the kinds of concerns I have raised. See McGrath, *Doctrine*, p. viii.

10. This is the title of chapter 3 of Torrance's book, *Reality and Evangelical Theology* (Philadelphia: Westminster Press, 1982), pp. 84-120.

11. See Torrance's essay, "My Interaction with Karl Barth" in Thomas F. Torrance, *Karl Barth: Biblical and Evangelical Theologian* (Edinburgh: T & T Clark, 1990), p. 123.

12. Torrance, *Evangelical Theology*, p. 84. In a personal letter to me in May of 1992, Torrance shared that,

> If I have anything to say about how I regard my own conception of the nature of doctrine, I would say that it cannot be separated from the divine events and realities of God's self-revelation, and our evangelical experience of it. As such it is a *sui generis* form of knowledge, although it overlaps with other forms in distinctive ways.

13. Of course, there will be those who will vehemently disagree with Torrance's construal of the constitutive structure of the Christian faith and his realist interpretation of God's self-revelation and who may yet think out their own position with equal rigor. Torrance mentions Schleiemacher's *The Christian Faith* as an example of a rigorously developed account, though he thinks that Schleiermacher's whole conception was wrong due to his fundamental presuppositions. See Torrance, *Karl Barth*, p. 121.

14. See Thomas F. Torrance, *Divine and Contingent Order* (Oxford: Oxford University Press, 1981), pp. 34-39 and Thomas F. Torrance, *Theological Science* (London: Oxford University Press, 1969; reprint, Edinburgh: T & T Clark, 1996), pp. 55-105.

15. See Thomas F. Torrance, *Space, Time and Resurrection* (Grand Rapids: Eerdmans, 1976), pp. 1-26 and Torrance, *Karl Barth*, pp. 136-41. What Torrance has in mind when he speaks of dualism or a deistic disjunction between God and the world is clearly illustrated by Ernst Troeltsch's principle of "interrelation" or "correlation" in which all historical events, including the religion of Israel and the rise of Christianity, are to be explained on the basis of "historical" causation (human agency) and "natural" causation (understood in physical, Newtonian cause and effect terms). See Ernst Troeltsch's article, "Historiography," in *The Encyclopedia*

of Religion and Ethics, ed. James Hastings (Edinburgh: T & T Clark, 1914), pp. 116-23. However, as William Abraham has pointed out, this excludes divine Agency by principle. See William Abraham, *Divine Revelation and the Limits of the Historical Critical Method* (London: Oxford University Press, 1982), pp. 108-10.

It is in this context that Torrance's statement that we cannot treat the event of Jesus Christ "as other historical events...as a fact of nature brought under general laws" becomes intelligible. Torrance, *Theological Science*, p. 322. This does not mean that Jesus Christ is not really historical, "but to claim that this historical event is more than it first appears, for in its inner happening there is a personal divine movement which gives it distinctive character without detracting from its nature as a fully historical event on the same plane as other historical events." Ibid., p. 323. Thus Torrance argues that unless we acknowledge this element of divine Agency, we are not able to adequately explain all of the historical evidence, but rather explain away those elements which do not fit our preconceptions. Ibid. The resurrection therefore, requires a judgement beyond what Troeltsch will, by definition, allow. Torrance maintains that, "Divine actuality and historical facticity are thus inseparably united in the ground of our knowledge and are not to be torn apart in our continuing inquiry into the fact of Jesus Christ." Ibid., p. 325. Yet McGrath's bracketing of the Jesus of history as doctrine's proximate referent unwittingly seems to have precisely this effect.

It should also be noted that it would be a grave mistake to interpret Torrance's understanding of God's interaction with humanity in Newtonian causal terms, for this is precisely where Thiemann went astray in his accusation that Torrance is a "foundationalist" who construes revelation in causal terms. See chapter 1, pp. 50-51, endnote 109 above. Torrance rejects this kind of causalism which is at the root of many theological problems, the relation between grace and human freedom being not the least of them.

16. Torrance, *Karl Barth*, p. 136. Also see Torrance, *Resurrection*, pp. 1-3. It should be noted that God's interaction is not limited to the space-time track that revelation has taken in the history of Israel and in the incarnation and Apostolic foundation of the Church and Scripture. God continues to interact with the world of space and time on the basis of the realities and events of God's self-revelation.

17. Torrance, *Evangelical Theology*, p. 85. Also see, Torrance, *Resurrection*, pp. 1-3. These last several statements should not be misunderstood to mean that Torrance first develops a certain God-world relation and then outlines a concept of revelation commensurate with it. Torrance sees the contingent relation that obtains between the world and God as rooted in Christian faith and revelation and injected into the thought-world of Western culture by Christianity. See Torrance, *Divine and Contingent Order*, pp. 13, 26-28, 32-33, and 63-64.

18. Torrance, *Evangelical Theology*, p. 85.

19. Ibid. This also includes communities of reciprocity–Israel and the Church–which serve as social coefficients in knowledge of God.

20. Ibid.

21. Ibid.

22. Ibid.

23. Ibid., pp. 85-86. Here we see again that for Torrance the mediation of revelation and reconciliation are inseparable. See Thomas F. Torrance, *The Mediation of Christ* (Grand Rapids: Eerdmans, 1984), pp. 34-56 and

Thomas F. Torrance, *Theology in Reconstruction* (Grand Rapids: Eerdmans, 1975), pp. 132-40.

24. Thomas F. Torrance, *Space, Time and Incarnation* (London: Oxford University Press, 1969; reprint, Edinburgh: T & T Clark, 1997), p. 72. See ibid., pp. 77-81; Torrance, *Reconstruction*, pp. 37-42, 49-53 and 222-23; and Thomas F. Torrance, *Theology in Reconciliation: Essays towards Evangelical and Catholic Unity in East and West* (London: Geoffrey Chapman, 1975; reprint, Eugene, Ore.: Wipf & Stock, 1997), pp. 253-66, where Torrance deals with this theme in Athanasius' theology. Here we see significant convergence between Torrance's position and that of what might be called the "ontological" Narrative theology of someone like Gabriel Fackre, which I would distinguish from the "Yale" school of Narrative theology that is cultural-linguistic and ambiguous concerning the relation of the narrated world of the Bible and reality. This is the essential point of the Greek patristic concept of *oikonomia*.

25. Thomas F. Torrance, *Reality and Scientific Theology* (Edinburgh: Scottish Academy Press, 1985), p. 139.

26. Torrance, *Evangelical Theology*, p. 86.

27. Ibid.

28. Ibid., pp. 86-87.

29. Torrance, *Scientific Theology*, p. 102.

30. Torrance, *Mediation*, pp. 16-17.

31. Ibid., p. 17.

32. Ibid., pp. 20-21. Torrance says that we see this conflict reflected throughout the Old Testament. Also see ibid., pp. 38-39.

33. Ibid., p. 18. Here again we see the interconnection in Torrance's thought between the mediation of revelation and the mediation of reconciliation.

It is also here that Torrance finds one of the roots of anti-Semitism, for the conflict between sinful humanity and a holy God mirrored in Israel, reflects the conflict between God and humanity in every human heart, a mirroring that humanity resents and in turn vents toward Israel. See ibid.

Torrance has an astonishing and suggestive discussion of Israel's vicarious role not only in the mediation of revelation, but in the mediation of reconciliation, in which God used the very hostility evoked in Israel in Israel's rejection of the Messiah to further God's purposes, and compares it with the role of the "scapegoat" in the Old Testament. See ibid., pp. 41-56.

Torrance also argues that "the vicarious mission of Israel in the mediation of reconciliation" to all of humanity does not end with the coming of Christ but "continues to have an essential place throughout all history in the reconciliation of the world to God." Ibid., p. 44. Torrance further maintains that the deep schism between Christianity and Judaism that developed in the early centuries of the Church and was perpetuated in history since has had a deleterious effect upon Christianity's attempt to understand the Gospel, especially the atonement. See ibid., pp. 47-56.

I find Torrance's discussion of the relationship between Christianity and Judaism, the continued place of Israel in God's economy, and the need for dialogue between Christians and Jews far more profound than the majority of material I have seen arising out of the ecumenical concern over Judaism, which often seems to reflect an experiential-expressivist orientation that tends to overlook or deny the deep continuities and differences between Judaism and Christianity. Torrance's book, *The Mediation of Christ*, has many discussions of the issues surrounding the place of Israel and Israel's relation to the Church. Torrance has also written a number of articles on the subject that can be found in a complete bibliography of Torrance's publications in Alister McGrath, *T. F. Torrance: An Intellectual Biography* (Edinburgh: T & T Clark, 1999), pp. 249-96.

34. Torrance, *Mediation*, p. 22.

35. Ibid., p. 25.

36. Ibid., p. 24. Here Torrance seems to be much more "historical" and "concrete" than either Lindbeck or McGrath who do not give enough attention to this kind of grounding of the biblical narrative. Torrance can even say that we cannot detach the Old Testament from the *land* of Israel, for when Israel itself was cut off from its land it suffered a radical detachment that tended to transpose Judaism into an abstract ethical religion, deformed through the loss of the priestly redemptive tradition. Ibid., p. 26. Torrance sees Judaism in Israel today as struggling to recover its lost concreteness. Ibid.

37. Ibid., p. 27. Torrance acknowledges that there are certainly transient and variable elements that are not of permanent value, even as the Holy Scriptures are characterized by features that are of a time-conditioned significance.

38. Ibid.

39. Ibid., p. 28.

40. Ibid.

41. Torrance, *Evangelical Theology*, p. 87.

42. Torrance, *Mediation*, p. 28.

43. Ibid. However, the problem, as Torrance sees it, is that Christianity, in its tensions with the Jews, has repeatedly tried to understand Jesus within the patterns of gentile culture, abstracting the Gospel from its context in Israel and Israel's mediation of revelation, as Albert Schweitzer showed in his treatment of the way the "historical Jesus" was repeatedly interpreted within the conditioning of modern European culture. Ibid., pp. 28-29. Also see Torrance, *Reconciliation*, pp. 24-28.

44. Torrance, *Mediation*, pp. 31-32.

45. Here Torrance can even assert that, "By its very nature Christianity cannot cease to be Hebraic or Jewish, for it cannot but be determined by the basic forms of thought and life created through the struggle of the Word of God with the soul and intention of the Jewish people in the progressive adaptation of them to the mind and will of God in his self-revelation through the law and the prophets." Torrance, *Reconciliation*, p. 28.

46. Torrance, *Mediation*, p. 32. In this regard Torrance suggests that the Old Testament Scriptures "proclaimed far more than they could specify at the time and so by their very nature they pointed ahead to the full disclosure of the divine reality they served." Thomas F. Torrance, *God and Rationality* (London: Oxford University Press, 1971; reprint, Eugene, Ore.: Wipf & Stock, 1997), p. 149.

47. Torrance, *Evangelical Theology*, p. 88.

48. Ibid.

49. Ibid. Torrance discusses the vicarious humanity of Christ in several places: see Torrance, *Evangelical Theology*, pp. 87-94; Torrance, *Rationality*, pp. 137-64; Torrance, *Mediation*, pp. 83-108; and in a variety of other briefer passages too numerous to list. The discussion found in *Evangelical Theology* is a summary and further development of the first half

of the chapter in *Rationality*. The chapter in *Mediation* is written for a wider audience and contains little that is not found in the other two places, though it draws out the soteriological implications much more fully than the treatment in *Evangelical Theology* and in this connection parallels the second half of the chapter in *Rationality*. Also see Christian D. Kettler, "The Vicarious Humanity as Theological Reality (T. F. Torrance)," Chapter 6 in *The Vicarious Humanity of Christ and the Reality of Salvation* (Lanham, Md.: University of America Press, 1991) for an able and insightful treatment of this theme in Torrance's theology.

50. Torrance, *Evangelical Theology*, p. 88. Elsewhere Torrance appeals to Athanasius who spoke of the two-fold ministry of Christ in which "'He ministered the things of God to man and the things of man to God.'" See Torrance, *Mediation*, p. 83. Also see Torrance, *Reconciliation*, pp. 227-31.

However, it appears that Torrance may have gotten it first from Barth in studying Barth's treatment of the theological couplet, *anhypostasia* and *enhypostasia*, which throws into sharp focus what Torrance calls, "the inner logic of grace," and which Torrance maintains is embodied not only in the incarnation but "with reference to which...all the ways and works of God in his interaction with us in space and time may be given careful formulation." See Torrance, *Karl Barth*, p. 125. I think that Torrance means this quite literally and its importance in his theology should not be underestimated.

Torrance clarifies the precise meaning he intends in the following passage: "By *anhypostasia* classical Christology asserted that in the *assumptio carnis* the human nature of Christ had no independent per se subsistence apart from the event of the incarnation, apart from the hypostatic union. By *enhypostasia*, however, it asserted that in the *assumptio carnis* the human nature of Christ was given a real and concrete subsistence within the hypostatic union–it was *enhypostatic* in the Word." See Torrance, *Reconstruction*, p. 131.

Thus, Torrance can say that,

> The Incarnation was wholly act of God but it was no less true human life truly lived in our actual humanity....In his obedient life he yielded the perfect response of man to the divine revelation which is revelation in human form. Here the doctrine of *anhypostasias* and *enhypostasias* applied to the incarnation applies equally to our understanding of revelation. Revelation is entirely God's action but within it, it is the concrete action of Jesus Christ that mediates revelation and is revelation. Revelation is supremely God's act but that act is incarnated in our humanity, giving the human full place within the divine action issuing forth out of man's life. The human obedience of Jesus does not only play an instrumental but an integral and essential part in the divine revelation....In revelation, therefore, we are not concerned simply with *anhypostatic* revelation and with human response, but with *anhypostatic* revelation and true human response *enhypostatic* in the Word of revelation.

Ibid. Also see Torrance, *Karl Barth*, pp. 125-27, 198-99, and 201-2; and Thomas F. Torrance, *The Trinitarian Faith: The Evangelical Theology of the Ancient Catholic Church* (Edinburgh: T & T Clark, 1988), pp. 146-90. Torrance applies this couplet to the sacraments, as well as other elements of Christian faith and response. See Torrance, *Rationality*, pp. 158-60;

Torrance, *Mediation*, pp. 99-102; and Torrance, *Karl Barth*, p. 135.

This whole discussion has implications, of course, for the charge of "actualism" or "occasionalism" sometimes lodged against Torrance and Barth.

Along similar lines, Christian Kettler answers Thomas Smail's charge that Torrance leaves out the importance of the personal response of faith that Smail thinks is part of Torrance's failure to distinguish properly between the work of Christ and the work of Spirit. Kettler rightly points out that Smail develops too much of a cleavage between the second and third Persons of the Trinity (I have found this to be a repeated temptation for those in the Charismatic movement), failing to acknowledge that the mission of the Spirit entails no incarnation, but rather enables us to participate by faith in the obedience of the Son to the Father, and in such a way that this does not destroy our human response, as when it is construed in mechanistic and causal terms of our response being the *effect* and Christ's obedience being the *cause*, but rather restores it. See Kettler, *Vicarious Humanity*, p. 139-42.

51. Torrance, *Mediation*, pp. 48-9. Also see Torrance, *Theological Science*, pp. 48-52; Torrance, *Rationality*, pp. 142-44; Torrance, *Reconciliation*, pp. 229-231; and Torrance, *Karl Barth*, pp. 103-5, 202-5 and 231-34.

52. Torrance, *Trinitarian Faith*, p. 161.

53. Ibid., pp. 162-68. Also see Torrance, *Mediation*, pp. 49-52.

54. Torrance, *Mediation*, p. 49.

55. Torrance, *Trinitarian Faith*, pp. 164-67.

56. Ibid., p. 166.

57. Torrance, *Evangelical Theology*, p. 88.

58. Ibid. Christ is God's exclusive language to humanity and he is humanity's language to God, for in developing this possibility others are set aside. Ibid. Torrance maintains that while God is free to create other possibilities, "this incarnation of the Word of God in Jesus Christ excludes all others and authorizes Jesus Christ as final ground, norm and law for all human response to God the Father," a point to which we will return in chapter 5. Ibid., pp. 88-89.

59. Ibid., p. 89.

60. Ibid.

61. Torrance, *Mediation*, p. 88. See Torrance, *Evangelical Theology*, p. 89, and Torrance, *Rationality*, p. 145. Here Torrance maintains that Christ's vicarious humanity "fulfills a representative and substitutionary role in all our relations to God, including every aspect of human response to Him: such as trusting and obeying, understanding and knowing, loving and worshipping." Ibid. Also see ibid., pp. 153-64 and Torrance, *Mediation*, pp. 91-108 where Torrance develops this in some detail.

62. Torrance, *Evangelical Theology*, p. 89.

63. Ibid. Torrance follows the same pattern of development in the chapter dealing with this subject in Torrance, *Rationality*, pp. 139-46 and 146-53, though the discussion in *Evangelical Theology* contains significant development of the second point beyond what is found in *Rationality*.

64. Torrance, *Evangelical Theology*, pp. 89-90.

65. Torrance, *Rationality*, p. 139.

66. Torrance, *Evangelical Theology*, p. 90. This is also why Torrance maintains that there must be a "significant area of overlap between theological science and natural science," for not only do both operate within

the same medium of space and time, but God entered the contingent universe of space and time and assimilated it to Himself in the incarnation of the Word of God as Jesus Christ, a physical, historical person. See ibid., p. 30. For Torrance's final discussion of this with Barth, see Torrance, *Karl Barth*, pp. 133-35 and 125. Because God reveals Himself through that which is not Himself (i.e., the created and contingent objectivities and intelligibilities of the universe–Israel and the completely human and physical, historical Jesus), and because doctrine must be related to the vicarious *humanity* of Jesus, as pointed out above, Torrance thinks that there must be even "a hidden traffic" between theological concepts and scientific concepts. Torrance, *Scientific Theology*, p. x. Also see Torrance, *Evangelical Theology*, pp. 21-34.

67. Torrance, *Evangelical Theology*, p. 91.

68. Ibid.

69. Ibid., p. 108.

70. Torrance, *Theological Science*, p. 160.

71. Torrance, *Reconstruction*, p. 129.

72. Ibid.

73. Ibid., p. 128. In this early article on "The Place of Christology in Biblical and Dogmatic Theology," Torrance argues that, "It is the incarnation of the Word which prescribes to dogmatic theology both its matter and its method, so that in its activity as a whole or in the formulation of a doctrine in any part, it is the Christological pattern that will be made to appear." Ibid. Torrance notes, however, that this "does not mean that all theology can be reduced to Christology, but because there is only one Mediator between God and man, the Man Christ Jesus, in the orderly presentation of the doctrines of the Christian faith, every doctrine will be expressed in its inner coherence with Christology at the center." Ibid.

74. Torrance, *Evangelical Theology*, p. 89.

75. Ibid., p. 91.

76. Ibid.

77. Ibid., pp. 91-92.

78. Torrance develops what he calls an "onto-relational" concept of person based on the doctrines of Christ and the Holy Trinity in which the *relations* between persons are an essential constituent of their being. See ibid., pp. 42-44; Torrance, *Scientific Theology*, pp. 171-74; and Thomas F. Torrance, "The Soul and Person in Theological Perspective," in *Religion, Reason and the Self: Essays in Honor of Hydel D. Lewis*, ed. Stewart R. Sutherland and T.A. Roberts (Cardiff: University of Wales Press, 1989), pp. 103-18.

79. Torrance, *Rationality*, p. 152.

80. Ibid.

81. Torrance, *Karl Barth*, p. 106.

82. Ibid.

83. Ibid.

84. Ibid., pp. 106-8. Also see Torrance, *Resurrection*, pp. 17-20 and 159-61.

85. Torrance, *Karl Barth*, p. 107. This is a summarative statement of what Torrance attempts to trace in the last chapter of *Resurrection*, pp. 159-93.

86. Torrance, *Resurrection*, p. 164.

87. Ibid.

88. Torrance, *Mediation*, p. 14.

89. See Torrance, *Reconstruction*, pp. 136-38, and Torrance, *Rationality*, p. 152.

90. See Thomas F. Torrance, "The Deposit of Faith," *Scottish Journal of Theology* 36, no. 1 (1983): pp. 1-28. Also see Thomas F. Torrance, ed., *Theological Dialogue between Orthodox and Reformed Churches* (Edinburgh: Scottish Academic Press, 1985), pp. 91-108.

91. Torrance, "Deposit," p. 2. Also see Torrance, *Theological Dialogue*, p. 92.

92. Torrance, "Deposit," p. 2. Also see Torrance, *Theological Dialogue*, pp. 92-93

93. Torrance, "Deposit," p. 14. See Torrance, *Theological Dialogue*, p. 102.

94. Ibid.

95. Ibid.

96. For Torrance, the character of Scripture is not simply determined by the inspiration of the Spirit so that one ends with an essentially oracular conception of the revelation embodied in Scripture. Nor is Scripture merely a human witness to a divine Word that is exclusively an event. Rather it must be understood in light of his realist view of God's self-revelation that involves full divine and full human agency. This clarifies what Torrance meant when he spoke of an exciting deepening of Scripture. See Torrance, *Karl Barth*, p. 122.

Here we see another point of difference between Torrance and fundamentalism (and some strands of evangelicalism) and some forms of Narrative theology, for they both view the character of Scripture in primarily literary terms. Fundamentalism construes the character of the Bible on the basis of its verbal inspiration and identifies the words of the Bible with the Word of God. Certain strands of Narrative theology speak of the Bible projecting a "followable world" that is rendered through the literary devices of narrative depiction, though the ontological reference of the narrative remains obscure or eschatological. I believe that it can be demonstrated that both are attempts to overcome the problems posed for Christian faith and Scripture by modern natural science and critical historiography, though attempts very different from one another in detail. Yet, in another sense, do they not both represent a retreat from science and history into the literary character of the Bible? As insightful as they may be, especially Narrative theology, is either an adequate response and a deep enough grounding of the doctrine of Scripture? Torrance's view has a theological and historical depth that I find missing in each of these other viewpoint.

97. Torrance, *Evangelical Theology*, pp. 92-93.

98. Torrance, *Theological Science*, p. 333. Torrance also notes that the ascension of Christ sends us back to the incarnation, the historical Jesus, and, of course, the Apostolic witness to Christ locked into Christ's self-witness. See Torrance, *Resurrection*, pp. 133-34.

99. Torrance, *Evangelical Theology*, p. 93.

100. Ibid. Once again, Torrance emphasizes that the humanity of Jesus Christ is the "real text" underlying the New Testament.

101. Ibid.

102. Torrance, *Mediation*, p. 32.

103. Torrance, *Evangelical Theology*, pp. 93-94.

104. Ibid., p. 94.

105. Torrance, "Deposit," p. 4.

106. Ibid., pp. 6-7.

107. Ibid., p. 7.

108. Ibid.

109. Torrance, *Theological Science*, p. 52.

110. Ibid. However, must this subjective realization not be thought out carefully and distinguished with reference to 1.) the vicarious humanity of Christ; 2.) the Apostolic foundation of the Church and Scripture; and 3.) subsequent knowledge of God in the Church, including doctrine? If these distinctions are confused or conflated, problems are bound to irrupt.

111. Ibid.

112. There are a number of places where Torrance discusses his understanding of the doctrine of the Holy Spirit. One must read all of them in order to get a balanced picture of Torrance's position. See Torrance, *Reconstruction*, chapters 11-14; Torrance, *Rationality*, chapter 7, "The Epistemological Relevance of the Spirit"; and Torrance, *Trinitarian Faith*, Chapter 6. Also see Torrance, *Theological Science*, pp. 52-54 and 349-52; Thomas F. Torrance, *The Ground and Grammar of Theology* (Charlottesville: University of Virginia Press, 1980), pp. 164-67; and Torrance, *Karl Barth*, pp. 208-12. There are two important secondary sources: Elmer M. Colyer, *How to Read T. F. Torrance: Understanding His Trinitarian & Scientific Theology* (Downers Grove, Ill.: InterVarsity Press, 2001), pp. 211-40, and Gary Deddo's article, "The Holy Spirit in T. F. Torrance's Theology" in *The Promise of Trinitarian Theology: Theologians in Dialogue with T. F. Torrance*, ed. Elmer M. Colyer (Lanham, Md.: Rowman & Littlefield, 2001), pp. 81-114.

113. Torrance, *Reconstruction*, p. 240.

114. Torrance, *Karl Barth*, p. 210. See Torrance, *Rationality*, p. 171, and Torrance, *Reconstruction*, pp. 214-16.

115. Torrance, *Karl Barth*, p. 210. Also see Torrance, *Rationality*, p. 171.

116. Torrance, *Karl Barth*, p. 210. Also see ibid., pp. 147-59.

117. Ibid., p. 211.

118. Torrance, *Reconstruction*, pp. 240-41.

119. Ibid., p. 242. Also see ibid., pp. 227, 231 and 235; Torrance, *Rationality*, pp. 171 and 173, and Torrance, *Karl Barth*, pp. 38-39 and 209-11.

120. Torrance, *Reconstruction*, p. 227.

121. See Torrance, *Karl Barth*, p. 209 and Torrance, *Reconstruction*, p. 243.

122. Torrance, *Theological Science*, p. 53.

123. Torrance, *Reconstruction*, p. 237.

124. Torrance, *Scientific Theology*, p. 186.

125. Torrance, *Karl Barth*, pp. 209-10. See Torrance, *Reconstruction*, p. 213.

126. See Torrance, *Theological Dialogue*, p. 82, where Torrance speaks of Love of God poured out and embodied in Jesus Christ, "in whom by the operation of the Holy Spirit divine and human nature were uniquely and hypostatically united in one Person."

127. St. Basil, *De Spiritu Sancto* 16.39. Quoted in Torrance, *Reconstruction*, p. 222.

128. Torrance, *Reconstruction*, p. 246. Also see Torrance, *Rationality*, pp. 167-68.

129. Torrance, *Reconstruction*, p. 246.

130. Ibid., p. 247. Torrance outlines the trajectory that this took within the earthly life, death and resurrection of Christ within space and time. See ibid., pp. 246-51.

131. Ibid., p. 247.

132. Ibid., pp. 147-49.

133. Ibid., p. 247.

134. See ibid., p. 248.

135. Ibid., p. 238.

136. Ibid., p. 250.

137. See ibid., pp. 130-32 and 237-39. Also see Torrance, *Rationality*, pp. 145-46, 153-54, 168-69, 172, 174, and 188-90.

138. Torrance, *Reconstruction*, pp. 251-52.

139. Ibid., p. 213. Also see Torrance, *Trinitarian Faith*, pp. 21-22.

140. See Torrance, *Reconstruction*, pp. 214-16. Also see Torrance, *Trinitarian Faith*, pp. 202-4; and Torrance, *Ground and Grammar*, p. 165.

141. Torrance, *Reconstruction*, p. 214. Also see Torrance, *Trinitarian Faith*, pp. 203-4.

142. Torrance, *Karl Barth*, p. 211. Also see Torrance, *Trinitarian Faith*, p. 203; and Torrance, *Rationality*, pp. 166-68. It is the fact that the Spirit is not cognoscible in His own mode of being, that He hides Himself in revealing the Father through the Son, and contributes to that knowledge in an essential but ineffable manner which makes it difficult to state precisely the contribution of the Spirit in our knowledge of God, including doctrine. See Torrance, *Reconstruction*, pp. 217 and 226-27.

143. Ibid., p. 215.

144. Ibid., p. 252. But of course, not without human testimony, as we have seen throughout this chapter. However, is it not at precisely this point that Barth's emphasis on the activity of God the Spirit seemed to undercut the validity of human testimony? While this may be a misunderstanding of Barth, might it not explain why some Barthian-oriented scholars have moved in the direction of a kind of Narrative theology in which the *narrative character of the text and its literary devices* are seen as so integral to the depiction of Jesus as the Christ? It is interesting that Thiemann admits that it is with reference to the doctrine of the Holy Spirit that he "is least satisfied with his own account of revelation." See *Dialog* 26, no. 1 (1987): p. 73.

145. Torrance, *Reconstruction*, p. 252.

146. Ibid.

147. Ibid., p. 253.

148. Ibid.

149. Ibid.

150. Ibid., p. 137.

151. Torrance, *Christian Doctrine*, p. 148

152. See Torrance, *Karl Barth*, p. 178. See Torrance, *Reconstruction*, pp. 132-34 and Torrance, *Mediation*, pp. 36-38. For Torrance, revelation and reconciliation proceed together through God's *oikonomia* in Israel, in the incarnation and in the life of the Church.

153. Torrance, *Scientific Theology*, p. 150.

154. Ibid., pp. 185-86.

155. Torrance, *Theological Science*, p. 52.

156. Torrance, *Scientific Theology*, p. 192.

157. Barth's emphasis upon the dynamic, event character of revelation could also be viewed as a way to circumvent all the problems created for Christian faith and theology by the historical/critical study of the Bible. The move of some Barthian oriented-scholars like David Ford, Hans Frei, and George Lindbeck toward a Narrative theology in which the followable world of the Bible (the correlary of Barth's "strange new world") is rendered through the literary devices of narrative depiction is an attempt to redress this event character of Barth's position which seems to some to mystify theological exegesis. This form of Narrative theology could be viewed as a way of restoring concreteness to theological exegesis by grounding it in the creaturely, in this case cultural-linguistic, structure of the Bible. The problem then, however, is the role of the Holy Spirit (as was noted with reference to Thiemann above) and the oneness between God and God's self-revelation, which, as we will see, is Torrance's concern. Furthermore, this form of Narrative theology (Thiemann's and Lindbeck's) abstracts the biblical narrative in its cultural/linguistic dimension from its grounding in the realities and events of God's *oikonomia*.

158. See Torrance, *Scientific Theology*, p. 189. While God is transcendent over Scripture and in that sense not bound to Scripture, God honors the structures God's self-revelation has assumed so that we are bound to Scripture.

159. Torrance, *Evangelical Theology*, p. 94. Elsewhere Torrance argues that, "The idea of a non-cognitive revelation, detached from the intelligible structures and the objectivities of space and time within which the Word was made flesh in Jesus Christ, is thus utterly inconsistent with the fundamental substance of the Christian Gospel." See Torrance, *Resurrection*, p. 2.

160. See Torrance, *Karl Barth*, p. 84.

161. Torrance, *Evangelical Theology*, p. 94.

162. Torrance, *Karl Barth*, p. 88. Also see ibid., pp. 83, 84, and 115.

163. Ibid., p. 88. Torrance can say that Scripture is so locked into God's self-revelation out of the dynamic yet concrete way in which it arose in coordination with God's revelation that it is correlated with that revelation in a sacramental manner. Ibid., p. 91. See Torrance, *Reconstruction*, p. 139.

164. Torrance, *Karl Barth*, p. 88.

165. See Torrance, *Evangelical Theology*, pp. 96 and 162-63. Torrance argues for a "dynamic" concept of verbal inspiration, which takes into consideration the fact that Christ assumed our sinful humanity, healing and creating it. He also redefines inerrancy and infallibility in light of this. See Torrance, *Karl Barth*, pp. 91-92 and 101-5, and Torrance, *Reconstruction*, p. 96.

166. Torrance, *Karl Barth*, pp. 90-91.

167. Ibid., p. 91.

168. Ibid., p. 92.

169. Ibid., pp. 91-92.

170. Ibid. Torrance maintains that revelation is not exhausted by this creaturely medium called into existence by the revelation. Ibid., p. 89.

171. Ibid., p. 95.

172. Ibid. Torrance relates this back to the incarnation and the Being of God in God's Act and the Act of God in God's Being. See ibid., pp. 95-98, though there is not space to discuss all of this here.

173. Ibid., p. 92.

174. Ibid.

175. Ibid., p. 98.

176. Ibid.

177. Ibid., pp. 98-99.

178. There is some basis for this criticism of Barth, as Torrance notes and addresses. See Torrance, *Karl Barth*, pp. 136-59, especially 155-59.

179. Ibid., pp. 87-88.

180. Torrance, *Evangelical Theology*, p. 96.

181. Ibid., p. 104.

182. Ibid., p. 99.

183. Torrance, *Karl Barth*, pp. 111-12. One must remember that for Torrance (and Barth), this worldliness is not accidental to God's self-revelation, but part of the astonishing fact that God does not stand aloof from human history, but actually interacts with us in space and time. See ibid., p. 110.

184. Torrance, *Karl Barth*, p. 90.

185. Ibid., p. 117. Also see Torrance, *Theological Science*, p. 192.

186. Torrance, *Evangelical Theology*, p. 96.

187. Ibid.

188. Torrance, *Karl Barth*, p. 116.

189. See Torrance, *Evangelical Theology*, pp. 96 and 99 and Torrance, *Karl Barth*, p. 112.

190. Torrance, *Karl Barth*, p. 113.

191. Torrance, *Evangelical Theology*, pp. 119-20.

192. Torrance, *Karl Barth*, pp. 117-18. Torrance indicates that this is, in fact, the manner which he, himself, has attempted to follow. He tells how from an early age, being brought up by godly, missionary parents in the Evangelical and Reformed Faith, he learned from them how read the Bible this way. See ibid., p. 83.

193. Torrance, *Evangelical Theology*, p. 17. Also see Torrance, *Resurrection*, pp. 7-8.

194. Torrance, *Evangelical Theology*, p. 108.

195. Torrance, *Theological Science*, p. 192.

196. Torrance, *Evangelical Theology*, p. 109.

197. Torrance, *Karl Barth*, p. 117.

198. See Torrance, *Theological Dialogue*, p. 96.

199. See ibid., p. 93.

200. Torrance, *Theological Science*, p. 343.

201. Torrance, *Reconstruction*, p. 129.

202. Ibid., p. 134.

203. Torrance, *Evangelical Theology*, p. 107 (my emphasis added).

204. Ibid.

205. See George Lindbeck, *The Nature of Doctrine* (Philadelphia: Westminster Press, 1984), p. 94.

206. Thomas F. Torrance, "Theological Realism," in *The Philosophical Frontiers of Christian Theology* , ed. B. Hebblethwaite and S. Sutherland (New York: Cambridge University Press, 1982), p. 185. Torrance would see Lindbeck's approach as methodologically and ontologically deficient, for Lindbeck prescinds from consideration of any intelligibility within the subject matter in question, in order to develop a formal theory of doctrine (and religion) which is religiously and theologically neutral.

207. Torrance, *Karl Barth*, p. 118.

208. For an in-depth treatment of how the doctrine of the Trinity arises in Torrance's theology, see Colyer, *How to Read*, pp. 286-301.

209. Torrance, *Karl Barth*, p. 119.

210. Torrance, *Scientific Theology*, p. 164.

211. Ibid., p. 165.

212. Ibid.

213. Ibid.

214. Ibid.

215. Ibid., p. 169.

216. Torrance *Christian Doctrine*, pp. 75 and 82.

217. See ibid., pp. 93-94 and Torrance, *Scientific Theology*, pp. 183-86.

218. Ibid., pp. 183-86.

219. Ibid. Also see ibid., pp. 187 and 192.

220. Torrance, *Christian Doctrine*, p. 298.

221. Torrance, *Scientific Theology*, p. 185.

222. Torrance, *Christian Doctrine*, p. 107.

223. Ibid., p. 108.

224. See Colyer, *How to Read*, pp. 301-21.

225. Torrance, *Scientific Theology*, p. 161.

226. Ibid.

227. Ibid., pp. 161-62.

228. Ibid., p. 162.

229. Ibid. This is what Torrance means when he speaks of "object/object" relations mentioned earlier in this chapter.

230. See Torrance, "The Deposit of Faith," p. 7.

231. Ibid.

232. Torrance, *Scientific Theology*, p. 162.

233. Torrance, *Evangelical Theology*, p. 109.

234. Ibid.

235. Ibid., pp. 97-99.

Chapter 5
Doctrine and Truth

Introduction

It should be clear by now that Torrance's understanding of the nature of doctrine bears a marked similarity to the cognitive-propositionalist theory, since doctrine for Torrance is a form of knowledge, though a *sui generis* form. One could say that Torrance's understanding of the nature of doctrine is cognitive, but not propositionalist.[1] Torrance's view is rather deeper and more complex than this, as discussed in the preceding chapter on Torrance's "realist" interpretation of God's self-revelation and its relation to doctrine and the nature of doctrine.

Torrance's understanding of the nature of doctrine cannot be separated from his construal of the divine realities and events of God's self-revelation and self-communication to us through Jesus Christ in the Holy Spirit and our evangelical and doxological apprehension of that revelation through the biblical witness in the midst of the Church. In examining Torrance's presentation of God's self-revelation, one is led to the Trinity as a paradigmatic instance of doctrine and the nature of doctrine. Indeed, for Torrance, the doctrine of the Trinity is "the **ultimate ground** of theological knowledge of God, the **basic grammar** of theology, for it is there that we find our knowledge of God reposing upon the final Reality of God himself, grounded in the ultimate relations intrinsic to God's own Being, which govern and control all true knowledge of him from beginning to end."[2] On this point, Lindbeck and Torrance are quite different, as is evident by the very dissimilar status of the doctrine of the Trinity in their respective positions concerning the nature of doctrine.[3]

It is evident that doctrine, for Torrance, is a form of knowledge. As such it makes truth claims, though what kind of truth claims? According to Torrance, what does it mean for a doctrine to be true? These are the questions that this chapter will address.

This chapter will outline the significance of Torrance's approach to theology for his understanding of truth in relation to doctrine and the nature of doctrine. While his position has certain affinities with cognitive-propositionalism, there is significant divergence as well, as will become clear in the course of this discussion.

In order to properly understand Torrance's notion of the stratified structure of truth it is important to grasp the stratified structure in which knowledge of God arises as an integration of form, since this is determinative for his conception of doctrine as a disclosure model, which in turn defines the way in which doctrines are related to the realities they intend. The opening section of the chapter deals with this stratification in our knowledge of God before discussing doctrine as integration of form in disclosive relation to the reality it intends. The third section of the chapter treats Torrance's stratified understanding of the nature of truth in relation to doctrine. The final section will deal with the justification and authority of doctrine in Torrance's theology.

The Stratified Structure of Knowledge of God

Torrance argues that our knowledge of the Triune God assumes a "stratified structure" on the ground of God's self-revelation to us.[4] Torrance thinks that this stratified structure is not all that different, at least formally, from the stratified structure that arises in the course of rigorous scientific activity in any field of inquiry.[5] This stratified structure comprises three levels of thought coordinated with one another.

The primary reason for this stratification is that in this *Self*-revelation, *God* interacts with *our* creaturely world of space and time. This interaction cannot but involve the level of God's own Trinitarian life, the trinitarian pattern within the saving events of God's self-revelation (the *oikonomia*), and our evangelical and doxological apprehension of God through those saving events in the Gospel. If we consider the stratification in terms of the *order of knowing* (*ordo cognoscendi*), our knowledge of God in the Gospel begins at the evangelical/doxological level of our basic relationship with God within the life of the

Christian community, moves through what God has done for us through Christ in the Spirit in the history of salvation (God's *oikonomia*), to who God is in God's own eternal Being and trinitarian Life.

The Evangelical and Doxological Level

The first level of thought in this stratified structure is what Torrance calls "the evangelical and doxological level" in which "we encounter God's revealing and reconciling activity in the Gospel."[6] As noted in earlier chapters, this takes place within the life and mission of the Church where we share with others in the common experience of coming to Christ as Lord and Savior via the Holy Spirit (the evangelical element) and respond together in faith, worship and obedience (the doxological element). Torrance describes it as "the level of our day-to-day worship and meeting with God in response to the proclamation of the Gospel and the interpretation of the Holy Scriptures within the fellowship of the Church."[7]

Here Torrance thinks that we find empirical and theoretical factors, form and being, structure and substance, inseparably interwoven, indivisibly united, both in the realities with which we are concerned (form in being) and "in our rational and experiential response" (integration of form in knowing) from the very start.[8] This is the level of incipient theology or what Torrance elsewhere calls theological instinct or spiritual discernment in which one becomes so steeped in the biblical witness, indwelling its message, that the truth of divine revelation becomes built into the fabric of one's mind.[9]

This entails implicit or tacit elements that are acquired, as we saw in chapter 3, within the evangelical and doxological life of the Christian community that serves as a social coefficient in our knowledge of the Triune God. As also noted in previous chapters, we rely on these implicit or tacit elements in all our explicit or formal cognitive activity.[10]

Through transforming encounters with the love of God in the Gospel through Christ and in the Spirit we find ourselves personally, spiritually and intellectually involved and shaped by the patterned activity of the evangelical (economic) Trinity, not through an analytic, logical or speculative process, but rather in a holistic, spontaneous and informal manner.[11] Our thinking, our worship, our life all begin to reflect the love of God the

Father, the grace of Jesus Christ, and the communion of the Holy Spirit at a tacit level. We learn to think of God in a godly manner.

As noted in chapter 2, it is at this evangelical and doxological level within the matrix of the Church that we first acquire the insights and clues that are developed into explicit doctrines through theological inquiry. Torrance could not be more emphatic about this point: "this ground level of evangelical experience and apprehension remains the necessary basis, the *sine qua non*, of the other levels of doctrinal formulation developed from it."[12]

The Theological Level

The second level is the theological level. Here, Torrance argues, "we direct our inquiries to God in this field of evangelical and doxological experience" and we attempt to cultivate the incipient insights or clues into the objective patterns or intrinsic intelligibility of that field, as we saw in chapter 2 above.[13] The goal or purpose is to penetrate into the interior connections in the evangelical and doxological level that ground and control our basic encounter with God's revealing and reconciling activity in the Gospel, and render these patterns of interconnection more explicit and precise by formulating concepts and conceptual models to express these realities and relations.[14]

The concepts and relations (doctrines) deployed at this level are refinements or extensions of that basic level of knowledge and experience. Their function is to enable us to grasp and understand that common knowledge and experience in light of the intelligible relations intrinsic to it, but which are not necessarily directly known or experienced.[15] For Torrance, scientific theology and explicit doctrinal formulation can never be more than an extension and refinement of the knowledge that arises at the evangelical and doxological level and would therefore be empty of content and irrelevant if cut from that level.[16] The task of theology and part of the role of doctrine is to clarify and unify such knowledge of God and thereby bring theological order into our everyday knowledge and experience of God so as to further and deepen our understanding of God.[17]

This task is accomplished by selecting a few primary ideas or convictions as close to the ground level as possible and organizing them into a preliminary "model" (doctrine or complex of doctrines) through which we seek to trace something of the intrinsic intelligibility or inner relations of the field of inquiry.[18] Often ordinary forms of speech are appropriated and transformed under the impact of God's self-revelation and take on quite different meanings in this theological process, as in the case of "Father," "Son," and "Holy Spirit" when used with reference to God. At other times, new terms have to be developed ("Trinity" or "hypostatic union" for instance) in order to explicitly articulate what we discern at this theological level.[19]

The doctrinal model we develop is a revisable, flexible axiomatic instrument in the service of this end. We continue to refine it, or select another if it proves inappropriate, until we find a model that enables us to probe deeply into the intrinsic relations of the field and we discern something of its orderly pattern.[20] Examples of clues or primary ideas that arise under the impact of God's self-revelation, which when clarified constitute disclosure models, flexible axioms that bring the inner constitutive relations of that revelation to articulation, include the doctrines of the hypostatic union and *homoousion* discussed in chapter 2 above.

As inquiry proceeds in this manner on the theological level, Torrance thinks that what we find is that God "reveals himself to us as Father, Son, and Holy Spirit, in a three-fold movement of his love in revelation and redemption."[21] The most basic constitutive relations implicit in the Gospel itself at the evangelical and doxological level are trinitarian in character: the Gospel has to do with the love of God that comes to us through the grace of Christ in the fellowship of the Spirit and elicits a movement of faith and worship in the Spirit through the risen Jesus Christ to God the Father.[22] It is, of course, the *homoousion* that expresses this oneness of activity and being between the Father, the Son and the Spirit in the economy of salvation (*oikonomia*) and underscores the fact that it is *God* whom we encounter through Jesus Christ and in the Holy Spirit, as we saw in chapters 2 and 4.

Thus it is on this second theological level that the economic Trinity comes to theological expression, articulating the orderly pattern or constitutive relations (form in being) in God's self-revelation and communication to us in space and time that are the basis of our evangelical and doxological encounter with the Gospel. This also underscores the fact that for Torrance, this kind of theological activity on the theological level is not a speculative movement of thought beyond the evangelical and doxological level, but rather one that gives precise and faithful expression to the trinitarian pattern of implicit relations embedded in the Gospel itself.[23]

The Higher Theological or Scientific Level

Torrance calls the third level a higher theological and scientific level where we inquire even more deeply into God's self-revelation in the saving activity of Christ and in the Holy Spirit.[24] Here Torrance is concerned with what he calls "the epistemological and ontological structure of our knowledge of God," for it is here that we find the ultimate ground of our knowledge of God; the actual intrinsic relations in God's redemptive self-revelation to us are grounded in God's own ultimate trinitarian reality as God, relations that are the actual basis and that provide the content of our knowledge of God.[25]

We can grasp things with our thought, Torrance argues, only if they entail intrinsic differentiations and internal interconnections that are in some sense constitutive of what they are in themselves independent of our perceiving and conceiving of them; yet differentiations and interconnections that are inherent in their relations toward us, for this is what enables us to pierce through the appearances in our relations with a particular field of inquiry and apprehend the intrinsic structures that control those appearances.[26]

Torrance finds Martin Buber's critique of the "conceptual letting go of God" in modern Protestant thought illuminating on this point. Buber faced the difficulty of how he could in some sense know God, if God is the ineffable, unnameable One God of Judaism.[27] Torrance points out that Buber surmounted this difficulty by appealing to "relations of love within the Being of God," a concept Buber appropriated from Spinoza.[28] For Buber, it is as knowledge of God is coordinated with these internal relations within God that knowledge of God attains at least some kind of conceptual grasp of God in accordance with God's intrinsic nature.[29]

This discussion of Buber is helpful in grasping the third level in this stratified structure in our knowledge of God, for Torrance indicates that this structure entails a movement from the second level of God's self-communication in the redemptive activity of Jesus Christ and the Spirit (the economic trinitarian relations in all that God is toward us in self-revelation) to the third level where we discern the trinitarian relations immanent in the Godhead, relations which are the ultimate ground of and reason for the relations of the economic Trinity.[30] For Torrance, this is a passage of thought "in which we are compelled, under the pressure of God's self-communication, to acknowledge that what God is toward us in the three-fold economic activity of his revelation and redemption, as Father, Son, and Holy Spirit, he is antecedently in his own Being in the Godhead."[31] It is here that Torrance finds the epistemological (integration of form in knowing, the intrinsic pattern that explains how our knowledge of God arises) and ontological (form in being, how our pattern of knowing is finally grounded in a pattern in being) structure of our knowledge of God, for it is here that we discover the constitutive ground of our knowledge of God in which we can come to know God in accordance with God's nature as triune.

Of course, it is the *homoousion* (Torrance sometimes calls it "the ontological and epistemological linchpin of Christian theology"[32]) that brings this epistemological and ontological structure to articulation, for the *homoousion* states with utmost precision that what God is for us and toward us in the grace of our Lord Jesus Christ and the communion of the Holy Spirit, God is inherently and eternally in God's own Reality and Life. There is a oneness of being and activity between God for us in the evangelical Trinity and God in Himself in the ontological Trinity.[33] Thus our evangelical and doxological apprehension of God in the Gospel is finally rooted in and sustained by the very Being-in-Communion God is. In the Gospel, God loves us with the very Love that God is.[34]

Through this application of the *homoousion* to the Son and the Spirit in appropriate ways, Torrance maintains that "our thought is lifted up from the level of the Economic Trinity to the level of the Ontological Trinity."[35] In so doing, Torrance thinks that we are forced to develop additional concepts like *perichoresis* to express, in an admittedly inadequate manner, the mutual indwelling of the trinitarian Persons in their co-activity and in the one Being of God, the "ultimate constitutive relations in God, in virtue of which he is who he is as the Triune God."[36] If God is, in fact, Triune in God's very nature, then to know God is to know God in accordance with God's nature as Triune.[37]

Furthermore, Torrance sees *perichoresis* as leading to a further "onto-relational concept of person" in which the relations between persons are real and constitutive of who and what persons are.[38] The communion between the divine Persons is as real as the Persons and belongs to what they are as Persons.[39]

Torrance admits that it would be "sheer theological sin" to identify this trinitarian doctrinal model (our conceptual structures) with the constitutive relations in the Godhead, for when we know God, we know that God is greater than we can ever conceive (*Deus semper maior*).[40] The trinitarian God is more to be worshiped and adored than semantically designated.[41]

Our theological concepts or doctrines fall short of the God to whom they refer. Yet, Torrance thinks that this inadequacy is essential to the precision and truth of doctrines, for they point away from themselves, effacing themselves before the reality of God that they seek to disclose.

Now what is of decisive significance in this discussion for Torrance's conception of theological science, and thus for his understanding of the nature of doctrine, particularly in relation to truth, is the movement between these levels in knowledge of God, for Torrance has a corresponding stratified understanding of truth that further clarifies the nature of doctrine.[42] In Torrance's perspective, this movement from level to level in theological knowledge, coming to expression in doctrinal formulation, is grounded in the free and gracious movement of God condescending in the outpouring of His love to be one with us in the incarnation of Jesus Christ, and through Jesus Christ and in the Spirit to "raise us up to share in his own divine life and love that he eternally is in himself."[43]

That is to say, the movement between levels is grounded in relations inherent in realities and events of God's self-revelation and our actual knowledge of God as it arises within the life of the Church on the evangelical and doxological level. While by their ineffable character they "defy anything like complete formalization," these relations are still the "ground upon which the intelligibility and objectivity of all our knowledge of God finally repose."[44]

It is on the basis of these relations that doctrines can have a claim to truth. Furthermore, it is the character of these relations in the cross-level coordination in knowledge of God discussed above that defines the essential nature of doctrine in Torrance's theology as an integration of form within the Christian community and grounded in the realities and events of God's self-revelation and self-communication with a claim to truth commensurate with the character of these relations.

These constitutive relations are also the reason that Torrance views the doctrine of the Trinity as "the *ultimate ground* of theological knowledge of God, the *basic grammar* of theology," since it is here that knowledge of God is "grounded in the ultimate relations intrinsic to God's own Being which govern and control all true knowledge of him from beginning to end."[45] Thus we come to where we ended the last chapter, the doctrine of the Trinity (a refined disclosure model with a small cluster of basic concepts), which arises out of our evangelical and doxological apprehension of God in the Church, and which allows us to explicitly articulate the implicit intrinsic and constitutive relations in that apprehension of God and thereby deepen and clarify the faith of the Christian community.[46] This brings us to the heart of the subject-matter of this chapter: the relation between language and being in Torrance's theology, and therefore to the nature of the truth-claims doctrines make.

Disclosure Model: The Relation of Language to Being

For Torrance, doctrines are cognitive, but not strictly propositional, for a propositionalist construal of the nature of doctrine and the relation of doctrine to Christian evangelical and doxological apprehension of the divine Realities of faith (God's activity in Jesus Christ and the Spirit and God's own trinitarian life) is too simplistic. The relation between doctrines and the experiences and realities they intend cannot be reduce to the kind of relations that obtain between ideas. Rather doctrine arises out of the tacit, holistic and participatory knowing that occurs in everyday evangelical/doxological apprehension of God in the Gospel. Theological inquiry (and the doctrines it entails) is simply a way of rendering explicit, clarifying and deepening that knowledge.

Furthermore, this process is not fully formalizable, for it relies on the implicit or tacit elements (what Torrance calls "theological instinct" or "spiritual discernment"), which we discussed in chapter 2 These implicit elements of spiritual discernment are learned in discipleship.[47] This, of course, bears a marked similarity to Lindbeck's emphasis on "catechesis."[48] But there is a fundamental difference rooted in Torrance's "realist" interpretation of God's self-revelation. For Torrance, in discipleship or catechesis one does not simply learn a grammar, one comes into intimate and personal experience and knowledge of God.

According to Torrance, it is at the evangelical and doxological level in the life of the Christian community, "living in empirical contact and communion with God," that our thought and our lives are molded by God's self-revelation.[49] We engage in tacit knowing where we come to know more about God than we can explicitly formulate at the time.[50] It is here that we find the "all-important level of intuitive intellective contact with divine reality which is the source of our basic convictions and primary concepts and relations" that arise as we let our minds dwell in this field of inquiry through hard exegetical activity, as well as prayer, worship, etc.[51]

Doctrinal formulation occurs as convictions and concepts arise not by logical deduction or abstraction, but out of the cognitive activity of tacit knowing that is personal and informal, though nonetheless rational.[52] The significance of this discussion for the relation between language and being is that Torrance is adamant that there "is not and cannot be any logical bridge between concepts and experience."[53] This means that there is no logical bridge between doctrines and experience or the realities they intend. Rather doctrines are correlated with the realities they intend through the tacit coefficient out of which they arose.

This is why Torrance calls for a modification in how we define knowledge. Furthermore, since knowledge cannot be construed simply in terms of what is explicit, reality cannot be defined in terms of what can be correlated with explicit concepts and statements. All of this deeply influences Torrance's understanding of the truth claims of doctrine that we will discuss in the final two sections of this chapter.[54]

What is of importance here is the disclosive relation that obtains between doctrines as disclosure models and the realities they intend. Since doctrines do not arise by deduction or abstraction from the Scripture or from propositional statements distilled from the Bible, the application of doctrines to the realities they intend requires unformalizable acts of judgement or spiritual discernment not basically different than those out of which they arose, for it is a relation between our concepts and reality that cannot be resolved into the relations that obtain between ideas.

This is why Torrance argues that "dogmatic structures

[doctrines]...cannot be complete in themselves if they are to be meaningful and consistent."[55] Torrance maintains that in all theological inquiry at every level we must always be careful to maintain evangelical and doxological participatory knowledge of God, for it is this knowledge and worship of God "that determines its [doctrine's] cognitive value."[56] This extra-logical participatory relation to God is critical in all doctrinal formulation, though it is a relation that cannot, itself, be formalized.[57]

Yet, the significance of the kind of doctrinal disclosure model, and the character of its relation to the realities of Christian faith, is that it clarifies and simplifies our knowledge of God. It allows the informational content of God's self-revelation to come to expression with greater precision and force in the form of doctrine.[58] This is what brings theological order into our everyday experience and faith in God, promoting further and deeper understanding of God.[59]

Thus the stratified structure discussed above (that arises in our thought as we probe into the inherent intelligible relations of the realities and events of God's self-revelation and our evangelical and doxological experience) serves this clarificatory truth function. We need cognitive instruments in order to grasp and express the relations inherent in the realities of the Christian faith. Doctrines serve that purpose. As such they are, of course, subject to continuous revision in light of God's self-revelation.[60] Doctrines arise out of, articulate and disclose real relations upon which our knowledge of God depends. But doctrines are not themselves the realities or relations they disclose.

As fluid axioms, doctrines occupy an important place in Torrance's theology, serving knowledge of God in a disclosive relation to the intelligible interconnections inherent in our apprehension of God's self-revelation, as in the case of Torrance's conception of the doctrine of the Trinity and its place in his theology. We are now in a position to discuss Torrance's understanding of truth as it relates to the nature of doctrine.

The Nature of Truth and Doctrine

As we have seen throughout the preceding discussion in this chapter and the others, Torrance advocates a critical realism in which the objective pole of the knowing relation, as it is grounded in the inherent relations and intrinsic intelligibility of reality (divine and contingent), is allowed to play a dominate role in knowledge through an integration of form that nevertheless involves the personal (and social) being and agency (coefficient) of the knower from beginning to end. Torrance maintains that this does not necessarily imply a compromise of the objectivity of theological science. But it does underscore the fact that personal being is the bearer of objectivity in knowing and in doctrinal formulation and that, therefore, it is important that there is a strong critical element involved so that the subjective elements of the knower, including uncritical preconceptions, do not obtrude in interpretation and doctrinal formulation.[61]

Yet, Christians do not always agree in their understanding of Scripture or in their theological and doctrinal formulation. How do we test interpretations and doctrinal formulations in Torrance's perspective? How does he conceptualize truth and the truth claims of doctrine in this context? This is especially important since disagreements are not always overcome simply by appealing to Scripture.[62]

Here Torrance turns to John Calvin and his preface to the *Institutes* of 1536 in which Calvin defended the doctrine that he outlined in it by an appeal not simply to biblical citation or ecclesiastical authority, but to *the Truth of God*, for it is there that Calvin (and Torrance) finds "the supreme Authority" for all doctrinal formulation and testing upon which everyone is dependent.[63] Torrance asserts that the Truth of God must retain its priority over our interpretation of the Bible and our doctrinal formulations, for authority finally resides in that Truth and not in a set of doctrines or even in the Bible itself.[64]

This is not all that different, Torrance thinks, from the orientation found in Einstein's conception of natural science, since he held that: 1.) the ultimate reference of scientific concepts is traced back to the mysterious reality of the intelligible universe, for that is where they have their final ground; and 2.) since the being of the universe has an ineffable quality, it manifests a depth of comprehensibility that eludes complete understanding on our part, and therefore is always the final authority in scientific formulations.[65]

Torrance maintains that all of this applies with greater force to our knowledge of God and doctrinal formulation.[66] God is not just "Object-being" over against us, but "Subject-being" who interacts with us personally and who personalizes us and establishing intimate reciprocal relations with us.[67]

As we saw in the last chapter, Torrance thinks that this even includes an element in which our knowledge of God through Christ and in the Spirit "is allowed to share in God's knowledge of himself."[68] Yet at the same time, God confronts us as a transcendent and majestic "Thou" whose Truth and Intelligibility are infinite and inexhaustible.[69]

Thus while God does not change and therefore remains the unchanging source of all of our doctrinal formulations of his self-revelation, those doctrinal formulations must be ever open to further clarification, amplification and change in light of further disclosure from God.[70] As Torrance repeatedly asserts throughout his writings, "We may apprehend God but we cannot comprehend him."[71]

The implication of this for Torrance's understanding of the nature of doctrine in relation to truth is that insofar as our doctrinal formulations are derived from God's self-revelation and self-communication, "there is much more to them than the concepts themselves, more than the formal truths of conception, for the Reality conceived transcends conceptual control."[72] Before the ineffable Reality and Majesty of the God whom we know through Jesus Christ, all of our doctrinal formulations are at a rather elementary level and are but a relatively insignificant reflection of the Truth.[73] It is in this context that Torrance's understanding of the stratified nature of truth further reveals the nature of truth and the truth-claims of doctrine.

The Stratified Structure of Truth

In its most basic and primordial sense, which Torrance thinks is in line with the patristic tradition, *truth* signifies a state of affairs existing prior to our knowing it and our truthful statements about it. Torrance calls this the *truth of being*, which simply means reality in its intrinsic relations.[74] Truth is "the reality of things" independent of us.[75]

Since Torrance advocates, as one of his fundamental premises, that things must be known in accordance with their nature, this understanding of the truth of being demands a corollary understanding of truth in our knowledge in which all our concepts and statements must yield to the truth of things and their ontic necessity of being what they are and not something else.[76] Only as we know things according to this rationality of truth of being (*ratio veritatis*) and embody this rationality in our discourse can we claim true knowledge.[77] Drawing on the work of Anselm, Torrance makes several additional distinctions in order to further clarify his understanding of truth.

First there is the distinction between *the supreme Truth and the truth of created realities*.[78] God, of course, is the supreme Truth in that all other beings have their truth only with reference to God who is the one self-existent Being. As such, Torrance maintains that God cannot be recognized or known by reference to anything else, but only in the power of God's own self-evidence.[79]

In calling the universe into being, God has given created beings truth of their own that must be respected and thus known in accordance with their inner intelligibility as contingent beings sustained by God in their reality independent of God. Created realities have their own created truth of being that must be acknowledged if we are to know them and conceive of them correctly.[80]

Torrance further distinguishes between *truth and truthfulness*, that is, the truth of being and the truth of relation.[81] Truthfulness means an openness on our part to the truth of being and a rightness of relation to it, for the truth of being is what it is in itself before we know and is also the ground of our apprehension and articulation of it.[82]

Finally, Torrance draws a distinction between *the truth of being and the truth of statement*, including doctrinal statements. Here, in a point that recurs many times throughout his writings, Torrance contends that: "It is impossible to picture how a picture pictures what it pictures, for that would involve the absurdity of reducing to a picture the relation between the picture and the reality pictured. No more can we state in statements how statements are related to being, without reducing the relation of statements to being entirely to statements."[83] Of course, as noted above, this does not mean that the truth of statement is not objectively grounded in the truth of being. But it does mean that there must be a clear distinction between the truth of statement and the truth of being.

While there is no logical bridge between language and being, statements serve the truth of being by directing our minds to reality so that the reality itself shows through.[84] Torrance contends that when our statements serve the truth of being in this way, our statements are true, but when they impede our apprehension of the truth of being, they are false.[85]

In light of these distinctions, Torrance outlines a stratification of truth comprising several levels.

On the first level there are *two truths of statement.*[86] This refers to 1.) the syntactical element whereby a statement functions in a consistent and coherent manner with other words; and 2.) the semantic function in which a statement refers to a state of affairs beyond itself.[87] Strictly speaking, a statement is true only when it is true in both of these ways, when grammatically correct and used to rightly reference the truth of being.[88]

This leads to the *truth of signification* where the syntactic and semantic ingredients function together so that they disclose the truth of being (form in being).[89] However, since this is dependent on the nature of the reality signified (the form in being must condition the integration of form in knowing), the truth of signification is located not strictly in the statement, but in the proper relation to the truth of being.[90]

This is a critical point in Torrance's understanding of truth. The truth of being is always prior to the truth of statement, which is dependent on the truth of being for its content, a content that arises out of the interaction of the mind with that which it comes to know as an integration of form.

Thus the truths of statement and signification presuppose the *truth of being.*[91] As noted above, the truth of being is its reality; what it actually is and ought to be. But it is not a self-subsistent truth for the truth of being is a contingent truth dependent on the supreme Truth of God for its existence.[92] For this reason the truth of created being points beyond itself to an ultimate Ground (God) by its very nature as contingent (it has to be contingent on something).[93]

Of course, the ultimate level of Truth is the *supreme Truth* of the self-existent Being of God. Here there is a difference between the Truth of God and all other truths, for while the other truths are true only by reference beyond themselves, the Truth of God is Truth without reference to anything else.[94]

The Stratification of Truth and Doctrine

This stratification of truth, Torrance points out, is an *a posteriori* reconstruction of how human knowledge is coordinated with what we seek to know and does not focus on the actual participatory heuristic process of inquiry (how form is integrated),[95] which we discussed at length in chapters 1 and 2. Yet he finds this "stratification of truth" of great significance.

Since the truth of statements lies in their referring beyond themselves, and the truth of signification is found in signifying that which is what it is, it is clear that it is improper to reduce "the truth of statement simply to its truth-function in discourse and it discloses the objective depth that a true statement must have beyond itself."[96] The truth of the reality signified remains whether it is signified falsely or not signified at all.[97]

Furthermore, since the truth of created being is grounded in a transcendent reference beyond itself in God, this stratification of truth reveals that we cannot define truth in terms of "agreement with the laws of human understanding," for things are true whether we think them or not.[98] There is thus an "irreversible relation" between the truth of statement and the truth of the reality stated, "for the truth of human statements is the consequence of the existence of things."[99]

In light of the stratified structure of truth, Torrance contends that doctrinal formulations are only properly made as we seek to penetrate through the created speech and truth of the biblical witness, which has arisen in the course of the events and realities of God's self-revelation and self-communication in space and time, to the "solid ground of the Truth, Speech, and Rationality of God" upon which the biblical witness rests. Torrance's concern here is that all doctrinal formulation must be "understood and expounded in the light of the Truth that God himself is...for its [doctrine's] real content is not the signifying truths of the Scriptures but the Truth of God revealed in and through them."[100] While the Holy Scriptures are the mediate source of doctrine, when true, doctrinal formulations are (or ought to be) objectively grounded in God's own self-revelation which resounds through Scripture as God continues to address us through the biblical witness.[101] In this way doctrine does greater justice to the Holy Scripture, for it seeks to establish its truth not in the signifying truth of the biblical statements but in the solid Truth of God which Scripture serves.

It is also crucial to remember that the actual process of inquiry through which apprehension of God takes place and out of which doctrines arise in this stratified manner is a personal, participatory and redemptive process. Torrance contends that in genuine theological inquiry and doctrinal formulation, "we are brought face to face with God in his own ultimate Truth and Reality" so that we cannot "undertake these tasks without a living, personal experience of that Truth."[102] This is why

Torrance contends that genuine theological inquiry and doctrinal formulation include repentance, forgiveness and reconciliation, for people (including theologians) have to be reconciled to the Truth in order to really know the Truth.[103]

Torrance can even call theology "a kind of ecstatic passion, in which–under the sheer impact of God's own Being in Word and Act–we are called to think of and to know him...in such a way that it cuts across the grain of our natural desires and mental habits and creatively reorients them."[104] This means that the truth-claims of doctrine cannot be truly known in an "impersonal" manner.

Of course, for Torrance, knowing the Truth of God is quite impossible apart from God's condescension to be one with us in our creaturely conditions and therefore to sustain our knowing and our doctrinal formulation that arises out of it.[105] This is what God has done in the incarnation of the Word or Truth of God within our contingent existence in Jesus Christ. Thus Torrance thinks that the claim of Jesus Christ, according to John's Gospel, to be "the Way, the Truth, and the Life" has implications for the nature and truth-claims of doctrine.

In that majestic "I am" of "the self-subsistent Truth of God meeting us face to face on our side of the creature/Creator relationship," Torrance finds that "the truth of signification, the truth of created being, and the ultimate Truth of God, without being confused, are indivisibly united in the oneness of his divine-human Person."[106] As such Christ is the Truth of God to humanity and the truth of humanity to God, and therefore, "the standard and norm for the formulation of all truth about God and his interaction with man."[107]

As the Way, Jesus Christ is not just a Teacher, for he himself is the Way to which he refers in his own personal Being.[108] Torrance thinks that this has the effect of prohibiting doctrinal formulation from straying into "timeless and spaceless generalities or abstract possibilities" and demands doctrinal formulation to be correlated with Christ's personal Being if it is going to be truthful.[109]

Since Jesus Christ is the Truth of God, Christ is the crucial embodiment of God's Truth in our world of space and time and thus the authoritative and final Judge of truth and falsity to whom all doctrinal formulations submit.[110]

As the Life, Jesus Christ indicates that he is the actualization of the creative life of God among humankind, and as such, the sole source of salvation and life. Torrance thinks that this demands a "living theology, a way of thinking which is at the same time a way of living, that cannot be abstracted from the life-giving acts of Christ in the depths of human being," as noted above.[111]

This fact that Jesus Christ is the supreme Truth requires an intensely personalized conceptualization of Truth of God, the Truth that God *is*.[112] This is Truth in the form of Personalizing Being that not only radically transforms the subjective pole of our knowing relation, but also Personalizing Being that retains its own essential mystery even in self-revelation, as noted earlier in several other contexts.[113] Torrance thinks that the more we know of the Truth of God, "the more we realize the ineffable and infinite fullness of his Reality which...reaches out infinitely beyond our apprehension."[114] What we know of God in this personalizing, participatory and redemptive encounter is polyvalent and far more than we can ever tell. This means that our knowledge, which we attempt to bring to articulation in doctrinal formulation, is more than can ever be fully specified or reduced to clear-cut propositions.

However, the revelation of the Truth of God in Jesus Christ is not an unintelligible Mystery, for though it reaches out beyond our comprehension, it is a Truth that we may apprehend. As we do so it increasingly brings intelligibility and meaning to ever increasing areas of our experience and knowledge.[115] Insofar as doctrinal statements are true, they will manifest a persistent fertility in their openness to the Truth embodied in Jesus Christ, as in the case of the *homoousion*, the doctrine of the Trinity, and the Niceno-Constantinopolitan Creed which have played such important roles in the history of Christianity.[116]

Since it is the very Truth and Word of God whom we encounter in Jesus Christ, doctrinal formulations are true only as they derive from, are grounded in, and refer to the Truth embodied in the divine-human personal Being of Jesus Christ.[117] Doctrines must refer away from themselves as truths of signification through the truth of Christ's human and creaturely being to the supreme Truth of God revealed in and through Christ.

In so doing, Torrance maintains that it is of utmost importance that we recognize the inadequacy of doctrinal formulations, an inadequacy that is, in fact, part of their precision, for the Truth of God in Jesus Christ is far more than can be expressed in creaturely verbal and conceptual expressions.[118]

Doctrinal formulations would not be truthful if this element of impropriety were not acknowledged, for then they would be placed on the same level as the supreme Truth, rather than functioning through a cross-level reference that is primarily denotative.[119]

Nevertheless, this impropriety does not mean that doctrines are necessarily false, for it is precisely their impropriety that helps us not to confound them with the realities they intend so that they fulfill their truthfulness as they direct our attention to "the objective self-signification of God's Truth in Jesus Christ."[120] We use doctrines correctly and truly when we do not simply think concepts or statements (doctrines) themselves, but rather utilize them in such a way that we think the realities to which they direct our attention.[121]

It is the very fact that, in Jesus Christ, God communicates not simply truths about Himself but the Supreme Truth of God's very Self that, in turn, implies that doctrinal formulations, insofar as they are true, are relativized by the Truth and indicate far more than they express. Torrance thinks that this is epistemologically consistent with the proper realist function of words and statements within his understanding of the way in which form is integrated in the day to day life of Christian faith and in scientific theology.[122] Despite their inadequacy to the Truth of God, doctrinal statements, under the impact of the Word and Truth of God upon them, can enable the human mind to apprehend the living Truth of God so that the Church effectively thinks and speaks of God on the basis of God's own self-revealing and self-evidencing Reality.[123]

Justification and Authority in Doctrine

In other words, Torrance thinks that theological concepts and doctrinal formulations find "their justification through the Grace of God alone."[124] Doctrines have their proper truth not by a process of verification that we enact, as if we could coerce God to be the truth of our formulations, but simply because of God's self-communication in Jesus Christ.[125] For Torrance, justification by the grace of God has an epistemological application as well as an ethical one, and it calls into question all our attempts at "epistemic self-verification."[126] To attempt such self-verification, in Torrance's mind, is to falsify the Gospel at its very root. We dare not boast of the truth of our doctrinal formulations.

Furthermore, Torrance argues that the doctrine of justification serves to further reinforce the point discussed above that doctrinal formulations are truthful not when they claim to possess truth in themselves but when they refer away from themselves to the Truth of God in Jesus Christ.[127] Of course, out of respect for the Truth of God revealed in Jesus Christ, the Church is called to think and speak faithfully and correctly about God through its doctrinal formulations. Torrance thinks that this is the essential meaning of orthodoxy and humility before God.[128] Still we must confess that we are "unprofitable servants," that what we say falls short of God's Truth, and that in the end, since we cannot force the supreme Truth of God to be the content of our statements, the intrinsic character of this Truth demands, "verification and action by the Truth Himself."[129] This, of course, is in keeping with Torrance's dynamic, ontological understanding of revelation, in which he is concerned to affirm the oneness between the content of revelation and the Being and Truth of God.

Yet, it is precisely at this point that Torrance finds the Church's true freedom in theological inquiry and doctrinal formulation. This is not the modern notion of freedom as self-determination, for Torrance thinks that we are unable through free will to escape our self-will and self-centeredness. Rather it is an objectively controlled freedom, manifesting itself in an openness of being and thought in response to the compelling claims of the ultimate Truth incarnate, a freedom that finds its own final ground in the "self-subsistent Authority or Freedom (*exousia*, *autoexousia*) of the Lord God."[130]

Since God does not overwhelm us with an unmediated self-revelation, the *oikonomia* of God's self-revelation and self-communication is one in which God has created a profound reciprocity with us within our space/time world and our creaturely existence and rationality. This corporate medium of relations and structures that God has called into contrapuntal relation to God's self-revelation and self-communication in Israel, and then in Jesus Christ and the Apostolic foundation of the Church (a reciprocity given expression in the Holy Scriptures) is the continuing creaturely medium through which God's self-revelation and self-communication still meets us.

Since God honors this creaturely medium, Torrance acknowledges "secondary authorities or delegated authorities whose function it is to serve his [God's] supreme Authority...in such a way as not to obscure it but let it appear in all God's Prerogative and Majesty."[131] The Holy Scriptures are certainly authoritative for doctrinal formulation, though Torrance accords primacy to divine revelation that resounds through Scripture and not simply to the Bible,[132] as noted in the previous chapter.

Furthermore, while the ultimate authority for doctrinal formulation and verification is the *autoousia* and *autoexousia* (the self-being and self-authority) of God, when this authority is given its rightful place, "then the way is open in the Church for an authoritative exercise of the *magisterium* in serving the inherent and ultimate authority of the Truth of God itself."[133] According to Torrance, the Church and its tradition also carry authority, so long as its structures and doctrines remain open to the objective Truth and Authority of God's self-revelation and self-communication through Christ and in the Holy Spirit.[134] This is why Torrance maintains that "the more ecumenical" doctrines are, "i.e., the more they are formulated within the openness of the members of the whole community to one another before God, the more likely they are to escape distortion...and to be properly open toward God."[135] The Church and its tradition constitute the indispensable social coefficient for knowledge of God and doctrinal formulation.

However, since the Church interacts with the surrounding society, it has tended to allow the cultural divisions and ideological passions present in the world to cut back into its own existence, so that the Church comes to reflect the fragmentation and pluralism of secular culture.[136] Torrance thinks that this has led to an inappropriate multiplicity of beliefs and doctrines in the Christian community.[137] Many belief and doctrines derive from unending questions posed by different cultural ages and contexts, reflecting transient frames of reference, rather that "the deep invariances" in our relationship with God.[138]

In light of this, Torrance believes that the recovery of the stratified structure of truth and authority, in which the truth of being is given priority over the truth of signification, could have a purifying effect through the discipline of doctrinal criticism, opening the way for significant clarification and simplification of the Church's doctrinal heritage.[139] What is needed is

> a rigorously scientific examination of the whole corpus of theological knowledge in which we try to isolate the core of basic and central theological

> concepts and relations, as few in number as possible, distinguishing them from derived notions of an intermediary and secondary nature, in order to grasp something of its inner coherence and unity, and then use it as an instrument with which to comb through the whole corpus of accumulated beliefs and doctrines in the service of clarification and simplification.[140]

In this way, knowledge of God can be organized into various levels of thought with fewer and more natural concepts or doctrines having wider applicability.

This is the kind of constructive epistemological activity and doctrinal formulation that Torrance advocates. It must entail

> such a penetrating grasp of the organic structure of our knowledge of God in its inner unifying core that we are able to discriminate what is relevant from what is irrelevant, what is central from what is merely peripheral...what is permanent from what is only of transient significance.[141]

Torrance thinks that this cannot but serve an ecumenical function, for in focusing on what is central, it is possible to attack the differences between Churches from behind by working out from the center, exhibiting doctrinal formulations that may elicit common agreement.[142]

When this is undertaken, Torrance thinks that theological knowledge and doctrinal formulation will bring into focus the "controlling ground-structures of our knowledge in the incarnation, creation and the Trinity, within which the obedient humanity of Jesus Christ and his filial relation to the Father will inevitably occupy a critical and constructive place in our thought,"[143] for it is here in Jesus that the truths of statement and signification, the truth of created being and the Supreme Truth of God all coincide. Torrance maintains that the more profoundly the Church's attention is focused on this controlling center in the Truth of God in Jesus Christ, the more the Church will be free from sociological pressure to compromise the truth of the Gospel in its life and in its doctrine.[144]

Notes

1. See Thomas F. Torrance, *Reality and Evangelical Theology* (Philadelphia: Westminster Press, 1982), pp. 16-19 and 65-71.

2. Thomas F. Torrance, *The Ground and Grammar of Theology* (Charlottesville: The University of Virginia Press, 1980), pp. 158-59.

3. See George Lindbeck, *The Nature of Doctrine: Religion and Theology in a Postliberal Age* (Philadelphia: Westminster Press, 1984), pp. 93-95 and 106-7, where it is clear that while Lindbeck's rule theory "does not prohibit speculations on the possible correspondence of the Trinitarian pattern of Christian language to the metaphysical structure of the Godhead," such interpretations should not be "made communally normative for the way Christians live and think." Ibid., p. 106. Furthermore, Lindbeck makes it clear he is uncomfortable with such interpretations, seeing them as finally "unanswerable this side of the Eschaton." Ibid.

4. See Torrance, *Ground and Grammar*, pp. 155-78, and Thomas F. Torrance, *The Christian Doctrine of God: One Being Three Persons* (Edinburgh: T & T Clark, 1996), pp. 73-107.

5. Torrance, *Ground and Grammar*, p. 156.

6. Ibid.

7. Ibid., pp. 156-57. Also see Torrance, *Christian Doctrine*, pp. 88-89.

8. Torrance, *Ground and Grammar*, p. 157.

9. Ibid. Also see Thomas F. Torrance, *Karl Barth: Biblical and Evangelical Theologian* (Edinburgh: T & T Clark, 1990), pp. 83 and 117-18.

10. Thomas F. Torrance, "Theological Realism," in *The Philosophical Frontiers of Christian Theology*, eds. B. Hebblethwaite and S. Sutherland (New York: Cambridge University Press, 1982), p. 192.

11. Torrance, *Christian Doctrine*, p. 89.

12. Ibid., p. 90.

13. Torrance, *Ground and Grammar*, p. 157.

14. See ibid., pp. 156-57 and 169-70.

15. Ibid.

16. Thomas F. Torrance, *Reality and Scientific Theology* (Edinburgh: Scottish Academic Press, 1985), p. 86.

17. Ibid.

18. Ibid.

19. Torrance, *Christian Doctrine*, p. 93.

20. Torrance, *Scientific Theology*, pp. 85-86.

21. Torrance, *Ground and Grammar*, p. 157.

22. Torrance, *Christian Doctrine*. p. 82.

23. Ibid., pp. 76 and 98.

24. Torrance, *Ground and Grammar*, pp. 157-58.

25. Ibid.

26. Ibid., pp. 149-50 and 161-62. This is something Kant unfortunately ruled out as discussed in chapter 1. Furthermore, it should be evident now that the kind of knowledge of the intrinsic relations of reality that Torrance

advocates is inseparable from his reformulation of how form is integrated.

27. Ibid., pp. 149-50.

28. Ibid., p. 150.

29. Ibid.

30. Ibid., p. 158.

31. Ibid.

32. Ibid., p. 160.

33. Torrance, *Christian Doctrine*, p. 99.

34. Ibid., p. 108.

35. Ibid., p. 166.

36. Torrance, *Ground and Grammar*, p. 166.

37. Ibid., p. 148. Of course, for Torrance, it is the fact that God is Triune in nature (there are intrinsic relations in God) that is the ground of God's knowability.

38. See ibid. and also Torrance, *Scientific Theology*, pp. 186-200. Torrance also maintains that this concept of person can have an important impact on how we understand human persons and social relations.

39. Torrance, *Christian Doctrine*, pp. 103-4.

40. Torrance, *Ground and Grammar*, p. 167.

41. Ibid.

42. Ibid., p. 159.

43. Ibid., p. 161

44. Ibid., pp. 167-67.

45. Ibid., pp. 158-59.

46. Torrance, *Scientific Theology*, p. 161.

47. Torrance, "Theological Realism," p. 192.

48. Lindbeck, *Doctrine*, p. 132.

49. Torrance, *Scientific Theology*, p. 83.

50. Thomas F. Torrance, *Transformation and Convergence in the Frame of Knowledge* (Grand Rapids: Eerdmans, 1984), p. 93.

51. Ibid.

52. See ibid., pp. 92-96 and Torrance, *Scientific Theology*, pp. 72-86.

53. Ibid., p. 76.

54. Torrance, *Transformation*, pp. 112-13.

55. Torrance, *Scientific Theology*, p. 93.

56. Ibid.

57. Ibid., p. 123.

58. Ibid., p. 86.

59. Ibid., p. 85.

60. Ibid., p. 81.

61. Ibid., p. 134.

62. Torrance, *Evangelical Theology*, p. 122.

63. Ibid.

64. Ibid., pp. 122-23.

65. Torrance, *Scientific Theology*, p. 135.

66. Ibid., p. 138.

67. Ibid.

68. See ibid., pp. 139 and 186.

69. Ibid., p. 139.

70. Ibid.

71. Thomas F. Torrance, *God and Rationality* (New York: Oxford University Press, 1971), p. 22.

72. Torrance, *Scientific Theology*, p. 139.
73. Ibid.
74. Ibid., p. 141.
75. Ibid. Also See Torrance, *Evangelical Theology*, p. 126.
76. See Torrance, *Scientific Theology*, p. 141.
77. Ibid.
78. Ibid.
79. Ibid., p. 142.
80. Ibid.
81. Ibid., pp. 142-43.
82. Ibid.
83. Ibid., p. 143.
84. This is why Torrance questions both correspondence and coherence theories of truth, for "whenever we try to develop knowledge by abstractive processes some type of correspondence view of truth is forced upon us by the prescinding of form from being, and then as the form assumes an independent status of its own, it is some standard of inner consistency or coherence view of truth that becomes uppermost." Ibid., p. 49.

In a similar manner, Torrance argues that when the "realist" relation between idea and reality or between sign and thing signified is damaged, though not completely severed, "there seems to be a regular tendency, as one extreme position is corrected in respect to another, for each to pass over into the other, so that idealism sometimes passes over into a form of realism and realism passes over into a form of idealism." Torrance, *Evangelical Theology*, p. 59. We saw an instance of this in the shift in the integration of form from Newton to Kant discussed in chapter 1 above. Also see Torrance, "Theological Realism," pp. 169-76, for a detailed discussion of this.
85. Torrance, *Scientific Theology*, p. 143.
86. Ibid., p. 144.
87. See ibid., p. 144 and Torrance, *Evangelical Theology*, p. 128.
88. Torrance, *Scientific Theology*, p. 144. Also see Torrance, *Evangelical Theology*, p. 128, and Torrance's massive discussion of "The Nature of Truth" and "Problems of Logic," chapters 3 and 4 of Thomas F. Torrance, *Theological Science* (London: Oxford University Press, 1969), pp. 141-280.
89. Torrance, *Scientific Theology*, p. 144.
90. Ibid.
91. Ibid., p. 145. Also see Torrance, *Evangelical Theology*, pp. 128-29.
92. Torrance, *Scientific Theology*, p. 145.
93. Ibid.
94. Ibid. Also see Torrance, *Evangelical Theology*, pp. 129-30.
95. Torrance, *Scientific Theology*, p. 146.
96. Torrance, *Evangelical Theology*, p. 130.
97. Torrance, *Scientific Theology*, p. 145.
98. Ibid., p. 146. Torrance contrasts this with Kant's view of truth. See ibid., p. 159.
99. Torrance, *Evangelical Theology*, p. 130.
100. Ibid., p. 135.
101. Ibid., pp. 134-35.
102. Ibid.
103. Torrance, *Scientific Theology*, p. 150.
104. Torrance, *Ground and Grammar*, p. 155.
105. Torrance, *Evangelical Theology*, p. 136.

106. Ibid., p. 137.
107. Ibid.
108. Ibid.
109. Ibid., p. 138.
110. Ibid.
111. Ibid.
112. Ibid., p. 139.
113. Ibid., pp. 140-41.
114. Ibid., p. 141.
115. Ibid.
116. See Thomas F. Torrance, *The Trinitarian Faith: The Evangelical Theology of the Ancient Catholic Church* (Edinburgh: T & T Clark, 1988).
117. Torrance, *Scientific Theology*, p. 142.
118. Ibid.
119. Ibid., p. 146.
120. Ibid., p. 142.
121. Ibid., pp. 146-47.
122. Ibid., p. 144.
123. Ibid., p. 147.
124. Ibid., p. 148.
125. Ibid.
126. Ibid.
127. Ibid., pp. 148-49.
128. Ibid., p. 149.
129. Torrance, *Theological Science*, p. 198
130. Torrance, *Evangelical Theology*, p. 151.
131. Ibid., p. 154.
132. Ibid., p. 96.
133. Torrance, "Theological Realism," p. 180.
134. See ibid., pp. 180-81.
135. Torrance, *Rationality*, p. 190.
136. Torrance, *Scientific Theology*, p. 151.
137. Ibid.
138. Ibid., p. 152.
139. Ibid., pp. 152-53.
140. Ibid., p. 154.
141. Ibid., p. 156.
142. See Thomas F. Torrance, *Theology in Reconciliation: Essays towards Evangelical and Catholic Unity in East and West* (London: Geoffrey Chapman, 1975; reprint, Eugene, Ore.: Wipf & Stock, 1997), pp. 8-9.
143. Torrance, *Scientific Theology*, p. 156.
144. Ibid., p. 157.

Conclusion

The Church and academy owe George Lindbeck a debt of gratitude for precipitating the debate concerning the nature of doctrine through the publication of his important book, *The Nature of Doctrine*. Lindbeck's proposal is significant not only because it has stimulated theological discussion concerning the character of doctrine in theology, but also because it raises fundamental questions regarding the nature of theology and indeed Christian faith and life. While these questions have never been the primary focus of the preceding pages, they are lurking behind many of the discussions above.

Thus Lindbeck calls not only for a "rule theory of doctrine," but also "a post-liberal way of conceiving religion." The reason for this is that "theories of religion and doctrine are interdependent." Furthermore, Lindbeck judges that "all standard theological approaches are unhelpful."[1]

The result is that Lindbeck's theory of religion (and the nature of doctrine) is neither "specifically ecumenical, nor Christian, nor theological," but rather derives from linguistic philosophy and the social sciences, though Lindbeck admits that "the motivations for this book are ultimately more substantially theological than purely theoretical."[2]

Yet, it is precisely this attempt at religious and theological neutrality that elicits Alister McGrath's strong assertion of "the right of living history over and against artificial theoretical constructions," for living history "subverts the neat analyses of those who synthesize the past, imposing a preselected pattern upon its flux."[3] In other words, a generic paradigm for religion and doctrine, as insightful as it may be, is inadequate to the character of religion and doctrine as historical phenomena. The contrasting titles of McGrath's and Lindbeck's books ("The *Genesis* of Doctrine" contra "The *Nature* of Doctrine") underscores this difference of opinion concerning how one ought to develop a theory regarding religion and the nature of doctrine.

According to McGrath, it is in the *genesis* of doctrine "as an historical phenomenon" that we will find "a depth and richness" regarding the nature of doctrine that "cannot adequately be captured by redüctive theories of the nature of ."[4]

Nevertheless, while McGrath concedes that historical analysis is inadequate for developing a normative theory, he does not really analyze and develop the necessary "creative dialectic between the historical and descriptive...and theological and prescriptive."[5] This is precisely what Torrance attempts to do. Torrance grounds his understanding of the nature of doctrine in the realities and events of God's self-revelation and our evangelical experience of that self-communication, thus providing a descriptive and normative delineation of the nature of doctrine. Yet is so doing, he also gives attention to the kinds of issues and insights found in Lindbeck and McGrath. Here Torrance redresses two critical and interrelated problems in Lindbeck's proposal.

The first is that the position that Lindbeck advocates seems to lack a critical principle or an element of critical realism. Or to put it still another way, Lindbeck's project neglects a proper movement of epistemic inversion in which once the subjective and social coefficients have served their roles of semantic intentionality, there is an inversion of the knowing relation so that the self-presentation of reality (in theology, God's self-revelation) in turn informs, corrects and even transforms the subjective and social coefficients, leading to ever more adequate integrations of form. Where in Lindbeck do we find that kind of inversion? Even McGrath, though he speaks of epistemic realism, never delineates what it entails.[6]

It is at just this point that Torrance has made one of what I consider to be his greatest contributions to theology and the discussion of the nature of doctrine: a carefully developed philosophy of the science of theology or an *a posteriori* delineation of critical epistemic realism in theological epistemology. Yet it is a delineation not abstracted from, or developed without reference to, actual knowledge of God as it arises in the day to day evangelical and doxological encounter with the realities and events of God's self-revelation within the Christian community, which that self-revelation has called into existence as its correlate.

Thus, Torrance has carefully worked through the modern discussion concerning the integration of form from Descartes and Newton to Kant, which underlies both experiential-expressivism and Lindbeck's cultural-linguistic theory. Torrance concludes, as discussed above in chapter 1, that there must be a different and more adequate account of how the theoretical and empirical elements condition one another and how they are combined in knowledge. Here Torrance discovered that theology (as in Barth) and modern science (Einstein and Polanyi) have had to cope with a parallel set of epistemological problems owing to the received dualist (cosmological and epistemological) framework of thought within the modern Western cultural context.

In developing his own constructive response, Torrance enters into dialogue with major areas of the histories of theology, philosophy and natural science. Yet, as Daniel Hardy points out, Torrance "proceeds by *reflecting critically* upon the knowledge which has achieved in the past and the means by which it has been achieved, in order to discriminate between achievements and distortions."[7] Thus, as Hardy also correctly notes, Torrance's positive position and historical reflection are subtly interrelated: "his positive position is established by reference to his historical work, while he judges what history is important, and interprets it, with criteria which employ his positive position."[8]

In other words, Torrance's approach entails the kind of sophisticated and "creative dialectic" between the historical and normative that McGrath intimates, but does not fully develop.[9] This involves a further correlation between a "double activity" in which thought conforms to the mode of rationality afforded by the reality being investigated as we actively respond to reality as it progressively comes into view in the course of inquiry, as chapter 1 outlined above. Torrance operates with a coinherence of form and being both in reality and our knowing of it. This is what leads him to an integrative and holistic perspective.

Chapter 2 above traced the implications of this epistemic conversation for the nature of doctrine in Torrance's theology as an integration of form arising as one indwells the conjoint semantic focus of the biblical witness within the evangelical and doxological life of the Church. Torrance sees the *homoousion* as an example of doctrine arising as an integration of form in a *disclosive relation* to the reality that the biblical terms point out and convey. As such, doctrine is a form of knowledge that is cognitive, though not strictly propositional.

Yet Torrance grants the difficulty of genuine knowledge,

which is rooted in the fact that we are all conditioned by the cultural-linguistic matrix of life and thought into which we are born as children of specific families and particular cultures and languages, something that Lindbeck has taken into consideration with the seriousness that it deserves in developing his theory of religion and doctrine. This whole complex of issues revolving around the relations between doctrine and the Church, including the way the Church shapes doctrinal formulation, the roles of doctrine in the Church and wider culture, and the need for doctrinal criticism was discussed in chapter 3.

Torrance conceives of the Church as the social coefficient in knowledge of God. Doctrines are rooted in interrelated forms of life in social-conceptual fields. Yet, because the Church interacts with the social coefficients of the surrounding culture, there is the ever-present danger of doctrinal deformation. This demands doctrinal criticism, a point at which Torrance's position is close to that of McGrath.

Still, Torrance conceives of doctrine as having an essentially positive role to play in the Christian community, helping the community refer its thoughts beyond itself to God, as well as guiding and interpreting experience, and demarcating the Church as a specific community.

This brings us to the second point at which Torrance redresses a problem, or at least an unanswered question, in Lindbeck's proposal: that is the relation of the Christian idiom and *Lebensform* to the realities they intend. As we saw in chapter 1, even after Bruce Marshall's careful clarification of the crucial distinction between the *nature* of truth and the *justification* of truth, and his defense of truth claims within the cultural-linguistic paradigm, Lindbeck's position still invites a further step, which his theory, as it stands, does not permit.[10] Lindbeck could have unequivocally stated his acceptance of Marshall's important clarification of the need for a "*crucial link* between *prima veritas* and *a Deo revelatum*."[11] However, Lindbeck did not.

This elicits McGrath's question of whether the Christian idiom reposes on human insight or on a revelation of God in the "Christ-event." But this is a very real problem for "postliberals" like Lindbeck who accept so much of modernity's critical moment with reference to the foundational documents of the Christian faith and who accept the historical and cultural relativity of the human condition, including all of humanity's noetic claims. The historicized ghost of Kant's synthetic *a priori* (Lindbeck's quasi-transcendental or culturally formed framework) still seems to haunt much of postmodernity.

Here even McGrath has not gone far enough since he seems to erect a very modern boundary in the discussion of the nature of doctrine at doctrine "considered as a historical phenomenon," which is generated as an attempt to "demarcate the significance of Jesus" and the "Christ-event he embodies," "without prejudice to the question of what the *ultimate* external referent of doctrinal formulations might be,"[12] as noted in the beginning of chapter 4 above.[13] But why bracket the discussion at that point? An adequate theory of the nature of doctrine cannot be developed without coming to terms with character of the Christ-event and the intelligible relations embodied in that event.

This is what Torrance attempts, as described in chapter 4 above. It is Torrance's axiomatic refusal to accept a dualist division between form and being in, 1.) the realities and events of God's self-revelation and in our evangelical and doxological knowledge and experience of it (that together are constitutive of Christian faith and life); and also 2.) in developing appropriate methods for investigating and ways of expressing this revelation in theological investigation that will not let Torrance rest content with any theory concerning the nature of doctrine that prescinds from the intelligible relations inherent in those realities and events and in our knowledge and experience of them.

Hence, for Torrance, doctrine and the nature of doctrine are conditioned by the realities and events of God's self-revelation and our evangelical and doxological encounter with them. According to Torrance, it is as we attend to those realities and events through the Scriptures (which were called into being by God's self-revelation) that doctrine arises as a *sui generis* form of knowledge. As the Church reaches deeply into the heart of its intellectual encounter with God as God makes Himself known through Jesus Christ in the Holy Spirit, the Church finds that the economy of redemption has a trinitarian structure, reflecting God's trinitarian Reality.

Thus the doctrine of the Trinity arises on the ground of intelligible relations inherent in God's self-revelation and is implicit in the Church's knowledge of that revelation from the beginning. Though incomplete and inadequate to the *Reality* of the trinitarian God, the doctrine of the Trinity is still disclosive of God's Triunity. As such, it is a paradigmatic instance of doctrine and the nature of doctrine, as well as "the *ultimate ground* of our knowledge of God, the *basic grammar* of theology."[14]

Here we see that, for Torrance, doctrines are true when they are in a disclosive relation to the realities they intend. Torrance maintains that one cannot state in statements how statements are related to reality, for to do so is to substitute a logical or linguistic relation for a real relation. Yet reality shows through.

Thus doctrines are neither propositions, nor nondiscursive expressions of inward experience, nor second-order rules governing the Church's first-order discourse. In Torrance's view, doctrines are *disclosure models* through which fuller disclosure of the Truth of God in Jesus Christ witnessed to in Scripture can take place. It is this relation to that Truth that is determinative for Torrance's understanding the truth claims of doctrine, as discussed in chapter 5.

Despite the dense and occasional character of Torrance's publications that, at times, impede readers from entering the horizon of his thought and has probably curtailed the impact of his theology, Torrance has developed his position with remarkable rigor. All of the elements of Torrance's theology that bear upon the nature of doctrine are carefully integrated in his thought, as I have tried to show throughout this monograph.

Nevertheless, it is at precisely this point of rigorous integration that Torrance has made a real contribution to theology in general and the debate concerning the nature of doctrine in particular. Those who want to improve on Torrance's reflections (or take exception to elements of his thought) in developing an adequate theory concerning the nature of doctrine will need to engage in an equally rigorous delineation and integration as Torrance has in his understanding of the nature of doctrine. Anything less, I believe, will prove inadequate to the depth and polyvalent character of doctrine in Christian faith and theology.

Notes

1. George Lindbeck, *The Nature of Doctrine* (Philadelphia: Westminster Press, 1984), pp. 20-21.

2. Ibid., pp. 7 & 10.

3. Alister E. McGrath, *The Genesis of Doctrine: A Study in the Foundations of Doctrinal Criticism* (Cambridge, Mass.: Basil Blackwell Ltd., 1990), p. ix.

4. Ibid.

5. Ibid.

6. McGrath admits that he only provides preliminary clarification and promises a more substantial engagement in a future work. Ibid., pp. viii-ix.

7. See Daniel W. Hardy, "Thomas F. Torrance," in *The Modern Theologians: An Introduction to Christian Theology in the Twentieth Century*, ed. David F. Ford (New York: Basil Blackwell Inc., 1989), I:73.

8. Ibid.

9. McGrath, *Doctrine*, p. ix.

10. See chapter 1 above, pp. 45-46, endnote 65.

11. Bruce Marshall, "Aquinas as Postliberal Theologian," *The Thomist* 53, no. 3 (July 1989): pp. 373-75.

12. McGrath, *Doctrine*, pp. ix, 2, 28 & 32.

13. See pp. 129-33 above.

14.Thomas F. Torrance, *The Ground and Grammar of Theology* (Charlottesville: University of Virginia Press, 1980), p. 158-59.

A Selected Bibliography

The most complete bibliography of Thomas F. Torrance's publications is in Alister E. McGrath, *T. F. Torrance: An Intellectual Biography* (Edinburgh: T&T Clark, 1999), 249-96.

Books

Calvin's Doctrine of Man. London: Lutterworth, 1949.

Conflict and Agreement in the Church, vol. 1. London: Lutterworth, 1959

Theology in Reconstruction. London: SCM Press, 1965. Reprint, Eugene, Oreg.: Wipf & Stock, 1997.

Space, Time, and Incarnation. London: Oxford University Press, 1969. Reprint, Edinburgh: T&T Clark, 1997.

Theological Science. London: Oxford University Press, 1969. Reprint, Edinburgh: T&T Clark, 1996.

God and Rationality. London: Oxford University Press, 1971. Reprint, Eugene, Oreg.: Wipf & Stock, 1997.

Theology in Reconciliation: Essays towards Evangelical and Catholic Unity in East and West. London: Geoffrey Chapman, 1975. Reprint, Eugene, Oreg.: Wipf & Stock, 1997.

Space, Time, and Resurrection. Edinburgh: Handsel Press, 1976.

Christian Theology and Scientific Culture. New York: Oxford University Press, 1980.

The Ground and Grammar of Theology. Charlottesville, University of Virginia Press, 1980.

Divine and Contingent Order. New York: Oxford University Press, 1981. Reprint, Edinburgh: T&T Clark, 1998.

Juridical Law and Physical Law: Toward a Realist Foundation for Human Law. Edinburgh: Scottish Academic Press, 1982.

Reality and Evangelical Theology. Philadelphia: Westminster Press, 1982.

Transformation and Convergence in the Frame of Knowledge: Explorations in the Interrelations of Scientific and Theological Enterprise. Grand Rapids, Mich.: Eerdmans, 1984.

Reality and Scientific Theology. Edinburgh: Scottish Academic Press, 1985.

The Hermeneutics of John Calvin. Edinburgh: Scottish Academic Press, 1988.

The Trinitarian Faith: The Evangelical Theology of the Ancient Catholic Church. Edinburgh: T&T Clark, 1988.

The Christian Frame of Mind: Reason, Order, and Openness in Theology and Natural Science. Colorado Springs, Colo.: Helmers & Howard, 1989. New and enlarged edition.

Karl Barth: Biblical and Evangelical Theologian. Edinburgh: T&T Clark, 1990.

The Mediation of Christ: Evangelical Theology and Scientific Culture. Edinburgh: T&T Clark, 1992. New edition.

Preaching Christ Today: The Gospel and Scientific Thinking. Grand Rapids, Mich.: Eerdmans, 1994.

Divine Meaning: Studies in Patristic Hermeneutics. Edinburgh: T&T Clark, 1995.

The Uniqueness of Divine Revelation and the Authority of the Scriptures. Edinburgh: Rutherford House, 1995.

The Christian Doctrine of God: One Being Three Persons. Edinburgh: T&T Clark, 1996.

Articles

"Faith and Philosophy," *The Hibbert Journal* 45 (1948-49)

"The Place of Word and Truth in Theological Inquiry according to St. Anselm." In *Studia medievalia et mariologica: P. Carolo Balic OFM septuagesimum explenti annum dicata*, ed. R. Zavalloni, 131-60. Rome: Editrice Antonianum, 1971.

"The Framework of Belief." In *Belief in Science and in Christian Life*, ed. Thomas F. Torrance, 1-27. Edinburgh: Handsel Press, 1980.

"The Place of Michael Polanyi in the Modern Philosophy of Science." *Ethics in Science and Medicine* 7 (1980): 57-95.

"Ultimate Beliefs and the Scientific Revolution." *Cross*

Currents 30 (1980): 129-49.

"Theological Realism." In *The Philosophical Frontiers of Christian Theology: Essays Presented to D. M. MacKinnon*, ed. B. Hebblethwaite and S. Sutherland, 169-96. Cambridge: Cambridge University Press, 1982.

"The Deposit of Faith." *Scottish Journal of Theology* 36 (1983): 1-28.

"The Substance of the Faith: A Clarification of the Concept in the Church of Scotland." *Scottish Journal of Theology* 36 (1983): 327-38.

"The Historical Jesus: From the Perspective of a Theologian." In *The New Testament Age: Essays in Honor of Bo Reicke*, ed. William C. Weinrich, 2:511-26. Macon, Ga.: Mercer University Press, 1984.

"A Pilgrimage in the School of Faith—An Interview with T. F. Torrance," by John I. Hesselink. *Reformed Review* 38, no. 1 (1984): 49-64.

"Karl Barth and the Latin Heresy." *Scottish Journal of Theology* 39 (1986): 461-82.

"Karl Barth and Patristic Theology." In *Theology beyond Christendom: Essays on the Centenary of the Birth of Karl Barth*, ed. John Thomson, 215-39. Allison Park, Penn.: Pickwick Publications, 1986.

"The Legacy of Karl Barth (1886-1986)." *Scottish Journal of Theology* 39 (1986): 289-308.

"My Interaction with Karl Barth." In *How Karl Barth Changed My Mind*, ed. Donald K. McKim, 52-64. Grand Rapids, Mich: Eerdmans, 1986.

"The Reconciliation of Mind." *TSF Bulletin* 10, no. 3 (1987): 4-7.

"The Goodness and Dignity of Man in the Christian Tradition." *Modern Theology* 4 (1988): 309-22.

"Interview with Professor Thomas F. Torrance." In *Different Gospels*, edited by Dr. Andrew Walker, 42-54. London: Hodder & Stoughton, 1988.

"The Soul and Person in Theological Perspective." In *Religion, Reason and the Self: Essays in Honour of Hywel D. Lewis*, ed. Stewart R. Sutherland and T. A. Roberts, 103-18. Cardiff: University of Wales Press, 1989.

"The Distinctive Character of the Reformed Tradition," in *Incarnational Ministry: The Presence of Christ in Church Society, and Family*, ed. C. D. Kettler and T. H. Speidell.

Colorado Springs: Helmers & Howard, 1990.
"The Christian Apprehension of God the Father." In *Speaking the Christian God: The Holy Trinity and the Challenge of Feminism*, ed. Alvin F. Kimel, Jr., 120-43. Grand Rapids, Mich.: Eerdmans, 1992.
"Incarnation and Atonement: Theosis and Henosis in the Light of Modern Scientific Rejection of Dualism." *Society of Ordained Scientists*, no. 7, Edgware, Middlesex (spring 1992): 8-20.
"The Atonement: The Singularity of Christ and the Finality of the Cross: The Atonement and the Moral Order." In *Universalism and the Doctrine of Hell*, ed. Nigel M. de S. Cameron, 225-56. Exeter: Paternoster Press, 1992; Grand Rapids, Mich.: Baker Book House, 1993.
"Ultimate and Penultimate Beliefs in Science." In *Facets of Faith and Science,* vol. 1: *Historiography and Modes of Interaction*, ed. Jitse van der Meer, 151-76. Lanham, Md.: University Press of America; New York: Pascal Center for Advanced Studies in Faith and Science, 1996.
"Einstein and God." *Reflections* 1 (spring 1998): 2-15.

Secondary Works

Books

David Hume. *A Treatise of Human Nature*. London: Longmans, Green, 1909.
Immanuel Kant. *Critique of Pure Reason*, trans. N. Kemp Smith. London: Macmillian, 1933.
Albert Einstein. *The World as I See It*, trans. Alan Harris. London: John Lane, 1935.
Albert Einstein. *Out of My Later Years*. New York: Philosophical Library, 1950.
Isaac Newton. *Optics*, 4th ed. New York: Dover, 1952.
Isaac Newton. Philosophiae Naturalis Principia Mathematica, trans. by A. Motte (1729), rev.and ed. by Florian Cajori. Chicago: Encyclopedia Britannica, 1955.
James Brown. *Subject and Object in Modern Theology*. New York: Macmillian, 1955.
Michael Polanyi. *Personal Knowledge*. Chicago: University of Chicago Press, 1958.

Hans Frei. *The Eclipse of Biblical Narrative*. New Haven: Yale University Press, 1974.
E. L. Mascall. *Theology and the Gospel of Christ*. London: SPCK, 1977, 46-50.
Herwi Rikhof. *The Concept of Church*. London: Palmos, 1981.
William Abraham. *Divine Revelation and the Limits of the Historical Critical Method*. London: Oxford University Press, 1982.
Charles C. Hefling, Jr. *Why Doctrines?* Cambridge, Mass.: Cowley Publications, 1984.
George Lindbeck, *The Nature of Doctrine: Religion and Theology in a Postliberal Age*. Philadelphia: Westminster Press, 1984.
Ronald F. Thiemann. *Revelation and Theology: The Gospel as Narrated Promise*. Notre Dame, Ind.: University of Notre Dame Press, 1985, 32-43.
Garrett Green, ed. *Narrative Interpretation*. Philadelphia: Fortress Press, 1987.
Alexander Thomson. *Tradition and Authority in Science and Theology*. Edinburgh: Scottish Academic Press, 1987.
Edgar McKnight. *The Post-Modern Use of the Bible*. Nashville: Abingdon Press, 1988.
Michael H. McCarthy. *The Crisis of Philosophy* Albany: State University of New York Press, 1990.
Alister E. McGrath. *The Genesis of Doctrine: A Study in the Foundations of Doctrinal Criticism*. Cambridge, Mass.: Basil Blackwell Ltd., 1990.
Christian D. Kettler. *The Vicarious Humanity of Christ and the Reality of Salvation*. New York: University Press of America, 1991, 121-55.
Alan G. Marley. *T. F. Torrance: The Rejection of Dualism*. Edinburgh: Handsel Press, 1992.
Colin Weightman. *Theology in a Polanyian Universe: The Theology of Thomas Torrance*. New York: Peter Lang, 1994.
Roland Spjuth. *Creation, Contingency, and Divine Presence in the Theologies of Thomas F. Torrance and Eberhard Jungel*. In Studia Theologica Lundensia Series. Lund, Sweden: Lund University Press, 1995.
John Douglas Morrison. *Knowledge of the Self-Revealing God in the Thought of Thomas Forsyth Torrance*, vol. 2, *Issues in Systematic Theology*. New York: Peter Lang, 1997.

Robert K. Martin. *The Incarnate Ground of Christian Faith: Toward a Christian Theological Epistemology for the Educational Ministry of the Church*. Lanham, Md.: University Press of America, 1998.

Alister E. McGrath. *T. F. Torrance: An Intellectual Biography*. Edinburgh: T&T Clark, 1999.

Elmer M. Colyer. *How to Read T. F. Torrance: Understanding His Trinitarian and Scientific Theology*. Downers Grove, Ill.: InterVarsity Press, 2001.

Elmer M. Colyer, ed. *Promise of Trinitarian Theology: Theologians in Dialogue with T. F. Torrance*. Lanham, Md.: Rowman & Littlefield, 2001.

Articles

Thomas A. Langford. "T. F. Torrance's Theological Science: A Reaction." *Scottish Journal of Theology* 25 (1972): 155-70.

Bryan J. Gray. "Towards Better Ways of Reading the Bible." *Scottish Journal of Theology* 33, no. 4 (1980): 301-15.

Robert J. Palma. "Thomas F. Torrance's Reformed Theology." *Reformed Review* 38, no. 1 (August 1984): 2-46.

Frank D. Schubert. "Thomas F. Torrance: The Case for a Theological Science." *Encounter* 45, no. 2 (spring 1984): 123-37.

Edward O. De Barry. "Review Article." *Saint Luke's Journal of Theology* 27, no. 3 (1984): 209-13.

Frederick W. Norris. "Mathematics, Physics, and Religion: A Need for Candor and Rigor." *Scottish Journal of Theology* 37, no. 4 (1984): 457-70.

Walter R. Thorson. "Scientific Objectivity and the Listening Attitude." In *Objective Knowledge: A Christian Perspective*, ed. Paul Helm, 59-83. Leicester, England: InterVarsity Press, 1987.

Walter Jim Neidhardt. "Thomas F. Torrance's Integration of Judeo-Christian Theology and Natural Science: Some Key Themes." *Perspectives on Science and Christian Faith* 41, no. 2 (1989): 87-98.

Daniel W. Hardy. "Thomas F. Torrance." In *The Modern Theologians: An Introduction*, ed. David Ford, 1:71-91. Oxford: Basil Blackwell, 1989.

C. Baxter Kruger. "The Doctrine of the Knowledge of God in

the Theology of T. F. Torrance: Sharing in the Son's Communion with the Father in the Spirit." *Scottish Journal of Theology* 43, no. 3 (1990): 366-89.

Richard A. Muller. "The Barth Legacy: New Athanasius or Origen Redivivus? A Response to T. F. Torrance." *Thomist* 54 (1990): 673-704.

David F. Siemens, Jr. "Two Problems with Torrance (reply to W. J. Neidhardt. *Perspectives on Science and Christian Faith* 43, no. 1 (1991): 112-13.

Kang Phee Seng. "The Epistemological Significance of *Homoousion* in the Theology of Thomas F. Torrance." *Scottish Journal of Theology* 45, no. 3 (1992): 341-66.

Stephen D. Wigley. "Karl Barth on St. Anselm: The Influence of Anselm's Theological Scheme on T. F. Torrance and Eberhard Jungel." *Scottish Journal of Theology* 46, no. 1 (1993): 79-97.

P. Mark Achtemeier, "The Truth of Tradition: Critical Realism in the Thought of Alasdair MacIntyre and T. F. Torrance." *Scottish Journal of Theology* 47, no. 3 (1996): 355-74.

John D. Morrison. "Thomas Forsyth Torrance's Critique of Evangelical (Protestant) Orthodoxy." *Evangelical Quarterly* 67, no. 1 (1995): 53-69.

Elmer M. Colyer. "Thomas F. Torrance." In *A New Handbook of Christian Theologians*, ed. Donald W. Musser and Joseph L. Price, 460-68. Nashville, Tenn.: Abingdon Press, 1996.

John D. Morrison. "Heidegger, Correspondence, Truth, and the Realist Theology of T. F. Torrance." *Evangelical Quarterly* 69 (1997): 139-55.

Paul D. Molnar. "God's Self-Communication in Christ: A Comparison of Thomas F. Torrance and Karl Rahner." *Scottish Journal of Theology* 50, no. 3 (1997): 288-320.

www.ingramcontent.com/pod-product-compliance
Lightning Source LLC
Chambersburg PA
CBHW060336100426
42812CB00003B/1010

* 9 7 8 1 4 9 8 2 4 6 8 0 4 *